GUTS

Combat, Hell-raising, Cancer, Business Start-ups, and Undying Love: One American Guy's Reckless, Lucky Life

ROBERT NYLEN

RANDOM HOUSE • NEW YORK

This is a work of nonfiction. Some names and identifying details have been changed.

Published in the United States by Random House, an imprint of The Random House Publishing Group, a division of Random House, Inc., New York.

Random House and colophon are registered trademarks of Random House, Inc.

Library of Congress Cataloging-in-Publication Data

Nylen, Robert.
Guts: one American guy's reckless, lucky life / Robert Nylen.
p. cm.
ISBN 978-1-4000-6776-3
1. Nylen, Robert. 2. Journalists—United States—Biography.
3. Vietnam War, 1961–1975—Personal narratives, American.
4. United States—Social life and customs—1945–1970.
5. Massachusetts—Biography. I. Title.
CT275.N84A3 2009
959.704'3092—dc22 2008041269

Printed in the United States of America on acid-free paper

www.atrandom.com

2 4 6 8 9 7 5 3 1

First Edition

Book design by Susan Turner

This Is Dedicated to the Ones I Love

Humbly, I offer this book to America's muses, sages, and patrons. Denigrators may call you "critics," "buyers for large national retailing chains," "publishers," or "independent booksellers." These are harsh terms for thoughtful people who *help* the rest of us. I love you guys. Sure, you're strangers to me, but frankly, some of my closest friends have already given me more help than I needed. My pals somehow misheard my pleas for praise. Instead, they provided detailed criticism.

My friends, right and wrong, include Dan Okrent, Lee Eisenberg, Bill Broyles, Geoffrey Precourt, Barry Werth, Sara Nelson, Scott Gray, Jon Harr, Kathy Goss, Tracy Kidder, Marty Wohl, Marisa Labozzetta, Lisa Newman, and Stephen Harrigan, and to each of them, I offer my gratitude, albeit somewhat grudgingly.

Without reservation, I thank my brother and sister, John and Sue, who gave me nothing but love. Kit Nylen, my wife, and Cassie Gray, our daughter, are not only forgiving, they're both first-rate editors and fine nurses. I'm intensely indebted to Chris Jerome, Richard Todd, David McCormick, Jon Jao, and Kurt B. Andersen, who cared more than they should have. Any one of you, including Dan and Becky Okrent, may borrow my Kubota tractor or slightly scuffed Honda scooter any time you please.

In our time [the sixties], we were clamorous and vain.

I speak not only for myself, but all those with whom I shared the era and what I think of as its attitudes. We wanted it all; sometimes we confused self-destructiveness with virtue and talent, obliteration with ecstasy, heedlessness with courage.

Worshiping the doctrines of Hemingway as we did, we wanted constant grace under constant pressure, and stoicism before a disillusionment that somehow never went stale. We wanted to die well every single day, to be cool guys and good-looking corpses. How absurd, because nothing is free, and we had to learn that at last.

—ROBERT STONE, *Prime Green*

Contents

GUTS

1.

Black Ice

A warm day in late December 2007 proved me nuts, and an idiot, again. I was in a hurry. Had to drive 190 miles south from our western Massachusetts home to take a meeting in Manhattan and then go to a party. Hastily, I gassed my car at Neighbors convenience store. As I sped away, a pretty girl at the next pump was trying to tell me something . . . important. She waved frantically, signaling me to stop. Too late! My lurch separated the gas line from the pump, the nozzle still lodged in my tank.

Gasoline spewed sideways. My sweet Samaritan retrieved her barefoot toddler and ran away to avoid being blown up. Mortified, I tried to reconnect the line to the pump. It was like trying to cap Old Faithful with a saucer. Gas soaked me, making me a potential torch. One spark and I'd be a one-man Hindenburg. I raced inside to rinse my stinging eyes with tap water. Blearily, I watched volunteer firemen assess the risk. Mere seconds after my SS *Valdez* had breached on dry ground, they determined that there wasn't much chance of an explosion. The dry air had sped evaporation. The damage: roughly five hundred dollars for the pump, four bucks' worth of kitty litter to absorb runoff, and a day out of service for Neighbors' regular pump.

Went home. Threw away my parka, rabbit-fur hat, and mittens. Bathed. Sniffed. Bathed again. Changed into fresh clothes. Rushed to Manhattan, eyes oozing. The sublime Taconic Parkway blurred by, its lovely scenery unseen. Stopped a couple of times to slather ointment on my aching face. Dabbed tears every few minutes.

Over tea in the Soho Grand Hotel, my face afire, I told a young woman that I usually didn't look like a molting chameleon. Not knowing my baseline of ugliness—it was our first meeting—she lied, sweet Charlize Theron to my grotesque Hellboy.

"You look fine!"

Next, it was party time. Beliefnet's directors and bankers nestled in a posh Greenwich Village restaurant to celebrate the sale of the company. Steven Waldman and I had started Beliefnet in 1998 (after we couldn't find money to start a print magazine). We changed the fledgling project into an online medium, got plenty of money, then even more money, and then we went bankrupt. I'd quit before the company declared Chapter 11 after discovering I was both irreligious and aspiritual. Long after I'd left, Steve had reorganized, raised more money, and led the pared-down company to success.

On May 1, 2007, Beliefnet won a National Magazine Award for Online Excellence—despite never having published a real print magazine. Steve graciously thanked me before 2,300 bejeweled, bedecked media mavens, John Waters, Edie Falco, and K. T. Tunstall in Lincoln Center. Meanwhile, I was attending to my busted ostomy appliance in the men's room. Every unpleasantness is a learning opportunity. A double-breasted tuxedo and a big, wide cummerbund effectively disguise one's failed artificial plumbing system. (Perhaps I should wear a cummerbund everywhere: Whole Foods, Target, the Ashfield Hardware Store, and evenings with friends: festive!) Six months later, Rupert Murdoch's Fox Entertainment had paid us a pretty penny—tens of millions of pennies—for Beliefnet, but then again, they'd paid sixty-five times more for *The Wall Street Journal.*

That evening, I explained my horrid face to seven fellow board members, one by one. Like young Charlize, they pretended not to notice my ruddy, scaling skin from a potion of incendiary and toxic drugs that Estée Lauder doesn't sell. Alone, each ingredient makes you peel in red, scabby slabs. Mixed, you look insane, too.

Back in western Massachusetts the next week, I asked Neighbors' proprietor, Phil Nolan, how much I owed him. He said: "It's all taken care of, Bob. Don't worry." That's what he'd said when I pulled the same stunt several years earlier. (I'm easily distracted.) Therefore, I'll buy gas, Budweiser, Berkshire Ale, and donuts at Neighbors as long as Phil lets me. Though my ruddy face was molting like snakeskin, it was no longer as painfully fire-truck red as on Gasoline Day. I might have been healing from a bad sunburn. Having slathered cocoa butter over my sore, frazzled mug, wearing a ski mask, I walked our retrievers into the woods, singing with Fountains of Wayne on the Nano:

The snow is falling down
On our New England town
And it's been falling all day long . . .

Scaring the wildlife, I felt so darned good I would have clicked my heels if it wasn't so hard in snowshoes. Brought the dogs back home. Invigorated, I took a spin on the handy-dandy Honda all-terrain vehicle. Fading winter sun lacquered the ground in a glowing pink-yellow. In the gloaming, the landscape looked like Taos, not the icy environs of Berkshire East. Four-wheel drive would get traction on the trail.

Wrong. Two hours later, Environmental Police officers riding big Arctic Cats pulled the ATV from the snowbank where I'd lodged it, close enough to our cozy house for me to have slogged back for a shovel and wasted an hour trying to dig free. The ATV was irrevocably stuck. It was dark and the temperature was sinking when Trooper Dave Unitas and his sidekick reminded me that ATVs aren't meant to go through snow deeper than eight inches. Four feet of snow and sleet had fallen in the last month, compacting into a thick, slick ice shelf.

Weirdly, I was reprising a wintry day two years before. Back in early January 2006, my suicide vehicle had been a little truck. Snow blanketed our little town, a fine, rare powder that seldom lasts long. A shimmering gossamer quilt had floated and drifted for days. In austere New England, such lily-pure, fluffy stuff rarely cossets us, so we expect to be quickly punished by sheets of nasty gray sleet, ice, and slush. On January 20, the weather had turned predictably bad, but I can't blame frostbite or snow blindness for my misjudgments. Warming wind had brought chilly rain. The temperature was rising, but the ground was still frozen. On impact, the rain became glare ice.

My scary slither that morning to my truck would have convinced a wiser person to go back inside. The driveway was an ice rink. Propelled by chronic ants-in-pants, I sought coffee and newspapers. Sure, the road was a toboggan run that might send me helter-skelter, but the rain was tolerable. The temperature had reached 42 degrees. Summer!

We find negotiating our winter roads no harder than pioneers found crossing the Sierra, so I began my journey cheerfully. My wife, Kit, knows I'm not much of a planner. Well, that's kind: I have no long-range thoughts. I'm impulsive: slow to think, quick to act, lousy at risk assessment, and incapable of forward thinking. Oblivious, in a word—that's me. Normal people are risk-averse. I like driving fast and partying heartily. Still, this morning, I was wary. The military crest of Bug Hill Road is 1,750 feet. That may not rival the Rockies, but Neighbors store sits in a low glen. Dropping down to the paved state road, Bug Hill falls four hundred feet in six-tenths of a mile: steep. So what I did was creep, shimmy, and skate across coarse black ice. The hump in the middle of the road that lets slush run off also makes vehicles slip-slide to the flank. I put the little 4x4 into low gear. Descending a few feet at a time, I stood on the brakes. The road's sloped shoulders made my plow burrow into the snowbank. (We wriggle from trouble by shifting into reverse, then going forward, rocking gently, hoping the transmission holds up.) A small electric motor turned the hydraulic plow into a pry-bar, aiding the tranny.

However, the third time the truck lodged in a deep bank, I started rethinking my plan, such as it was. Our driveway needed salt and sand. So I thought: forget papers and caffeine: get winter road mix from the town warehouse to help UPS, DHL, Airborne, FedEx, and George Propane deliver our woolens, Polarfleece, Gore-Tex, and natural gas. The steepest stretch behind me, I was committed. At some point, the road crew would come in a yellow truck strewing grit, making the road passable. When? I could wait. Sure. I could be patient. (As if!) Lifelong attention deficit disorder precludes me from simulating patience. Where was Ritalin when I was coming up? I have no off switch. When I'm not walking or running, I'm not still. Never. My body agitates and jiggles.

Anyway, a town truck might not come for hours. Crews clear bigger roads first. At a curve in the steepest stretch of Bug Hill Road, my Tacoma skidded again. Brakes grabbed erratically. Suddenly I saw a little station wagon inching uphill toward me. For every two feet it climbed, the wagon skittered a foot back. Up, down, slide. Me, I was going down. I flashed my lights in warning, but our neighbor, nineteen-year-old Kit Adams-Henderson, was aiming for her warm hilltop chateau.

This was the precise patch of road on which our own sturdy wagon had jackknifed in a late-night ice storm in 2003. After my wife and I had abandoned our Saab wagon, we traipsed home and called a tow truck. At two A.M., the wagon led a vehicular slide-a-thon with the tow truck and town police cruiser, all going downhill exactly where young Kit was now spinning her wheels. Her wagon sliced across the road and stopped precariously as my rusty plow slid into the right bank. I clambered out the passenger door, where crunchy snow offered traction, unlike the glassy road surface. Reaching Kit's car, I shoved. She rocked. I grunted. She shifted, accelerated, and reshifted. Pushing and shoving was unwise; my second dumb decision that morning. With each shove, a chunk of intestine protruded farther through a jagged aperture in my belly.

My twelve-day-old abdominal hole, as big as a Susan B. Anthony dollar but less shapely, was my second ostomy. An earlier stoma had been reversed in a false recovery. (I'd get another one, a keeper, a year later.) This one hadn't hurt all that much.* Compared to my first five-hour operation for colorectal cancer—no, *rectal* cancer, let's not be coy—this was nothing, a tummyache. However, my exertions pressed guts into my two-piece semidetached personal Tupperware, my stoma appliance.

* From *The U.S. Army Survival Manual:* "Pain is your body's way of telling you that you have an injury. Pain, in itself, is not harmful, but it does make you uncomfortable. You may not notice pain if your mind is concentrated on other matters. But if you let it, pain can get the best of you. It can weaken your will to survive. You can tolerate pain, however, if you—

Understand its source and nature
Recognize that it's something to be tolerated
Concentrate on things you need to do (think, plan, keep busy)
Take pride in your ability to take it."

Regardless of his wounds, a knight's duty is to rescue distressed damsels, so I pushed up, slipped, fell down, got up, moved to the front, and pushed again, hard. Nothing. I got behind her car again, shoving upwards. Nada. Then in front, pushing down. Kit moved her car a teeny bit, sliding to and fro, until finally she lodged her car in the snowbank on the right shoulder. Traffic could pass. Whew. Peter Adams, her dad, arrived, jabbing a cross-country ski pole into the ice to stay precariously upright. When he reached our slick patch, he fell, hurtling, laughing, and sliding on his hip until he stuck like a dud torpedo in the left bank. He got up, and we all tried to rock my truck free. No use.

Peter loaned me his ski pole. I trudged home, soaked, clammy, and shivering. I told Kit (Nylen, my wife—not every woman who lives on the upper reaches of treacherous Bug Hill Road is named Kit) what had happened. She said: "You loved that, didn't you, you old fool?"

You know what? She was dead on. I'm our town's Don Quixote, or Sancho Panza. Yes, they're opposites: yin/yang, idealist vs. pragmatist, delusional dreamer and hardheaded realist, but Cervantes' characters were the human contradiction writ large. The good Don obsessed about doing the right thing. So do I, with similar results: quixotic. And just as Sancho mocked everyone, more or less fondly, well, so do I.

WHY AM I NOT DEAD?

Slogging back to the house, I wondered: why do I take such dumb risks over and again? Perhaps my restive ways could be cured, or at least understood. Why was I recapitulating previous mishaps, presaging new fixes to come? Was I an unusually demented American guy, or a typical pre–baby boomer? Mulling my busted gut, I pondered the other kind of gutsiness: toughness. Americans are famously aggressive and infamously unaware. Like both presidents Bush, we don't like doing the introspection thing. We make war like belligerent sixteenth-century Spaniards, yet we think we're peacemakers. I've mongered war myself. I'm one of a tiny, bloody band of Americans who've both been shot and who've killed in turn. My brethren? Crazy Horse, George A. Custer, John Dillinger, Bonnie and Clyde, Audie Murphy, Lee Marvin, John Kerry, and Tupac Shakur.

Even if you're unscarred, perhaps you, too, act tough. You're not alone. We love goofy, thick-skulled, get-'er-done obduracy. Sports pages, ads, TV shows, and magazines promote toughness with relentless fervor. We prefer gut checks and head butts to nuance. Americans like politicians who might have given Torquemada a tussle had they been contemporaries. The head of the Spanish Inquisition used torture to root out heretics. Torquemada was fond of subtle interrogation techniques like foot roasting, suffocation, waterboarding, and the rack. Although Richard Cheney's interrogation tactics didn't achieve inquisitorial ingenuity, tough he was. The late David Halberstam described Cheney this way: "Seemingly, he was the toughest of the tough." In 2006, Cheney was photographed grinning crookedly as he squeezed a copy of *U.S. News & World Report*. The cover featuring his mug was headlined "Tough Guy."

In 2008, Bill Clinton argued that Hillary Clinton was tough enough for the job, and he, Hillary, and John McCain said that Obama was too soft. After she knocked back a Canadian whisky at a Pennsylvania bar, and after a RAW wrestling spoof depicted her pantsuited doppelgänger stomping on a cocoa-colored skinny dude with big ears, Senator Clinton won the Keystone State handily.

As root words go, "tuff" is a fittingly compact fortress: four chiseled Anglo-Saxon letters, three consonants. However, "tough guys" evokes contemporary menaces like mafiosi, gangbangers, Ultimate Fighters, Hell's Angels. A dozen current TV programs are devoted to working tough guys like ice truckers, Arctic crab fishermen, and lumberjacks. Me? I've never kick-boxed, tattoed my face, or yanked off anyone's fingernails.

While I was losing my blasé independence, I realized that I'd striven for crusty self-sufficiency since I was a feeble kid. My efforts were inept, even laughable. I finally understood that I'd been on a quest only when I could no longer do what I'd always done so cavalierly. Sure, I always played sports—I'm an American—but I never went into a chain-link cage. Like my dad, I'm a toiler, not a brawler, usually. Like my dad, I've fallen short of my goals. Reach should exceed grasp, right? Aren't men destined to overreach? Underachieve? Sometimes, even would-be tough guys turn off our little minds and mosey along. I don't pretend to know what motivates daring devils* like Evel Knievel, Jackie Chan, Steve Fossett, or the guys who hurtle over Niagara in barrels, except this: they don't do it for the pain. They don't *plan* to hurt themselves. They want to be thrilled by *evading* pain, by tempting fate, taking flight and landing safely, not suffering broken bones. They're unable to envision the most awful consequences of their actions. Instead of emergency rooms, they see headlines in the offing. I say this as a chronic bone breaker, emergency room guest, small-bore entrepreneur, and part-time madman.

Last summer, as I was building a bridge on the back trail, I stepped on a loose board, somersaulted, fell through the beams, and hit my left shin. The accident left a fibrous knot below my knee. The resulting blood clot dispatched a chunk of itself into my bloodstream. The next day, my left arm swelled like a clown's appendage. Now, I inject Lovenox, a blood thin-

* She doesn't completely fit the tough-guy mold, but ultra-swimmer Lynne Cox has bested the nearly frozen waters of the Arctic and Antarctic, whose salinity makes them barely navigable at 27.6 degrees Fahrenheit.

ner, into my stomach every day. I also prick my fingers four times a day to read glucose levels, and administer shots of insulin accordingly. What could be worse than nine, ten daily stabs? No pricks, no stabs, and no metabolism. So I'm happy. No fooling. I mean it. This isn't Dr. Bernie Siegel talking: it's Slopey Shoulders, Automatic Bob, and Upside Down. (You'll see.) Trust me. Life is good.

A super-duper five-hour operation for cancer in 2004 was a total success, except that two huge infections ensued, requiring more surgeries. On April 13, 2008—four years and eleven days after a team of doctors had stuck a super-scary cancer diagnosis in my file that said Careful! Mortality Ahead—I broke my right ankle. At the time, I wasn't doing anything dangerous, just going down our stairs and missing the last riser. Something other than my balance was off: these were the fifth and sixth bones I'd broken in a four-year period at a time when a more prudent person might have been taking it easier. (In 2005, I broke two bones in my right foot. In 2006, I broke two ribs in a very, very short ATV ride.) During those years, my first ostomy was reversed, oops, too soon, and then re-created, not once but twice. I herniated myself—twice—had one hernia fixed, gave up on the other. All the while, I took enough painkillers to supply half of Asia's nineteenth-century opium dens, with leftovers for Samuel Taylor Coleridge and Eugene O'Neill's mom.

Between 2004 and 2008, I had eleven operations all told, as well as three hundred hours of chemotherapy, thirty-six radiation treatments, and a dozen emergency room visits. Then, for good measure, last spring I broke six bones at once (motorbike mishap), a personal record.

Travel back in time with me to the summer of 1968, that tumultuous, legendary, terrible year. The day is as brightly lit as an Arizona solarium. My bedraggled platoon is slogging over a sere rice paddy far, far away from the continental United States. In Vietnam, snow is unimaginable and ice is a luxury item. As we patrol Southeast Asian boondocks, in balmy Miami the sun also shines more benignly. Republican conventioneers are nominating Richard Nixon and Spiro Agnew for high office. Hotel ice machines provide GOP delegates with pristine cubes at the press of a button, dropping into buckets with no straws stuck to them like the dirty chunks local kids sell us.

"One dollah! Cold Coca-Cola! Good ice, GI!"

Although it's hard to tell from the orderly, well-dressed conventioneers roaming Coconut Grove, the nation is boiling over. A nice Republican lady tells *Time* magazine that the GOP faithful should start protesting, too. What, exactly, will Republicans demand? *Time* asks. She says, we must resist government efforts to take money from our law-abiding pockets "to pay welfare people to watch TV all day."

Soon the Democratic Convention will begin in Chicago. Mayor Richard Daley's policemen will bust heads. War protesters, Yippies, reporters, and bystanders will bleed on network TV. Newsman John Chancellor will be arrested. Dan Rather and Mike Wallace will incredulously report live as they're roughed up and hauled away to the hoosegow.

We don't get TV in I Corps (except in hospitals), so the moment passes us by. Nothing new: for the first four months of Infantry OCS, newspapers, radios, and newsmagazines were forbidden outright. From the U.S. Army's viewpoint, all news was bad news from '67 onward, beginning with San Francisco's odious, un-American Summer of Love.

In 1968, the grunts' news source is *Stars and Stripes*, a tissue-thin paper that arrives in bundles, two or four issues at a time, every few days, by chopper. *S&S* reports that Soviet tanks are crushing a spontaneous Czech uprising in Prague. In a made-up nation once called Mesopotamia, the Arab socialist

Baath Party overthrows Abdul Rahman Arif. Arif isn't well known to Americans. A year later, Saddam Hussein Abd al-Majid al-Tikriti starts killing Iraqi people, especially his rivals, eventually muscling his way into the Iraqi presidency, to the ultimate regret of his nation and the world. That's not in *Stars and Stripes,* but it's true.

In Vietnam's northernmost, scariest combat zone, my men and I, Lieutenant Robert Nels Nylen, trudge to our bridge posting. Our sweat-blurred grunt's-eye worldview is less than half a kilometer, tops, from wherever we're slogging at the moment even when crossing open fields, as we do today. In jungles, we see twenty feet in daytime, max, and nothing at night. Marines are fighting near the DMZ thirty miles to the north. Do we care? Naaaaah. Hubert Humphrey, George Wallace, and Richard Nixon: Who are they? Some stiffs in suits.

Moving from point A to point B on another stifling day, we're patrolling, looking for trouble, hoping not to find it. In that malign sump, our mission is as mundane as our scalding coffee (warmed by a burning cube of C-4 explosive). Heat numbs us. Mindlessly, we put one jungle boot before the other. Then Private Dumbass Shithead Sumbitch Finder trips a rusted trip wire. Accidentally.

Blam. Clumsy, careless Finder—not his real name—triggers a Chinese Communist grenade. The Chi-Com booby trap rips off his right ear and drives shrapnel into his shoulder and forearm. Shards lacerate the arm, shoulder, and right hand of Pfc. Day, who's following Finder.

Instantly, the ground beneath our feet is rendered unsafe. It had always been so, but now it is more terrifyingly, unavoidably so. The rice paddy we crossed to get to the brushy dike where Finder and his ear became separated—terrain boringly parched and featureless moments ago—is now fraught with buried mines and unseen menace. I freeze. Can't move. Not a step. Not a millimeter. Where could I walk without setting off another trap? Would the next wire set off another grenade? Perhaps a 105mm howitzer shell, wiping out five men in a nanosecond? Would a huge, mother-humping 155mm shell pulverize a whole squad? Would the ground swallow us and spit back our bones and blood in a pink cloud of tissue and dirt? Would I stomp on a Bouncing Betty and kiss my nuts bye-bye?

Our new medic rushes to the vortex of the dike. Reddish smoke wafts. Finder screams. He isn't our most alert GI. A month earlier, watching Finder alight from a helicopter, Doc Froemming, our prior medic until he was blinded, said dismissively, "His shit is weak."

Descending, Finder looked at his new mates with dull, fearful eyes. It didn't take X-ray vision to tell he was a dud, a loser. Finder would endanger himself and his colleagues from the moment he hopped off the chopper. It wasn't his fault. He was a sad-sack member of Robert McNamara's Nearly-Special-Needs Army. Defense Secretary McNamara had lowered recruiting standards to permit borderline dopes into the service. In the late sixties, recruits were in demand, even dimwitted ones. The Army was the first employer of dropouts, kids with disciplinary problems, and low-grade criminals. Infantry standards had never been high. Now they fell under the limbo bar.

Smart guys avoided the draft. They got bone spurs and flat feet, lost or gained weight. They feigned illness, homosexuality, psychosis, or clinical depression.* They stayed in school, got married, and had babies. Few college grads volunteered unless they'd joined ROTC back in the mid-sixties for a semi-free

* In 1967, when Warren Zevon, the late singer-songwriter, got his draft notice, he asked his father to tell the Selective Service that his randy son was gay—comically untrue. For good measure, on the day of his physical, Zevon gobbled LSD and amphetamines, and smoked pot. He was classified 4-F.

ride. ROTC guys finessed themselves into noncombat branches like military intelligence and finance. Enlist? Ha ha ha.

Dumb guys weren't clamoring to get in but they resisted ineptly, if at all. They had few alternatives. They weren't going to Canada. They scarcely knew where it was. Before military service, these guys hadn't traveled more than a few miles from their blocks, farms, or counties, much less from the nation itself. Anyway, guys like Finder needed jobs. Before his encounter with a booby trap, we knew him as a guy who'd joined to get his brown teeth fixed. Military service was often a poor kid's first opportunity to see a dentist. Now Finder's face is no longer connected to his left ear. A chunk of his shoulder is gone, too.

"My ear! My ear! Is it gone?"

Personally, I can't move. My brain is soaking in a vat of molasses. Time stops. My job is to be up front, leading, calling in a medevac, dusting off Finder and Day, thwarting a ground attack that could follow the trap. But I'm stuck. My jungle boots have sprouted roots, sent tendrils into the baked soil. I'm glued, magnetized, inert. In combat, five minutes is forever. Destiny. It's always there.

Stories you'll read here revolve around a hot war, scalding firefights, a few tepid fistfights, and some risky start-ups. Sometimes when I was raising money, hives crawled like centipedes over my face, and strangers looked away from my swollen visage as if I were a leper. You'll encounter maladies that attacked me in a cold place, too. I should have died in 1952, 1968, 2006, 2007, and 2008. An intern saved me in '52. Luck saved me in '68. Recently, doctors Deborah Smith, A. Ron Miller, Joseph Wolfson, Jon Kurtis, and a bunch of good nurses kept me going. I mean to tell the truth here, but neurologists aren't sure that any of us understand what we see or do, much less remember our deeds accurately. Apparently, our brains craft plausible narratives from the unwieldy chaos that comprises human life. Then we retell ourselves these stories until they're imprinted. In other words, ultimately, perhaps there is no final truth to report. Our recollections, though unique, don't always work the way they should. Eyewitnesses often disagree about what they saw. Life is *Rashomon,* a movie in which every participant sees the same crime differently, or sees no crime at all.

Dr. Smith calls the faulty way that I reconstruct her medical advice "gestalt creation. You try to make sense of the senseless, Bob. We all do."

Ever since Homer, Virgil, and Herodotus created poems about legendary events, we humans have been telling stories about our misadventures. Yet even fresh memories may prove flawed, let alone decades-old recollections. Though the genre is as old as cave paintings—a way of saying: here's my mark! I killed a big thing with my spear!—a memoir is a strange thing that amalgamates navel-gazing, narcissism, and microfocus. A memoirist should humbly admit his self-absorption, apologize, and move on. I'm sorry, really sorry.

For safety's sake, I've corroborated facts and recollections with letters, journals, books, and an unpublished forty-year-old memoir, "Shooting Gooks and Other Stories"—whose ironic title was lost on contemporary editors in 1970—as well as an interview for Time-Life Books' *Vietnam Experience,* magazine articles, military histories, and the online grab bag, which is often right. I interviewed the only Delta Company man I could find, sainted Dennis Froemming, my platoon's fearless medic in 1968. You'll see through my prism, warped by mind-addling painkilling drugs. Why toughness? Guts? Well, I'm guessing that you admire people who face trouble with gusto, or you stumbled into the wrong book. Poor thing! You've been wandering, confused, and alighted on this page. Go away before you hurt yourself. Now!

Sometimes I think I'm tough or at least unnaturally aggressive. Mostly, I know how silly my boasts are. I'm not even the bravest person in the average doctor's waiting room. Despite bearing plentiful scars (roughly two hundred stitches) and two dozen busted bones (give or take) as well as having swooned under general anesthesia for many cumulative days, I'm a human meringue pie: a walking, talking, fluffy confection of hot air and cotton candy. A natural-born wussy, I didn't start misbehaving until I was, oh, thirteen or so. Like many underachieving boys who are overeager to become men, real men, I yearned to be tested one day. In the meantime, I exhibited nothing that even a compassionate observer could call "character." Only in delusional dreams was I brave. I lost myself in romantic books about chivalry and warriors.

Yet I led a platoon in Vietnam: got wounded, lost friends, and saw ghastly sights in that ugly war's most vicious year. After my riveting, hideous time in Vietnam, back in the Land of the Big PX, I decompressed, but every firm to which I applied for work found me a nutcase. I went to grad school because I was unemployable. The GI Bill and my sweet new wife, Kit Hopkins Nylen, paid for my marketing degree after my English B.A. had proven useless. Fortunately, the routine of school and Kit's affection screwed my head back on properly. My schoolmate the future junk bond king Mike Milken learned a lot at Wharton and got go-to-jail rich. For me, Wharton was a refuge, a halfway house. At night, I recorded combat experiences, still as fresh to me as the evening news.

Slowly, I readapted to my all-American life, joyfully getting, spending, and laying waste to my new petty powers, as M.B.A.s must. My middling career in interesting businesses—magazines, new media—entailed working with genuinely tough people. Businesspeople do hard things every day, like begging for start-up money, firing people, scrambling to make payroll, and of course, dissembling madly. A welter of sales plans, call reports, and budget spreadsheets buried my combat stories. Nobody wanted to hear from psycho Nam veterans anyway. We were caricatures, losers and killers. Happily, I was paid pretty well. Like my marauding Viking and Scots-Irish forbears, I traveled, gathering plunder, then started little companies: reckless, giddy entrepreneurial work.

A small town in New England captured our family. Now as I try to stymie diseases that should have killed me years ago, I pretend nothing's wrong. My obliviousness may be a gift. It's hard to become consumed by woe when your attention span is as blessedly short as mine is. Most of us try to display grit as we blunder through our lives. This isn't a guy thing: it's a human thing. Inspecting my own past, rereading history, I seek signs, portents, asking myself: Have I been tough enough?

Too tough?

And you?

What about you?

2.

Evidence that I'm No Tough Guy

In 2004, an ugly series of little Russian boxes opened in me, the bestial, slimy children of Sigourney Weaver's *Alien* nemesis. Infections in my viscera jumped up inside bigger, badder diseases, each one uglier than its vile predecessor. Between surgeries and atomic zappings, in surreal dreams, the nation's War on Terror and my tiff with cancer overlapped. In my addled brain, Salvador Dali's clock and Morley Safer's burning hut melded, white-hot, one. IED explosions in Baghdad in the flat-screen TV over my hospital bed set off Munch's *Scream*. For years, targeted and toxic drugs—never mind narcotics—produced pluperfect, perfervid nightmares. Leucovorin, Avastin, FOLFOX, Zofran, and Erbitux, with Xeloda and irinotecan on the side, roil sleep patterns like crazy. Bizarrely, I thought my medical travails gave me a window into the challenges a new generation of grunts faced, but my war was vicarious. Trying to buck up, it dawned on me that I'd been feigning courage forever, if deficiently. The facts, in chronological order, more or less:

1. ABANDONED MY HANDICAPPED SISTER

My older sister, Sue, walked into our local soda fountain. In 1952, Sue was fourteen. Harry Truman was in his last presidential September. Heroic Dwight David (Ike) Eisenhower would soon take over. Men wore fedoras. Women wore gloves. In our third year of war in Korea, Ike promised to visit the bloody Asian Peninsula. Never mind: this was a sunny, warm day in suburban Delaware. Two of Sue's schoolmates followed her to the counter. Eager for cold Cokes, the girls had alit from the yellow bus. The other girls weren't Sue's friends. They taunted her. Homely, ignorant teenagers, by mocking a cerebral-palsied kid, they flaunted their superiority for a change. Sue was cute and curly-haired. Her brown eyes sparkled. She laughed easily, heartily, and often. Adult neighbors doted on her, calling her "Suzie Q," knowing how tough her life would become. Her hope was to be accepted as a normal kid; fat chance. "Spaz," the girls called her. Walking erratically, haltingly, Sue trembled. Her lower lip jutted. Tears brimmed.

Sue was indeed spastic. A brain injury at birth had stiffened her muscles and impaired her coordination, making every step a shaky, risky adventure. The harder she tried to control herself, the more rigid she grew. The girls were cruel but technically correct. Sue didn't take an unaided step until she was eight years old. Friends and family joined in team-patterning sessions to reroute faulty neurons from her fingers to toes. Good-natured, glad for the attention, Sue lay quietly as adults stretched and kneaded her. Over the years, kind Indianans, Ohioans, Alabamans, Tennesseans, and Delawareans moved her limbs to ingrain proper movement into her haphazard nervous system.

She'd shucked her heavy metal leg braces a few years before: spaz, yes, was she. Therefore, I needn't intervene. Sue didn't know I was hiding behind the comic-book rack. I slunk from the store, pretending I hadn't seen her, shamed. Had I mustered the nerve to do the right thing, I'd have rewarded myself with my favorite snack, a chocolate milkshake and Ritz peanut butter crackers, bought with change I'd lightfingered from Mom's piggy bank. Either way was bad karma, but Delawareans in the fifties didn't know from karma.

I was a coward. My first big test proved me a weakling. I ran from bullies: worse, from girls. "Moron," they called Sue. That wasn't right. She wasn't a *re*-tard either, but I cowered and fled. I was eight years old. Maybe the girls would have yelled at me if I'd defended Sue. What was I afraid of? I don't know.

At the time, I loved King Arthur, Charlemagne, and *The Song of Roland*. I imagined myself as a page, then a squire, training to become a heroic knight like Galahad. American adventurers featured in Landmark Books held me enrapt, too. As I slunk away from the soda fountain, every step widened the gulf between my journey and the paths my heroes had chosen. By the time I got home, the gap was a canyon. I was no Jimmy Doolittle, John Paul Jones, or Davy Crockett. I couldn't carry Roland's tune or chain mail tunic. I was a sissy. Am I now, today, being too hard on a kid who happened to be me in a smaller version? No. I will regret forever what I didn't do. Sorry, Sue.

2. HEMORRHAGING: AN OMEN?

Later that year, I had a tonsillectomy, a common procedure then. I can still conjure the sickly sweet ether. Mom slept on a cot next to my hospital bed. As I recuperated, each swallow went down my sore gullet like a jagged rock. My tonsils and adenoids were gone, but the wound didn't heal. At home, I spat blood. In the hospital again, I gagged as the rubber tube went down my throat, but the doctor stanched the bleeding. I bled, wept, and threw up for another week. Was this my destiny? Whimpering? Retching?

3. DEEP-SEA FISHING, AGE NINE

Nels Nylen, my grandfather, was a shop foreman of the Cheney Brothers Silk Mill in Manchester, Connecticut, where his son Bert, my dad, worked too. Work reforms in the 1930s gave workers an extra day off. Nels built oceangoing dories, then a seaside cottage a hundred sandy steps from Long Island Sound. Behind Nels and Amelia Nylen's Cedar Beach property, a tidal marsh was stinky at low tide but smelled sweet at high tide. After he'd finished the garage and house (from Sears Roebuck kits) and the dory (from scratch), Nels rowed through the salt marsh to the sea. Years of fixing looms on the shop floor had given him the imposing muscles of a blacksmith. His handlebar mustache (that I've imitated, badly) was waxed and curled like a boardwalk boulevardier's—a look at odds with his prudent comportment. His heavy-lidded eyes and dark hair made him look Italian, not Scandinavian. Uncle Hube's wife, Mary, called our shared droopy mien "bedroom eyes." (Aunt Mary Cianciola Nylen, Sicilian American, knows from eyes.)

When Bert's younger brother was born, his parents asked their firstborn son to name his sibling. "I call him Bertil Carl Nylen," Dad said. "That's *your* name!" they protested. If the name was good enough for a Swedish king and himself, Bert thought, why not the kid, too? But they made him find an alternative. Imagination was not Bertil Carl's long suit: "Okay: Hubert Carl Nylen."

Today, Sweden is the placid home of inoffensive, socialistic blonds, people like Annika Sorenstam, ABBA, and cheerful indie rockers. Swedes send us nice Saabs, Volvos, and IKEA furniture. As nations go, it's harmless, a Nordic pussycat. Yet a thousand years ago, while Norsemen and Danish Vikings were plundering easy pickings on the British Isles, Svenskis sailed east to conquer Finland and Russia. Nels Nylen's fierce, bearded predecessors cut across the Baltic, looking for trouble and comely Lithuanians, pushing east. Swedish marauders got all the way to Persia.

When the tide ran out over the Connecticut coastal flats, Granddad, Uncle Hube, and Dad ventured over the undulating sandbars, carrying pitchforks and pails. They stopped at each bar, searching for air bubbles. My brother, John, and I tagged behind with toy shovels. Clams burble through little holes, venting air, water, and detritus through the sand. With luck, the men could grab five clams per forkful, but usually it was slow going, a single clam at a time. With pants furled above their knees, they waded out to the horizon. We lost them in shimmering evaporation. They'd fill a pail, leave it on a sand bar, keep going, then retrieve the pails on return. Shucked, doused with ketchup and horseradish, accompanied by oyster crackers, the provender was a tasty meal pillaged from the Sound. Mmmmm. Before pollution and red tides decimated shellfish for a generation, fresh clams were delicious even for an unadventurous diner like me once I got over the chewy, rubbery texture. One second they were alive, the next moment masticated into gritty lumps; brunch, executed with our molars. We were carnivores. We are.

Granddad and Dad took me on my first fishing expedition in Granddad's handmade dory. The planks seemed sewn together. Skimming over the marsh, I was safe. Granddad was as strong as a galley slave. Reassuringly, I could see the muddy bottom. Taking turns, Dad and Granddad rowed. We slithered over reeds that we left in our shallow wake. Oarlocks thunked rhythmically. Then we hit the chop. The roiling Sound collided with calm marsh water. I couldn't swim. The ocean and beasts lurking therein scared me. High tide. We were at sea. I couldn't see bottom. Below was a turbid, dark green-blue netherworld.

After the men rowed for a mile or so, they dropped anchor, showed me how to bait my line, and went about their business—catching bluefish, flounder, and haddock. Sticking a hook through a slimy, squirming, living worm frightened me almost as much as the sea did. The ocean was so deep that I couldn't think right. Soon the floorboards were alive with bluefish and flounder. Fish were big! They wriggled! They made squishy, yucky, flopping noises! They didn't cooperate! They resisted your grasp, shot from your fingers, slithered and flapped! They hated us! They gasped, drowning from oxygen overdoses! We were cruel! They were dying in our Martian atmosphere! The horror!

My line tautened. Something tugged. My tiny reel ratcheted and the rod twisted. Granddad netted my catch. A little fish flopped at our feet. I was pleased, sick, and scared. Grinning, Granddad said, "Pick it up." The greasy little bastard exploded like a balloon, inflating to three, five times its original size. I shrieked and let go, afraid that the sharp spines emerging on its flanks would puncture my hand.

"Blowfish," Granddad said enigmatically. "It blows itself up. Scares us. Works good, huh? Not so good to eat. Maybe we put him back where he wants to be."

He tossed the slimy changeling overboard. I didn't go fishing again for fifty years. Terrors lurked beneath the waves: creepy, writhing, oily beasts.

4. CUB SCOUT IN ROPES

Johnny Sparks and Buddy Haley tied me to a stool in our Cub Scout den mother's basement. I was ten. Johnny was my age, but solid. Buddy, eleven, was stronger. They tied me up and left me. A half hour later, Mrs. Marsh heard me hollering and freed me.

That year, I missed a hundred school days, but got straight

As. (Miss Dill pitied her wan, towheaded, bloodless, headachy, skinny pet.) But why couldn't I make a proper muscle? Why did my arms look like spaghetti with no biceps? Why was I sick all the time? Throwing up? I stayed home, listened to *Stella Dallas* on the radio (which I heard as *Stellid Alice*) and nudged toy soldiers across the hardwood floor. My dysphoria wasn't complete. I made model airplanes and stacked Lincoln Logs. When I felt up to it, I ran my Lionel locomotive off the tracks at top speed. I listened to the *Delaware Farm and Home Hour*. I knew poultry prices in Kent and Sussex counties. I read comics.

My salvation was the world's best medicine, a dream cure. For my throw-up migraines, the doctor prescribed elixir of Coca-Cola. Yes! A magical slip of paper granted me pure essence of Coke syrup, supersweet and hypercaffeinated. Elixir indeed. In the age of cod liver and castor oils, was there a finer medicine than a potion made from fructose, sucrose, and caffeine? My headaches diminished. On the other hand, the remedy taught me that sugar was health food. In a long, bittersweet farewell, forty years later, my now-diabetic pancreas said bye-bye after processing a million cakes, Cokes, and Hershey and Mounds bars.

Still, I was a sissy boy who'd ignored his crippled sister's plight. That's why I was sick. I was predestined to sin and suffer. I deserved punishment. That's what my Presbyterian Sunday school teachers were saying about our faith as I heard them: predestination was its core. I may have misunderstood Calvinism, but I thought fate had made me this way. Later, karma, kismet, fatalism, and predestination converged to cement my sophism. Fate had made me steal from my mom. Fate had made me impure. Fate made our grocer, Ed "Easy" Fine, call my mom to ask whether the silver dollar I'd given him was mine to spend. Busted. I'd tried to pass off an unusually ambitious theft as my personal savings. Easy Ed knew better. He doubted that a kid would spend such a grand coin without explaining how he'd earned it unless some evil deed had been done.

"Wait until your father gets home!" was the battle cry of the day. Dad didn't accept my alibi that our maid, Wanda, had been stealing from us, because Wanda hadn't given Ed Fine the coin. Dad didn't buy my backup story that it was a gift from a friend whose identity I'd sworn to protect. He'd never struck me before, but Dad spanked the devil out of me that day. When I tried to squirm free, he slapped my thighs and hips, because I'd compounded theft with false witness.

5. BLEW MY STAR TURN

Miss Dill selected me to play the only role in a single-act one-character play, *The Life of George Washington.* Wearing a powdered wig and a tricorn hat, I delivered my lines precociously, if I do say so myself, reading Miss Dill's script in a reedy alto. Four hundred Alfred I. DuPont Elementary School students and teachers applauded politely.

In the sixth grade, I had a single line in our class play. An audience watched, pointed, whispered, and giggled. I lost my nerve, froze, stammered, and blushed. Every ounce of blood left my brain and fell to my cheeks, which turned fiery red. I forgot every word. I was mute. The next day, Mrs. Flickinger reminded the class that Mr. Big Shot Student Council Member had asked for a big part but couldn't handle a walk-on. "Good work, Van Johnson," she said.

That stung. Van Johnson was the star of *Thirty Seconds over Tokyo,* the movie based on a book by Army Air Force Lieutenant Ted Lawson. He piloted one of a couple dozen B-25 bombers Colonel Jimmy Doolittle led in the first U.S. raid on the Japanese homeland. After crash-landing *The Ruptured Duck* in China, his leg shattered, Lawson and his crew evaded

Japanese capture. An infection turned the leg gangrenous. It was crudely sawn off. Blond, handsome Van Johnson played Lawson in the movie. How could I grow up like Lawson if I couldn't even ape the actor who'd imitated him? Much less win June Allyson?

6. FLUNKED FOOTBALL TRAINING CAMP

Dad's job entailed transfers. My mom, Sue, and Dad lived in seven states before I was born. In 1956, we left Wilmington, Delaware, for a suburb of Chicago. In the tenth grade, I went out for high school football: Illinois football, big-state football. Thirty-two hundred students attended Lyons Township High School's two campuses. Sputnik had just gone up. I had to do something manly for America, not just take advanced chemistry and trig. A hundred boys tried out for the frosh-soph team. I'd grown six inches in the last year. I'd carried my saxophone the prior spring, tweetling and oompahing with our junior high band in La Grange's Pet Parade, my gray woolen trousers stopping six inches short of my shoes, exposing white socks and pale shins. I was six feet one, 126 pounds. That fall it was time to leave band practice and become a jock like Dad, or die trying.

In a secondhand uniform, smelly oversized shoulder pads swallowed my sticklike limbs and bobbling Adam's apple. I was a skeletal adolescent Ichabod Crane with zits, a lousy football player, slow and squeamish. At the start of the second preseason week, we had our first contact: tackling drills. Coach gave us one instruction: Don't back up. Stand still and take the hit. It's easier. Are you ahead of me? Have you guessed that I was terrified? That a big guy was running at me, fast, about to hit me like a sawdust dummy? That I backed up a half step as a postpubescent bull moose tackled me? Awkwardly, I planted my right leg in the turf to brace myself. Clifford Lake hit me so hard that both bones in my lower leg broke above the ankle.

I looked down. The boot jutted at 45 degrees. My right leg had snapped above my black high-topped boot like an overcooked drumstick. In agony, I yanked turf from the field. Goggling at my bent, busted leg, Lake apologized. "Didn't mean to do that," he said. (Two years later, Cliff won the state discus championship.) "So sorry. Really sorry. Does it hurt?"

Trying not to bawl, I yanked clods of sod with both hands. Meanwhile, Coach hovered. "I told you not to back up, Nylen," he said. It was the only time he ever addressed me by name. Coach was a lean, flat-topped World War II vet. He'd seen worse than mere broken bones. "You stand still, Nylen, you don't get hurt. You back up, bad things happen."

It was my fault. At the hospital, an orthopedic surgeon came in from his Wednesday golf game to mend me. "Relax, young man," he commanded. "Relax, or I can't set your leg without anesthesia." Sure. Relax. I could no more loosen quivering, puny muscles as taut as hickory saplings than I could do differential calculus, shoot down a Russian MiG, or attract a girl who could see the finer points of my personality instead of pustules. Reluctantly, the orthopod anesthetized me, losing another half hour from his golf game.

For more than three months, I wore a cast from groin to toes. After the cast came off, revealing emaciated, hairy, unmuscled flesh, I limped for a year. My friends thought I was faking. For a while, I had no friends, clomping through empty hallways for the ten minutes I was granted to get to my classes before hormone-riddled kids hit the staircases. My right leg is still skinnier than my left. Subsequent wounds didn't help (until injuries in 2008 made my legs more symmetrical, if smaller).

7. ABANDONED MY CRITICALLY INJURED FATHER

Three months after my football career ended, on a frigid December night, I tossed and turned in the bedroom that Johnny and I shared. My cast was ungainly. I couldn't turn. The plaster casing was too heavy. I was half an Egyptian mummy. My upper body fidgeted. My twitchy, sweaty shape rutted the mattress. Yet that night I was glad for the excuse that plaster sarcophagus afforded when my father fell, hard. He'd made a wrong turn: from the den, he went left, not right into the powder room; a simple mistake, a catastrophe. He tumbled down wooden stairs onto a cold cellar floor. He broke his clavicle, smashed his right inner ear, fractured his skull, and lost his God-given grace. Instantly, his equilibrium and spiritual center were gone, forever.

The man who'd taught me to throw, catch, saw, hammer, and row moaned in agony. Dad was big: six feet two, 225 pounds, no steroids. Firemen wrestled his protesting bulk up the steps and into the ambulance. Dad shouted "No! No! No!" as they grunted upstairs with the stretcher. Dad didn't understand what had happened. Nor did he know why he hurt so much.

He'd ruined his excellent brain. Exploratory surgery on his cerebral cortex worsened matters and failed to find the cause of his grand mal seizures. Now the family had two head cases, Sue and Dad; three, counting me. Dad had spent thirty years as a DuPont executive. He drove a new Pontiac. My mom drove a shiny blue 1957 Cadillac with fins, an automatic antenna, and power windows. Dad made $40,000 a year, the equivalent of maybe three or four hundred grand today. Bert Nylen was going places. He didn't expect that that place would be a concrete floor. His ambitions and head were dashed together.

Despite his injuries, he was promoted to his dream job, helping run DuPont's biochemical lab at headquarters. We went back to Delaware, our best move. Wilmington had always been our real home even though Mom had grown to hate the DuPont Company's high-handed ways. However, Dad couldn't handle his new post. He took barbiturates to ward off seizures, but he fell again, this time in an icy parking lot. His busted inner ear threw off his balance. He slipped and broke an ankle. After the first fall, he teetered even standing still. Eighteen months after the cataclysm, the only place Dad could go was into early retirement. Mercifully, the company he loved granted him a lifelong pension. After DuPont found him unfit to work, he hated his unending dependence on The Company. In thirty-two years with DuPont, he'd gotten eighteen assignments in ten states. He'd met Enrico Fermi, Robert Oppenheimer, Niels Bohr, and Pierre S. du Pont, the stars of his solar system. He'd helped make the wondrous, terrible, hideous atom bomb. The Company got him through the Depression, promoted him, and paid him well, but let him dance with Vishnu ("Now I am become Death, the destroyer of worlds . . ."). The Company took every scintilla of his energy. Then DuPont stopped trusting him. Not without reason.

Dad tried to become a real estate agent. He worked for a while for a friend's little firm, but failed. Salesmen should have the gift of gab. Dad's chatter was gone. He sold his DuPont stock—The Company's stock—bought it back, sold it again, bought more; ditto, the cycle repeating itself many times until he died, after his final fall on wintry ice in 1996. A busted hip did him in. Plus pneumonia. During his last thirty-six years, Dad had puttered, carpentered, plumbed, and electrified. He crossword puzzled. He took up veterinary medicine as a hobby. When the family cat got an infection, Dad shaved her belly, made a cut to drain the infection, dabbed antibiotics, and sewed her together with needle and thread. (She died.) When he dented his car fender, he got under the housing and pounded the damaged bits with a rubber mallet. He filled a hundred pings with Bondo. When he finished, the Oldsmobile looked like it had suffered a bout of automotive pox. Dad proudly showed his handiwork to the neighbors with whom he was still speaking.

"Ahhhh," they said.

He devoted himself to his daughter. He wrote memos to Johnny and me on yellow DuPont stationery. After describing our failings in detail, he explained how we could make something of ourselves.

From the desk of Bertil C. Nylen . . .

You can make something of yourselves one day.

If.

Only.

You.

Will.

Listen.

And.

Wake.

Up.

Yours truly,

Dad

When his skull cracked in that frigid basement in 1959, Dad lost his balance, his coping intelligence, but much worse, he'd dashed roughly half his sense of humor, too. His charm had been the core of his persona. Then: *pooft.* Gone. He still told jokes: good jokes, bad jokes, dialect jokes; but witty Dad was gone. Spontaneously funny Bert Nylen, the life of cocktail parties in ten states, had vanished. New Dad didn't understand where Old Dad had gone. As time passed, New Bert grew bitter at Old Bert's absence. After the fall, Dad was easily vexed. His grand mal seizures frightened his family. When a spell hit, after he came to after several minutes of frenetic isometrics, New Dad didn't remember the fit that had knocked him out. Days later, another fit. In midspasm, we tried to slide a flat wooden depressor between his jaws so he wouldn't bite off his tongue. That wasn't easy. Even when impaired, Dad was strong. Midseizure, he was Samsonesque. Downers numbed him and staved off cranial lightning, but they didn't help him find work or make him funny again. When he wasn't dazed, Dad was irascible.

Turd by turd, he removed dog poop from our immaculate lawn. He hung plastic poop bags from the doorknobs of our careless neighbors. Our righteous poodle, Cutie, pooped in our backyard. Why didn't all dogs behave like Cutie? Why didn't the world still work as it once had? Dad wondered ruefully why our neighborhood, the DuPont Company, and the whole darned country were filling with doo-doo.

8. CANDIDATE UPSIDE DOWN: A PREQUEL TO TROUBLE IN THE JUNGLE

During the Summer of Love, I was in Georgia doing postgraduate work at the only school that would have my underachieving buddies and me: the Infantry Officer Candidate School in Fort Benning. In 1967, officers-in-waiting had no radios, newspapers, magazines, or TVs. We didn't hear the Grateful Dead, the Jefferson Airplane, Janis Joplin, or ex-paratrooper Jimi Hendrix's revolutionary guitar work. There were no flowers in our helmets. No one invited us to Human Be-Ins. We were learning to blow things up and kill people. Although I'd fired nothing more powerful than BB guns and .22 caliber rifles before enlisting (two weeks before my draft notice arrived), I was an excellent marksman, a sharpshooter.

When my OCS company went to the mortar range—easy duty—I was blasé. Ho hum: my normally jittery mind went into slumber mode. So it was a surprise when the drill instructor yelled at me—*"Don't drop it, Candidate!!"*—through my wispy daydreams.

"Stand back, Candidate, and keep hold! Now . . . pull it out! *Give it to me!*"

Inadvertently, mysteriously, terrifyingly, I'd reversed the mortar shell, upending it. The explosive charge at the shell's tip faced the bottom of my tube. The fins were sticking up. That's backwards. Still, nothing awful would have happened had I dropped the bomblet. Well, probably nothing. The round couldn't go anywhere.

That didn't appease the sergeant.

"Try it again, Candidate," he ordered. (Get back on the horse, cowboy.)

Ordinarily, accidents are most likely to occur on the grenade course (some men freeze rather than throw their lethal metal baseballs, a fact that makes grenade instructors nervous) and the firing range (where officers like future general Petraeus can be accidentally shot by a man who falls down with a round in his chamber and his safety off).

You know what I did? With the mortar round, that is? Consider: one 81mm mortar has the power to wipe out an entire squad. The first time I screwed up wasn't due to nerves. Worse: I'd been lazy. The second screwup was from sheer terror. Unnerved, I literally didn't know which end was up. Seeing my glassy eyes, the DI asked a calmer candidate to help me: a good thing, too. I was shaking. My buddy guided my numb hands. Like swim mates at summer camp, we dropped the shell together. My platoon began calling me "Candidate Upside Down," payback for the way I'd goaded them on double-time marches and overnight hikes. With too much stamina, I was a pushy jerk on long-distance ordeals. I'd become a self-appointed mini-member of the training cadre, a prison trustee working for the Boss Man. Softer guys, even stronger men who were cursed with fast-twitch muscles rather than long-distance stamina, resented me. My metamorphosis into "Upside Down" was sweet justice.

When I got to Vietnam, however, I never, ever placed a shell the wrong way in a barrel, tube, or magazine clip. Sometimes in combat, I performed well; sometimes not.

Time passes. Timid little boys compensate for their weakness. Frankly, though, I never became cool: the attitude affected by every young American male from the fifties on can't be faked. Dangling a Marlboro from your sullen lips isn't enough. If sneering sufficed, I'd be in the Cool Guys Hall of Fame: I smoked, smirked, and showed off. Ironically, the more effort you put into cool-guy posing, the more coolness recedes. Like Zen, cool comes only when one doesn't grasp or grovel for it. In fact, I overcompensated without becoming the stud I aspired to be. I played sports, drove fast, and took risks. In college, I became a hard-drinking, ill-behaved, smart-ass buffoon. Acting up and guzzling heroic quantities of beer were fun, but unwise. Once I was pummeled in a fraternity party fracas. Some football star had shown up with my girlfriend, Kit Hopkins. I made some offhanded remark at the bar while waiting for a plastic cup of beer. A jock friend of Kit's date invited me outside. He sucker-punched me as we walked to our duel. Before I could retaliate, a dozen guys separated us, and a general brawl broke out.

I staggered back to Lambda Chi Alpha seeking allies. There was no one home. I returned to Sigma Chi alone, seeking revenge, and landed one solid punch on the jaw of the guy who was trying to stop the scuffle. Spurned, the peacekeeper turned on me, too. At the end of the tussle, a dozen knots adorned my hard head. Oddly, Kit and I had been an on-again, off-again item until that night, when we became stuck to one another.

She became my pinmate, my fiancée, and then my life partner. Go figure.

This pugilistic evening took place a year or two after my most ardent college protest: I joined several hundred fraternity and sorority members who gathered in front of the university president's house. Our goal was to denounce his new policy shutting down keg parties at midnight. Fittingly, that night, I'd passed out in the bushes. Kit roused me and walked me home. I really don't know why some decent, sweet women are attracted to losers.

Bravado masked my qualms when I didn't marinate them. To camouflage my racing heart, disguise my quavering voice, and distract attention from my giganormous pimples, I adopted a calm façade. Vestigial courage? Beginner guts? Simulating bravery may be a halting first step on the path to real resolve. Maybe valorous people don't stifle fear. Perhaps nerve can be finessed: you pretend to be someone who doesn't succumb to craven impulses. It's an act, theater: fear lurks as we pretend otherwise. Bulging eyes, moist foreheads, and pulsing carotids betray us to anyone paying attention.*

Anxiety is natural. Portraits of Napoleon, hand in his vest, capture the world conqueror massaging his plebeian dyspepsia. He wants us to think he's implacable: his growling belly reveals his doubts. Aristotle believed that fear is universal, but he disapproved of rash, reckless actions and especially despised faking courage as unworthy. What does the real thing look like?

A quick, asynchronous fast-forward to western Massachusetts, 1995. Dwight Scott is building a house for his sister, ICU nurse Cindy Scott. Forty people gather on a crisp fall day to help him

* Falling to his knees in *Public Enemy Number One*, gut-shot gangster and grapefruit face-masher James Cagney mutters: "I ain't so tough."

raise and connect Dwight's lovingly tenoned posts to mortised beams in the time-honored way, no nails or screws. As unskilled friends like me lift, Dwight's carpentry team joins huge timbers, hammers dowels home by wielding big wooden beadles. (Popeye and Bluto used beadles when they were striking the circus bell, vying for Olive Oyl's affection.) Dwight's work embodied ancient Yankee know-how.

In a single day, a two-and-a-half-story frame rose, *shazzam,* and might stand for centuries. (Two, at least.) In the fading autumnal light, the temperature dropped fast as shirtless Dwight climbed a ladder, walked on the uppermost beam, and stuck a good-luck pine tree on the top. Finis. Dwight was fearless. As he came down, with night falling, we cheered.

"How did you stay so calm?" I asked. Holding his right hand between us, Dwight gazed steadily at me, but his hand shook like an aspen in a gale.

3.

Back in Asia, 1968; Among Things Un-Carried: No Camera, Thanks

If two parts of Earth differ as much as do Vietnam and New England, I haven't seen them. The Gobi and the Loire Valley? Siberia and Bali? Euro-Disney and Abu Ghraib? Vietnam made me a xenophobe. English-speaking countries are the only foreign lands I visit voluntarily. No one speaks unkindly in the olde Empire unless you don't say "please" and "thanks very much."

Wartime memories come often, never lineally, arriving unbidden at odd hours. Frankly, I was terrified in combat more times than I'll describe, but I wasn't a dud. My feet weren't always stuck in concrete. Unlike Navy Lt. JG John Kerry, though, I kept no film record of my prowess. Slogging in the grubby infantry differs from serving in the hygienic Air Force or spotless Navy. For one thing, a grunt has no place to stash a camera. Even a riverine vessel like Kerry's had dry cubbyholes. Moreover, our existential cavalry cinema would have been most riveting when we were shooting something besides cameras.

True, some grunts toted gadgets into the bush. By the late sixties, cameras, radios, and tape recorders had shrunk, and "portable" was a potent selling word. Transistors, godparents of computer chips, had reduced electronic gear to items so neat that a little plastic box held a wondrous universe. No more radio tubes. Our combat zone rocked and rolled, faintly, unlike the Victrolas that blasted Christmas carols over the trenches in Verdun. The Doors, Stones, Vandellas, and Supremes discreetly traveled with us into the highlands . . . at low volume, barely loud enough to reach a fire team, never penetrating the jungle. Triple-layer canopy is a damp, thick sonic sponge. We loved "We Gotta Get Out of This Place" and Sam Cooke's "Another Saturday Night." We, too, lacked weekend fun. The Beach Boys cranked up "Sloop John B":

Why don't they let me go home?
This is the worst trip I've ever been on.

Cigarettes were more likely to give us away than Radio Vietnam. Fortunately, smoke hangs innocuously in airless jungles, dying a quick, humid death. I smoked less than a pack a day at home, but in country, two nervous packs daily was my quota. Zippo lighters burned our thighs as fluid seeped out. Tim O'Brien explained the rich array we stuffed in rucksacks in *The Things They Carried.* He knew his mates' packs and the contents of their baggy pockets as well as Inuits know totems: amulets all. On our backs, we carried the equivalent of small, fully stocked contemporary college refrigerators. Most guys toting toys were dumb FNGs (Fucking New Guys, "cherries"). Short-timers didn't add to their loads. True, I was an Effing New Guy, my status given away by my gold second lieutenant's bar (actually, a dull bronze tab). My body hadn't adjusted to the ferocious heat. Every ounce I carried felt like a pound, every pound like a hundredweight. I emptied my canteens the first hour of our first trek. Immediately, I was as thirsty as if we'd spent days wandering in the desert. I shed stuff like a fledgling losing feathers. I'd packed light, I thought, but almost everything I carried was dispensable. You need ammo, water, salt, C-rats: that's about it.

More than a year had passed since Infantry OCS. At Fort Benning, grim tactical officers had whipped flaccid officer candidates into the best shapes of our slack American lives. We hardened by crawling, marching, running, chinning-up, sitting-up, and double-timing, packs flopping on our backs, M-14s held high. We slept four, five hours a night. Snacks were forbidden, disparaged as "pogie bait." We had no time to digest. Stuffing our faces, we ate "square meals." Our forks made right angles to our faces as hovering Tactical Officers admonished us not to talk, look at our plates, or pass our greasy eyeballs over their sanctified beings. While double-timing from the mess hall, half the unit threw up. The infantry was nuts about eliminating fat. We were lean or we were gone: "paneled," expelled by a panel of officers. After completing twelve weeks of the eighteen-week course, we were encouraged to tailor our fatigues. Our pants were darted like Zoot Suit trousers worn by Chicano gangsters in World War II. Our shirts were tucked tight to display our hard new physiques. Now gaining weight would require an expensive trip to the tailor.

For 62nd Company's prom in May '67 (celebrating our advance to Senior Candidate Status, allowing us to scream at junior candidates and wear spiffy blue helmet liners), I nominated Kit Hopkins for Company Queen. She placed runner-up, and was mortified. The nomination was the worst thing I did to her until 1975, when I sent her to Elizabeth Arden on Fifth Avenue as a surprise present. After being made up lavishly, her hair poofed like Debbie Reynolds in the fifties, she emerged through the famous red door weeping, mascara tracks dripping down her pink, pretty, embarrassed cheeks.

After graduating from Benning School for Boys, I taught

speaking and writing at the Army Ordnance School. Yes: before going to war, I taught new instructors how to teach. It wasn't fun. Army pupils feared school more than attacking pillboxes, or forwarding ammo for other people to use when attacking pillboxes. (Ordnance isn't a combat arm, unlike infantry, armor, and artillery: ordnance officers test and supply ammo. They don't shoot unless hard pressed.) The Aberdeen Proving Grounds felt homey. Helen Jamison, my mom, grew up on a Pennsylvania farm forty miles to the north. Baltimore and its infamous Block (starring stripper Candi Barr) was a short drive away. A dozen blue crabs, bay-seasoned, cost three bucks. We smashed them on BOQ (Bachelor Officer Quarters) floorboards with mallets.

Mr. Bender, my boss, a civilian, a G-14, wore short-sleeved shirts to work. His stumpy right arm had been mangled in the Normandy invasion. Short sleeves enabled him to move his stubs of radius and ulna like freaky arm fingers. Mr. B. didn't care whether I stayed in shape as long as I played lunchtime hearts and pinochle very poorly. I obliged. During that quasi-civilian year, exercise was optional. When I felt like it, I jogged around a cinder track or played intramural football. My tapered fatigues started clinging, but I could still button them.

Every two weeks, I led twenty fresh ROTC graduates on night patrol. I took my work seriously. ROTC wankers didn't. Their indolence infuriated me. Two hours into my first patrol, I screamed at the grousing, slovenly bastards, who complained that it was dark, they couldn't see, blah blah. They thought our night classes were dopey Army efforts to fuck with their splendid minds and punish their porcine bodies. Even if they did go to Vietnam, they'd work in headquarters so far back they might as well have been in Singapore. Why get in shape? I thought: You toads might have to lead counterattacks, like it or not. Shape up! Overnight, I became an angry hard-ass, the sort of putz I'd despised: a quasi-lifer. Startled, I realized why drill sergeants and tactical officers had yelled at me until their eyeballs bulged and their throats quit. *I'd been just as pathetic as these jerks were!* And might *always be*! Unless I talked *sense into them*! I yelled until I rasped, then croaked at the tubby REMFs (Rear Echelon Mother Fuckers), another dumb lifer dedicated to national defense. Suddenly I knew how vulnerable we were. These officers were . . . *ours*! Sad. The center would not hold.

Molding flabby REMFs into soldiers, I, too, dissipated. The muscles Fort Benning had tautened turned to suet. Drinks at the Aberdeen Officers' Club cost twenty-five cents a shot, as did a pack of Tareytons. A six-pack of Ballantine beer at the PX cost a buck and a quarter. Schmidt's, just $1.10. The Army of the sixties was a boozy, smoky boys' club. Today's coed all-volunteer military attracts well-toned, high-achieving, able people who hemorrhage far too often but otherwise lead exemplary lives with low rates of substance abuse (except when they get home missing limbs but gaining PTSD). Orders to Southeast Asia prevented me from emulating flaccid ordnance boys. I stood tall and pushed up. Sometimes.

JUNGLE EXPERTISE

Before we went to Southeast Asia, in late May 1968, the Panama Jungle Warfare School acclimated 160 officers to humidity and explosions. After we second looeys had gone to seed for a year, we humped through a Central American miasma, firing blanks at Green Beret "enemies." From Fort Sherman—today a high-end resort called the Meliá Panama Canal Hotel, no fooling, with several pools and a sushi bar—we patrolled through swamps, swatted bugs, rappelled down cliffs, and ate monkeys. Yes, they taste like chicken. So do rats, snakes, coatyls, jaguars, and tapirs. Wading through sluggish, critter-infested rivers, we evaded laid-back Special Forces who were recharging their own batteries. Billions of insects bit us. Zillions.

Jungle training put us back on a proper military track. However, inexplicably, having rehoned us into hot-weather killing machines, the Army sent us home on leave. For ten stateside days, we munched junk food and watched TV. The Beatles were back on Ed Sullivan. Robert Kennedy was shot: *ka-blam.* Ten weeks earlier, Dr. Martin Luther King, Jr., had been assassinated. The world was spinning off its axis. French kids rioted in solidarity with their disgruntled American brothers, or in solidarity with someone, somewhere, or merely because they were French: *je ne sais quoi.* American cities blazed. After burrowing into ghettos, Black Power penetrated Army ranks. Happily, Richard Nixon had a secret plan to bring peace with honor and fight crime. His running mate, former Maryland governor Spiro Agnew, had ruthlessly quelled Baltimore riots after MLK's death. (On WBAL-AM, I heard Agnew declare martial law in March.)

Discovering new cultures can edify, yes? The First Cavalry's incoming orientation included admonitions from Psy Ops officers. Don't call Vietnamese people "gooks," "slopes," "dinks," "slants"—all racist, derogatory, ugly names. Befriend them, win their minds. In the next class, an infantry instructor warned us: "Beware. Gooks are wily sons of bitches."

In early June 1968, I joined Delta Company in the highlands as it briefly defended a forward artillery base astride a ridge near the Laotian border. In radio communications, our battalion, the 2nd of the 12th Cavalry, affected a gambling motif. Our battalion commander was Roving Gambler, our artillery observer was Birth Control 69er, and sister companies were Aces High, Bad Bet, Wild Card, and Easy Winner. Stacked Deck was Delta Company's call sign. As Stacked Deck 1-6, twenty-four years old, I was my platoon's eldest man.

More-seasoned men had had their asses shot off before I arrived.

Four months before I joined Delta, our battalion had struggled to reinforce Marines in the heart of Hue, the Citadel, confronting murderous ambushes. Nine Delta Company men survived the ordeal unscathed. Nine! Ten were killed and ninety-five wounded, some badly. Two months later, the Cav reinforced jarheads who had endured a siege at the beleaguered fortress of Khe Sanh. Delta had taken fewer casualties preventing Khe Sanh from turning into Dien Bien Phu II, but had fewer men to lose. The company personnel roster was posted on a blackboard in LZ Jane, our battalion HQ. Chalked names were erased and added as men flitted in and out of the company like gypsies. In three months, our leaders included three company commanders, two first sergeants, eight platoon leaders, a dozen platoon sergeants, and countless squad leaders. Company strength dropped as low as 96 men and reached a high point of 130, averaging around 110. A few dozen men were shot, mortared, or mined, or got hepatitis, fungus, or malaria. Everybody had dysentery. A few lucky men got short and went home intact, except for the runs. A couple reenlisted, changed their occupational specialty to something less hazardous than 11 Bravo, infantryman, and got out of the field. One man—addicted to adrenaline—extended to stay in the field. Officially, twenty-six men in my company died in the last nine months of 1968. That's an odd way to win a war.

A day later, on my first combat assault (in radio code, a Charlie Alpha), we jumped from the skids of hovering helicopters onto tree stumps splintered by artillery and air strikes. We sheltered through the night, jumpily, hearing phantom enemy probes until daybreak, and then humped through steaming boondocks. Stumbled along, each vital but horrid can of ham and lima beans a brick. Every ounce of gear, every 5.56mm

M-16 round, and every swig of water was a dead weight,* but water was immeasurably precious. I hung three, then four rubbery half-gallon canteens from my pistol belt as well as seven clips of M-16 ammunition. Still, I was thirsty, and probably prediabetic, too. Soon dysentery added to my cravings for water. At night, I chopped vines as I'd learned in Panama, their meager, watery sap dripping into my steel pot, augmenting my slim takings from streams.

My shoulders slumped. My rucksack held a damp jungle blanket, soaked underwear, and clammy socks, as well as a hammock, buried within forty-eight hours† (because dangling in branches amid incoming fire doesn't help attain REM sleep), rations, *Time* magazine's light overseas edition, letters, a first-aid pack, malaria pills, iodine tablets (for purifying water), and grape powdered Kool-Aid (for making iodine-water drinkable). Also: a toothbrush, toothpaste, heavy K-bar knife, cigarettes, a two-ounce can of lighter fluid, several gluey tropical Hershey chocolate bars, and a warm can of 3.2% beer. The

* In *A Walk in the Woods,* Bill Bryson describes hiking the Appalachian Trail with his chubby friend, Katz. Hopelessly unfit, Katz has packed everything he can think of: spam, bologna, salami, rice, brown sugar, oatmeal, pots, stove, Sterno, utensils, plates, clothes, batteries, flashlights—so much gear that he can't close his backpack. He starts paring the excess before stepping into the woods. Within the first mile, Katz is shucking stuff willy-nilly. He discards so much gear that someone gathering his discards could open a small outdoor supply store.

"What happened to the pepperoni?" Bryson asks.

"Flung," Katz answers.

"The toilet paper?"

"Really flung."

† In the bush, soldiers buried unwanted gear so it wouldn't fall into enemy hands. Even though 230 American feet trampled the jungle floor, making our path hard to miss no matter how feverishly the drag squad brushed away evidence that our traveling circus had passed, we left no cans, plastic, or butts. Each Winston filter, Lucky Strike tobacco flake, and Kent microfilter was field stripped into tiny shreds.

ruck's exterior apparatus was festooned with smoke, fragmentation, and concussion grenades, flares, trip wires, and a spare machine-gun bandolier. I sometimes hefted a mortar round. We all did. Mortar platoon members carried the heavy base plate, tube, tripod, aiming mechanism, and two rounds apiece in addition to rifles and other gear.

On my fourth day in the highlands, dysentery spoiled my pants. In short order, I fouled my backups; jettisoning both foul sets, I trudged in my skivvies, slipping into the jungle when spasms hit. A mortar man gave me his extras: brotherly love.

In my wallet, I carried a good-luck talisman. Kit's dad, Bud Hopkins, promised me that his lucky silver dollar would bring me home, whole. His charm nearly worked. Trimmed with electrician's tape, my dog tags didn't jangle. Our aluminum mess kits were sound-deadened by spare socks. My pistol belt and all the stuff hanging from it chafed my hips raw, drilling four bloody holes into my pelvis. Had I strength for more stuff, I'd have added a clip, not a camera. I'd have more welts, gladly. Moreover, I didn't need to record one second of combat. Each moment etched itself into memory without technical aid. Impressions were indelibly seared by cerebral acid. Photos were redundant.

Forty years later, I see freeze actions involuntarily. I have few photos. My measly two souvenirs, a flag and a pith helmet, were stolen by moving men. It's okay. I was branded. My mental files comprise a ghastly PowerPoint presentation: executive producer, Beelzebub; director, Mephistopheles. My grim slideshow lives in 3-D. Cranial Polaroids flash at random, not when I punch a remote. *Zap:* here's a decapitated NVA corpse hanging from barbed wire along Highway One. *Pow:* a fatty chunk of pork, replete with bristles, floats in an unsavory stew in a service-station-restaurant-brothel near Chu Lai. *Wham:* There's Spec Four Whoever, shredded, bleeding. *Shazam:* Specialist Cloud's pale skin, never red, is turning ashen, his life leaking away second by second.

4.

More Jungle Trouble: Scrolling Down the Devil's PowerPoint

ARMY FIELD MANUAL 31–35: JUNGLE OPERATIONS

> 2–2. Jungle . . . is an area in humid tropics wherein land is covered with such dense growth of trees or other vegetation that it impedes military operations and obstructs lines of communication.
>
> 2–5. Climate . . . high, constant temperature, heavy rainfall . . . oppressive humidity.
>
> 2–8. Animal Life . . . abundant . . . pythons and anacondas, giant scorpions, beetles, ants, leeches, spiders, mosquitoes and other insects. The environment has five layers—canopy, middle tier, surface of the ground, surrounding low vegetation, as well as beneath the ground and under water: birds, monkeys, apes, sloths, iguanas, marsupials, squirrels, snakes, centipedes, deers, tapirs, wild pigs, all thrive.
>
> 2–22. Southeast Asia
>
> b. Climate . . . the temperature in Southeast Asia seldom falls below 64 degrees. The mean is around 80. The air is

> quite damp: over 90 percent humidity at night, seldom falling below 65% during the day . . . Annual rain is between 80 and 128 inches. Rain forests are dense. Tallest trees reach 150 feet. Undergrowth is complicated by liana (thick creepers) and palm rattan, making movement difficult. Closely spaced bamboo trees grow 40 feet high, like fences.
>
> d. Troops are exposed to many health hazards. Diseases include diarrhea, fungus infections, mosquitoes, flies, fleas, leeches, and other parasites. More soldiers are hospitalized from disease than wounds.
>
> e. The major military effect of the jungle environment is to restrict movement and slow tempo. Fighting is extremely short range with limited visibility. Jungle warfare requires specialized techniques and demands higher standards of training and leadership at lower levels than any other form of fighting.

A Light Observation Helicopter (LOH, affectionately known as a Loach) is flying so low that if we jump really, really high, its rotors could trim our fingernails. The lovable olive-drab eggbeater, an adorable, improbable two-man machine, looks cute in the glinting sunshine. It's ours, of course. We own the sky. North Vietnam will send no helicopters below the DMZ until Americans leave, though daily rumors warn us that the North Vietnamese Army is sending tanks and MiGs—Russian-made jets—to destroy us.

The rough network we're following, the Ho Chi Minh Trail, is no autobahn. It's a mesh of crude paths whacked higgledy-piggledy through jungle, vanishing in vegetative cul-de-sacs. The NVA could drive a two-ton truck in short lurches through the Trail, and a month later you'd see no evidence that anything but monkeys, snakes, and parrots had passed by. Sitting on ridgetops at night, we sometimes saw headlights flash below, taunting us. We'd call artillery. The truck headlamps could go off, then come on again, flickering fireflies, persistent, nagging.

Right before the Loach circled overhead, we'd stumbled on an NVA camp. Our point element—the small unit leading the company's sharp tip, comprised of a lead fire team within a lead squad within a lead platoon, four, nine, and thirty men, respectively—explored a recently abandoned tunnel network. The prize is an underground field hospital outfitted with cots, medicine, and plasma. On dirt floors, blood clotted on bandages and sheets. Rice cooled in pots. Charcoal embers were warm to the touch. The front half of Delta Company crawled into the bunkers, investigating. The rear of our reticulated column folded upon itself, catching up, a caterpillar expanding and contracting.

When the point man takes his first step, the drag man is still resting his rucksack against a tree, facing backwards. Five minutes later, the drag man steps off. Now the lead element stops to check noise and finds the bunkers. The midsection keeps moving, then stops. The drag element stumbles into the midsection, and then it, too, stops. The point steps off again, slowly, investigating. Sometimes the drag squad must jog to keep up. The tail rejoins the head in steady convulsions. In motion, in single file, our company strings out for a half kilometer. The jungle is dense. Machetes make noise, alerting enemies, so we send no flankers and limit the cutting commotion to a single chopping blade. Now the drag squad double-times to keep up. The last guy pauses nervously to brush away our presence. The head moves below ground into burrows. Ceaselessly, the centipede's body tries to catch up, never quite closing the gap. We're relieved to have the vicious little hummingbird circling above. We slow to admire it. Perhaps it'll escort us into hostile territory. We think warm thoughts, until its mini-gun opens up on us.

Zzzzzzzzz! Zzzzzz! Zzz! Americans riding an airborne Disney cartoon machine are shooting at Americans on the Trail. Half visible at best through thick foliage, we're indistinguishable from bad guys. Pilots assume all people near the Laotian border are enemies. We stop moving, confirming their suspicions. They see a column of men halting on the Ho Chi Minh Trail. Targets! We see a white star on Bambi's sweet fuselage. Ask no questions: shoot, get ready, aim, Americans believe. Maybe the indistinguishable ridges that run along the Mekong River from Laos to Cambodia confuse the Loach. Each ridge must seem identical to its neighbors. Perhaps the Loach doesn't know that we were dropped a few days ago. We'd leaped onto a hilltop (undefended), spent the night, and patrolled, making no contact for seventy-two beautiful hours. We'd walked through a ridge defoliated by Agent Orange. Mostly, we hacked the jungle. The Trail was a third-rate pedestrian highway. The clearing process had opened a dim view of the ground to pilots.

We're waving one minute. *Brrrrrrrrrrrrpppppp.* The minigun slashes through leaves, pulp, and flesh. In midwave, three, four, five guys are hit; one is hit several times. Unnervingly, my first experience with killing fire is the sort of malign accident known as friendly fire. There's nothing friendly about it. Our company commander frantically seeks the LOH's radio frequency. Searching a codebook isn't easy when you're taking six hundred bullets a minute.

Acting as one, with no command to do so, every man aims skyward. Tribal instinct trumps national interest. Do that again and you're coming down, you cuddly, multi-million-dollar piece-o-shit, you. The Loach makes another pass, holds its fire, swerves off, and returns. At last our CO gets through. Thank God. No showdown. We regroup. Wounded men are medevaced. The Loach flies above us contritely (if you can impute penitence to a machine). We slog off the trail, whacking bamboo, brush, liana, and wait-a-minute vines, then entering a meadow. However beguiling the eerily undulating elephant grass looks, the ten-foot-tall blades cut us as if we're wading through vicious knives. It's spooky, too, this wall of chlorophyll that stands high enough to cover a pachyderm. An enemy platoon could hide in here, waiting.

At dusk, we hastily arrange a makeshift perimeter before the forest swallows us. Night falls. We see nothing. Nothing. Not a bloody thing. We can't see two feet. Our defensive line is a crayon drawing of a circle. Men stagger out a few feet from their positions to take a leak and get lost, calling softly to their buddies for directions. Most of us stand and try to pee away from our shallow holes.

Flash. A few days later, company officers have gathered on a ridgetop. After several days patrolling in lower ground, we've reached an abandoned landing zone where we'll be resupplied for the first time in three days. It's unthinkable that anyone will follow us up the ridge, which is steep, muddy, slippery.

Whoooooosh. A B-40 rocket whizzes over our heads, sucking air on its trajectory precariously near my large, closely cropped skull. Vacuuming our brains, the rocket explodes below on the sheer ridge we've just clambered up and goes off with a hollow thunk. It's no biggie. It's nothing. It's horrifying. It's over. It'll happen time and again. Sometimes you flinch, or flop and cower. Sometimes you scarcely notice. Our company has wriggled, shoved, and dragged itself up a steep, slimy, seven-hundred-meter-high ridge. We're tired. U.S. Marines held this position once, leaving rude, cursory scoops dug into the red earth. (Marines intentionally don't dig deep or fight defensively.) Doggies and gyrenes have the same folding shovels, but we . . . *dig.* We're not burdened by a gung-ho tradition. We believe in General Patton's dictum. We don't want to die for the

USA. We want to make *them* die. Busily, we improve Marine foxholes.

Soon, a log bird (logistics ship) will deliver mail, hot chow, cold soda, and colder ice cream. Marines carved the landing zone by axe, artillery, and plastic C-4 explosives. We enjoy a commanding view of lush scenery. We can see kilometers into Laos. By contrast, North Vietnamese soldiers who nestle hidden within that view enjoy a better view of us than we have of them. Aside from November Victor Alpha, there's no helpful shorthand for NVA, unlike the radio code for Viet Cong: Victor Charlie, or just good old Charlie. Our enemy prefers cover to vistas. They burrow as we fly. They don't demolish jungles to create landing zones so that whirring machines can deliver creature comforts. They have no high technology, no edible goodies, no hot meals, no Hershey bars. They have rice and durable AK-47s whose banana clips are loaded with thirty bullets. Our clips are designed to hold twenty rounds, but the springs malfunction, so we actually carry only sixteen rounds or so, to preclude jamming the rifle's feeding mechanism.

Our supplies arrive ostentatiously by Huey 1-B supply helicopters. Hueys also come in two other varieties: gunships (for heavy fire) and slicks (for logistics or medical evacuation). Squat and menacing, Hueys look like horned toads. We also have Cobras (nasty, fast rocket-firing ships), Chinooks (transportation behemoths), and LOHs, of course. Some Marine units still fly the sort of green praying-mantis choppers that date back to Korea, ugly machines featured in *M*A*S*H*.

NVA troops carry bandoliers of dried rice in socks draped over their shoulders. They capture and use our ammunition. Our guns, mortars, and rifles can't reciprocate, however. Their barrels have been machined a millimeter bigger than ours, so our barrels are too tight to fire their slightly larger rounds. Our enemies try to neutralize our manufacturing advantage with ingenuity.

The rocket zoomed at us from the wood line at the clearing's border. Skirmishers have their AK-47s (the stolid automatic weapons invented by the Russian folk hero Mikhail Kalashnikov) in addition to their RPG (rocket-propelled grenade launcher). The whoosh reverberates in my addled head. Rounds buzz our way like vicious insects. Then they stop firing. Their hive goes silent.

Flash. A dumb-ass mortar man has decided to leave the shelter of his hole to dig into a thermos of cold ice cream. So we're in a firefight. So what? We get shot at every other day. Big deal. Vanilla? Still frozen? Soon to melt, lost forever? That's special.

Zap, thwock. Our mortar man has been shot through the thorax. Doc Froemming jumps from our foxhole to save the shithead, asshole mortar man, his sucking chest wound caused by a simpleminded craving for melting ice cream. Moron.*

The gunner crawls, slides, and burbles back to his hole. He's choking on his own blood. Doc ignores pings and buzzes, stanches bleeding, stops air from escaping the wheezing lung with a plastic sheet pressed over the gunner's heaving chest.

* When I tell this story today, friends say: "You can't mean that." You were *kids,* they remind me. You couldn't be so judgmental.

That's no defense. We had free will, like the generals and politicians we blamed for our plight. We let ourselves get tugged into war. We didn't dodge the draft. Honestly? We were half afraid, half thrilled. Every new testosterone-drenched generation tests itself. War gives a rush, although squalor arrives in its wake as surely as DTs follow drunken sprees. Chris Hedges's antiwar screed, *War Is the Force That Gives Us Meaning,* explains this giddy, sick complicity, this primal duality.

When I got back to the States, two of my former 1st Platoon mates somehow found me in Fort Dix as they processed out of the service. Gleefully, they told me how our company had caught the remnants of an NVA battalion near the Cambodian Parrot's Beak. The enemy soldiers were trapped, cowering in a giant cavity that had been created by B-52 strikes. My buddies evoked the bloody rapture of wasting bad guys by the score. All told, they killed two hundred human fish in that ghastly barrel. I understood their dark, guilty joy; Lord help me, I even envied them!

Doc is exposed. It isn't fair. Medics have it worst, except for medevac crews. As he works, our company lays down fire. Suppressive fire, we say, as if we shoot gentle, kind bullets that don't want to offend. Every fifth one of our outgoing rounds is a red tracer. Every fifth incoming round shot from NVA weapons is green, alien. All our 120 men fire something: M-16s, M-60 machine guns, mortars, antitank weapons, grenade launchers. Mortar rounds loop out close to our perimeter. A fiery all-American scythe shreds the knoll. Die, Commie mo-fos.

Only outgoing red tracers: no green, thank goodness. AK-47s are pitched lower than our chattering M-16s: their incoming sounds more menacing than our outgoing. Their guttural bursts differ from our tinnier ones. Doc drops into our hole, shaking. Who wouldn't? Watching Doc work, I shake with empathetic terror.

Gingerly, we patrol, finding no one. NVA have scooted. At twilight, another log bird drops more ammo and ferries away two wounded men. Night falls. Crickets, frogs, birds, and monkeys chatter. It's not as pitch-black as it was in the lower jungle, but we're too nervous to sleep. They know where we are. We don't know where they are.

Flash. The next morning, my platoon takes point, heading for where the NVA fire came from the day before. Cliffs border our LZ: this end of the zone encompasses one hundred meters of forest. We expect to make contact, to meet people we'd rather not encounter. This is my second point command, my first in a hot zone. On my very first, I got lost and climbed a tree to get my bearings as Lieutenant Rapier chuckled.

Spec Four Cloud leads our point squad. Cloud is a short-timer just back from his second R&R, he reminds me jumpily.

Unless I screw him over, in twenty-five days and a wake-up call he'll return to his honest-to-God Indian reservation. Cloud has a premonition. Never mind, I say. You short-timers get so nervous. I don't blame you, but you're good, Cloud, everyone says so. You're savvy, smart, and careful. We need a cautious man to keep us from trouble. Sergeant Schaefer, Cloud's squad leader, argues too, but my mind is made up. I've got twenty-four men, not forty-three as mandated by the Army's Table of Organization and Equipment. The best men get the worst duty—the punishment for competence.

Go slow, Cloud, I say. Slow. Slow as you want. We're in no hurry. The ridge is too narrow, too sheer for me to send flankers. We'll crawl after you when you say it's okay. Reluctantly, slowly, Cloud moves into the tree line. He's careful, a turtle, a snail—or rather a sloth, a slug, as he has no proper carapace.

Behind him, we creep, maintaining a few meters' space between each man. Protocol. The point man is alone in every respect. In a half hour, Cloud, low-crawling, has edged forty meters into the jungle. Seven men from our platoon (including me) are now inside the tree line. The bulk of the company dawdles nervously back on the LZ, fearing a mortar attack that might start on the only ones left on the bald ridgetop. No one wants to move. No one wants to stay.

People in the jungle expect a firestorm to erupt momentarily. We're right. Crawling ever so slowly for thirty infinitesimal minutes is enough time for Cloud to trigger the ambush he dreads. He's hit many times: six, seven shots through his slender chest, so close to the earth you wondered how they could have hit him at all. Right away, he's dying.

Sergeant Schaefer has been shot through both arms, both legs, and his gut. Our third man is shot in the ass. Doc is next, untouched. Our fifth guy is shot in the foot. I'm sixth, scared and bursting with shaky energy. Can someone die this fast? Like me?* Just three weeks in country? Our seventh through eleventh men form a hasty assault line on the narrow ridge. We move fast on automatic, as close to the cliffs as we can get.

At the ambush site, six, seven, then eight men jam in a tight row. Our elbows touch. We fire, toss spent magazines, reload, fire, throw grenades, and push ahead, maybe, oh, twenty seconds from start to finish. The ambushers don't resist. They're gone. We find spent shell casings on their crude defensive berm, a dirt mound a few inches high and a few feet across. Four men. We return to retrieve Cloud, whose eyes flicker. We get poncho halves to drag Cloud and Schaefer to the LZ. The other wounded guys limp, leaning on buddies, happy! They're going home! They'll live! As we wait for dust-off, Battalion HQ requests an Air Force jet to hit the far side of the hill where the NVA fled. We pop smoke, marking our position.

A jet screeches so low we see rivets, although he's flying 500 miles per hour. The pilot passes, ensuring that he sees us. He returns, thunderously, dropping jet fuel in twin canisters that explode in orange fireballs. The jellied brew lands half a football field from us. It's as hot as if we'd been barbecuing and our propane tank exploded.

We yell: "More crispy critters! Do it again!" We crave protection, even fake protection, and specious vengeance. We're in no hurry to chase the perps. Air Boy returns, dropping car-

* Three days later, I am hit, awakening in a Navy MASH unit in Quang Tri. Across from me in the air-conditioned Quonset ICU—a wonderful, terrible place—lies Sergeant Schaefer. His face is swollen. Casts and tubes are everywhere. He moans.

"Hi, Schaefer. Hi, Sarge. How ya doin?"

He focuses. "Hi, sir," he says. The exchange takes all our energy. We rest. Next to me is a critically wounded guy on a heart-lung machine that expands and contracts, giving cacophonous life support. The respiration machine and its patient emit rasping noises together. It could be worse for Schaefer, I tell myself.

tridges on us like hot brass hail, and releases a second inferno. The ambushers are probably a mile away already, tumbling down the ridge, exhilarated. The maelstrom burns plants, bugs, snakes, and trees. We feel better. That's something!

Flash. I'm in the White Elephant, the Da Nang Navy Officers Club. There's a movie tonight. Popcorn, too! A bar. Two bars! Cocktails cost thirty cents, and beer a quarter, I think. A dime? I'm on leave from the Navy hospital on China Beach as I recuperate from my second wound. Third? Who knows.

Navy Special Policemen guard the entrance. They stop two pistol-packing First Cav chopper pilots. "You can't bring in weapons," they say. The warrant officers are loud, oiled, greased, lubed, and itching for a fight, but the SPs insist. Grumbling, the chopper jockeys hand over their dinky pistols. Reaching the Elephant's belly, they announce that they'd saved the Marine Corps in both Hue City and Khe Sanh, after the remaining Marine pilots gave up and flew away.

They offer to kick the ass of anyone who disagrees. A jarhead major invites the young men downstairs, into the grotto, the sanctified bar, for congratulatory beverages of their choice. "Beer," they say. Accompanied by a couple of Marine captains, the major serves them beer from his pitcher, buys backup pitchers, too. He toasts the pilots' courage.

Everyone chug-a-lugs. Beers guzzled, the major offers a modest challenge: "You guys are good, for sure, so you may be strong enough to do something that I can't get any of my candy-ass officers to do," the major says. "See these bar stools? Can you lift them with one hand, holding one leg?"

"Shit, yes," the Cav says.

"Go to it, boys. Ten bucks if you shame my pogie-bait-eating pussies."

The pilots drop to the floor. Marines pour beer on their

heads. The chopper-flying dickheads, Cav brethren, sputter, leaving without throwing a punch.

Flash. On July 4, 1968, our company has been skirmishing for days. Enemies had ambushed us. We'd lost men. We found NVA bodies, red stars on their dark green caps, and left playing cards in their mouths, macabre warnings signifying—what?—I have no idea. Some of our senior guys were over the edge. Anyone with four months in country was considered tenured: especially anyone who'd been a chopper waist gunner, then had re-upped to become a ground-pounder, an earth-cruncher, a grunt, as two adrenaline freaks had done. In another week, I'd earn a CIB, a combat infantry badge, a matte black metal rectangle embossed with rifle and wreaths and worn over the left breast pocket, like jump wings. Wearing one meant "I'm the man"—*a* man—okay, a fool with moldy feet, facial crud, and worms. We endured much to earn these useless trinkets. In a war in which too many ribbons and medals were given for too few deeds, a CIB meant "I may be a moron, but I've seen some shit."

The longer dismounted grunts stayed in the field, the more likely we were to be shot, booby-trapped, intestinally compromised, and infected. Surviving unscathed for a year was rare. Leaders who rushed about jabbering on radios with whippy long antennae were vulnerable targets. On July 2nd, 1st Lieutenant William Rapier, Delta Company CO, left for medical care forever. Tapeworms had been eating his rations for months, sapping his energy. He'd been wounded, too. Boarding a chopper for a clean, cool hospital, he looked relieved. Who could blame him? We missed him. He'd been with the company since 1967. He'd fought in the A Shau Valley, Tet, and the relief of Khe Sanh. Our battalion, the 2nd of the 12th, was nearly wiped out helping Marines retake Hue. Three months after Tet, two months after our brigade relieved Marines at Khe Sanh, I arrived. Hoorah! The bad stuff was over, finis. The Cav, the First Team, had saved the jarheads' asses again. It'd be better now. The besieged outpost at Khe Sanh had threatened to emulate Dien Bien Phu's loss to the Viet Minh in 1954, when despite a heroic airborne rescue effort, France lost its outpost, soon afterward conceding defeat, and the country was partitioned. Historians say Hue was the war's turning point. If not Hue, then the inflection point was Khe Sanh's rescue. Which way the war turned at these crises depends on whether you buy the conventional wisdom—American public opinion soured on the war in 1968—or the revisionist view that post-Tet, U.S. forces confronted a crippled foe. We'd won, but didn't know it, because the defeatist news media didn't tell us!

Lt. Rapier's fey, dark view of military life had been as useful as extra bullets. Although he was entitled to a haunted thousand-yard stare (the walking-dead look that cartoonist Bill Mauldin and photographer Robert Capa captured in previous wars), Rapier functioned perfectly well. Suddenly, he was gone, though, leaving raw second lieutenants as company senior officers: another guy whose name I've expunged from memory, and me. Between us, we'd spent roughly seventy days in country. The other guy had a week of seniority on me. He became acting company commander. Phew.

On July 3 and 4, after the ambush killed Cloud, our company descended a ridgeline. Ground-pounders should send flankers to maximize frontal force, bringing as much firepower as possible to bear on potential enemies. We had too few men, and it was too hot to think straight. The jungle was too thick, so we walked slowly, in single file, down a ravine.

Rrrrrrppp. We hit a raggedy-ass ambush, a chance encounter, not a planned skirmish. Enemies simply saw us before we saw them, and they fired first. Fortunately, their fire, badly aimed, was not the sort of cruel, concentrated bursts that mark serious engagement. Apparently, we'd stumbled into equally surprised enemies.

Four platoon leaders awaited orders. The others were a staff sergeant, a four-striper, and two three-stripers, buck sergeants, both draftees who hadn't risen through the ranks in the traditional way. These instant noncoms had attended twelve weeks of leadership school before joining our children's crusade. They were known as "shake 'n' bakes" for America's miraculous chicken-cooking enhancement. As in most wars, adolescents did the fighting. We got no orders from our new leader. Minutes passed: that's an eternity if people are shooting at you, or worse, shooting at me. Delta Company stretched along the trail, squatting, trembling, eyes bugging. By osmosis, our point element spread itself into a short tee atop our immobile column. A throaty M-60 machine gun raked the valley before us.

Sergeant Rico Cololucci took command of 1st Platoon as I headed forward, hunched over. Rico had run the show just fine before I arrived. He was nineteen. Yes. Nineteen. The company's acting CO was twenty-three. He'd spent nineteen months in the Army. He was sitting behind the point element, immobile. His homely dark-rimmed plastic GI glasses and wide-eyed stare made him look befuddled. Perhaps he was. He was entitled. He wasn't a ring-knocking West Point grad: he was either OCS, like me, or worse, ROTC. Not that!

"What should we do, sir?" I asked. We'd suffered no casualties, but in a firefight, sitting men are fat targets.

"Well," he said. "Don't know, not for sure. What do you think?"

"What if I lead a squad up the slope, go east, then north, down that valley? Come from the side? See what's up? You know, flanking maneuver? Put more fire on 'em?" (Fire and movement are Infantry Tactics 101.)

"Okay," he said. I half-loped backwards, asking every other man after the point squad to join my berserker attack.

Asking no questions, five men accompanied me. Was I nervous? Well, I was ignoring a fundamental infantry rule by creating my own reconnoiter group. Adrenaline-soaked, I violated unit integrity as well as common sense. Yet acting was better than sitting, even if acting meant moving into a potential killing zone with strangers.

Scrambling through underbrush, my ad hoc crew climbed a little ridge and moved down, firing on descent. Green tracers were coming our way. We'd hit an observation post, a few men. Perhaps they'd radioed their plight. Probably not: our foes didn't carry much communications gear. Hurriedly our quintet set up an assault line. We fired a LAW (light antitank weapon—a wire-guided rocket) as well as a grenade launcher and M-16s. We tossed hand grenades, too.

Whoooosh! Something shot back.

Whamcrack! It exploded—close—too close to our lead guy, a big black dude from the 2nd Platoon. The Specialist Fourth Class was throwing a grenade at the bunker as a rocket charge blew into tiny, lethal shards. The hurler was as big as and strong as Bob Gibson, the fabulous Cardinals pitcher, and as vulnerable as Gibson as he fell from the mound after delivering heat. Something harder than a batted ball had come back his way.

I didn't know his name. We barely knew one another. Serving in different platoons, we'd had little contact before this moment joined us eternally. His nametag was embedded in his flesh along with his cotton fatigues. When I'd asked him to come along, he'd run forward, no questions. His reward for reflexive gallantry was to be shredded. Don't conjure up the surfing/snowboarding usage, shredding down the slopes or over the waves. My brave volunteer had been hamburgerized. Bloody tissue oozed from his forehead to his boots. B-40 rocket fragments had struck him with full force. How many? Two hundred? My ears were clanging as I walked to him, stunned. Pain shot up my shins. I crumpled.

The explosion had been so cataclysmic that I hadn't noticed shrapnel peppering my legs. No big deal. I was more shocked than hurt, yet the pain grew. I suppressed a yowl. The 3rd Platoon medic treated the brave Spec Four. A couple of minutes later, the 2nd Platoon medic lifted my right trouser. A thin, bloody stream squirted from my right calf. (This trick recurred later at the rear aid station: the battalion surgeon removed my bandage, sending blood like a water pistol across the tent. A befuddled medic got hit square in the face.)

I was bleeding, but Spec Four Whoever would die without urgent hospital care. Two more men had been hit, too. Back on the trail, a guy took a bullet. Our CO rallied, set up a defensive position, and sent a squad to reinforce us. Our Vietnamese Kit Carson scout yelled "*Chieu hoi*!" (Give up!) at whoever was in the bunker, now silent. The scout, a former NVA infantryman, had *chieu-hoi*ed himself in 1967, leaving the Communist side for better pay and a chance to see his South Vietnamese family without being arrested and tortured by our side. Now he faced the obverse problem.

"Okay," someone answered in weak Vietnamese.

We extricated an NVA soldier from the hole. His mates were dead. Three men, two dead—just three men all told—had caused this havoc. The survivor was badly wounded. Desperately, he had fired the B-40 rocket just as he was going down with a bullet through the thigh. (In an enclosed bunker, the rocket's back blast can kill.) His femoral artery gushed bright red. He was going into shock. Our medic applied a tourniquet. He loosened it now and then to prevent our prisoner from losing his leg.

When the shaking, skinny, gray-white, lucky man was stable, we gave him a cigarette. He puffed greedily. Nothing like American nicotine for severely wounded prisoners, World War II movies had taught us. After offering the gift, our scout pressed for information. No torture: we used kindness and medical care instead. It worked. "A battalion is up that ridge," our prisoner said. "They kill you."

After his gratuitous taunt, we told him to shut up and gave him no more excellent Marlboros. Four wounded Americans needed to be evacuated. However, the triple-canopy jungle, perhaps 150 feet high, didn't permit a helicopter landing. Clearing a suitable landing zone was out of the question. It was midafternoon: night would fall before we finished. Moreover, our forward position was intertwined with the enemy line.

Above the rain forest's tallest trees, a Huey dust-off helicopter hovered, but took gunfire. The pilot veered off and called gunships to suppress fire from the far ridgeline. Two sinister, sleek Huey Cobras swooped down, firing rockets and mini-cannons, pass after pass, at the far ridge. Another medevac ship arrived, hovered, and dropped a jungle penetrator, a tri-pronged seat like a small ship's anchor.

In the tiny clearing that the company had hewn from the jungle, I hopped onto the penetrator. Tracers kicked dirt and zipped by me. Confused, agitated, I noticed the heavy contraption had a seat belt. Weird: a seat belt on this thing was like donning a life vest before jumping into a vat of acid. I clicked the buckle anyway. Our guys signaled the crew chief: pull! I rose. My boots were inches from the ground when the penetrator detached from the cable. The metal contraption and I crashed to the soft jungle floor. Ascending, the connecting ring smacked my head, knocking me dizzier.

The crew chief sent the cable back down. Able-bodied men reattached the seat. Up I went, secure this time, if being pulled upward through thick foliage to a thinner, higher layer, under a fat, noisy target, can make one somehow safe. Centrifugal force sent me spinning. Fire zoomed by and pinged off the bird. Going up, I fired my rifle to the north—*brrrp, brrrp, brrrp.* I was woozy and my aim was lousy. NVA shot back. A few meters from the chopper's skids, a bullet slammed into my right thigh.

"Do I get *two* Purple Hearts?" I asked as the crew chief pulled me in. He grunted, yanked the rifle from my sweaty hands, hung a litter from the cable (to be wrapped around our Spec Four), and lowered the hoist. We waited in our spinning "Shoot Me" carnival booth for an eternity, or maybe five minutes, until the chief winched the poor shredded bastard up, dropped the penetrator again for the last two wounded men, retrieved them in one pass, and signaled "go" to the pilots by whirling his right hand in a manic circle.

The pilots had been trying to clip the tippy-tops of surrounding leaves to present the smallest possible target. Each time a new weight was attached to the hoist, they'd nudged their hand toggles and foot paddles, moving mere micrometers, maintaining altitude as the load increased and more fire came our way. After dropping us off, the ship would buzz off and rescue men who were bleeding elsewhere, again, going to hot landing zones time and again, again, and again, until they were shot down or DEROSed. (Went home . . . date of effective return from overseas.) All helicopter pilots were courageous kids, but flying unarmed, protected only by a red cross, medevac pilots were stupendously brave and two-thirds nuts. Inside the chopper, the din was akin to being next to a subwoofer at a Rolling Stones concert while Hell's Angels set off cherry bombs. The deck was slippery with blood and gore. As we zoomed away, I pressed the chief about my medal status, pointing to my holes.

Two hearts? Three? Exasperated, he said: "All wounds in one action, sir, that's just one heart. Don't make no never-mind how many holes you got. Tough shit, sir. Sit down, keep calm, and shut the fuck up. Please, sir."

This may not have been the first time he'd been presented with this inane question, but this was the first time I'd been wounded, and arguably the second, too.

5.

Nervous, Frowsy Nancy

In mid-August 1968, my company is defending a hard-baked, dowdy brown knob, Fire Base Nancy. Our encampments bear the names of commanders' wives or sweethearts. Cheery pep-girl descriptors are incongruous with our unlovely surroundings. (Marines used more apt terms, like "Rockpile.") Nancy was a big, sprawling old girl who might better have been called Brunnhilde. Slatternly Nancy should have accommodated a battalion. In the real world, three hundred bone-tired men defended old Nance.

Heat scorched us. We slept badly. Mosquitoes assailed us. You could douse yourself in pure DEET (100 percent insect repellent; technically, N,N-Diethyl-meta-toluamide)—reeking worse than a French courtier soaked in cheap cologne—but it didn't matter. Skeeters found you. You awakened with a puffy, misshapen face. No matter how hot the night, you swaddled in a jungle blanket to gain the scant protection afforded by its smelly poly-fabric.

Bursts of combat had afflicted Delta Company. Every other

day, it seemed, we lost someone, or two, to ambush, booby trap, illness, or some other catastrophe. We'd pile into Hueys, jump off in territory that promised a higher quotient of bad guys per square hectare, patrol and hump through boonies. The First Cavalry had so many helicopters that we could make combat assaults into interesting places every few days. Consequently, we were more likely than ground-bound infantry or even vaunted Marines to "make contact"—an anodyne term for getting our asses blown off. Repeatedly. Long-range reconnaissance patrols and SEALs were in greater danger, but not paratroopers, who are supposed to float on parachutes from planes—doing so in the jungle would have been suicide. The Frogs had reinforced Dien Bien Phu's scoured, bleak hills with paratroopers. We know how that worked out. The 101st Airborne, the Screaming Eagles, became air-mobile, like us, ignominiously, straight-legs with jump badges and boots.

On Nancy, our under-strength infantry company joined an undermanned company of artillerymen and a shrunken engineer company in guarding an oblong perimeter a couple of kilometers around. Our sparse force—half as many as Nancy was meant to hold—stretched as loosely as the spindly concertina coils that surrounded us in turn. Immediately to the south was an abandoned tea plantation. Below, southeast, a curving, muddy river. East was a village. West—who knew? Cared? Not us. We could see the Gulf of Tonkin: shimmering sea and sky blended in humid waves. Over there, west, unwatched, the Central Highlands were a thousand shades of green, freaking scary green.

Our fire base, a barren mesa, had been bulldozed. Sandbagged bunkers and concertina wire didn't improve the view, nor provide protection, we'd learn. We had reached Nancy after assaulting undefended rolling hills to the north, in No Man's Land, free-fire country, where we were pelted by rain seeping through our shelter halves for twenty-four hours. We encountered only intrepid women, gathering brush for cooking. We didn't shoot them, guessing right for once. Then, when rain cleared, we trekked and bushwhacked through withering heat. As we approached Nancy, our radiotelephone operator (RTO), a Baltimorean hugging a heavy slapover laden by spare batteries, said, "I'm done, sir," dropped his radio, and slumped to the ground. He was no longer sweating, a bad sign: heatstroke, inbound. I added his PRC-25 radio to my load. I was sweating like a wrestler, a good thing.

After he finished a rubbery canteen of Kool-Aid, the shamed RTO teetered to his feet, regained composure, and grabbed the radio back, cursing God, the Army, and me.

Helicopters landed on Nancy at unpredictable intervals. Rotors kicked up pebbles, dirt, and rocks, pelting us with debris in rapid-fire ka-chunks. Dust devils swirled as the choppers departed. When the air cleared, looking into the distance, we couldn't see our enemies. They saw us. How could they not? We were a third-world version of Teterboro Airport. On dusty, sun-cured terrain like Nancy, each bunker should be twenty-five meters (thirty yards) from its neighbors. By necessity, Nancy's bunkers were fifty meters away. Moreover, a unit commander, even a lowly platoon leader, should be behind the line his men form so he can direct or confuse them quickly. By necessity, however, my command bunker was on line. All our twenty-some men had to fight, even me. Fifty meters is one-half a football field. At night, stealthy people can crawl between these bunkers.

After haphazardly patrolling near the Street Without Joy, aka Highway One, to the east, staying on Nancy for a few days was a reward for that humping. Easy duty, Nancy promised. Showers (upended blivets—rubbery bags, warmed by the sun). Hot chow! A canvas mess hall! Wood floors! Latrines! Every other day, the poop that idly fermented in 55-gallon steel drums (cut in two) was burned by a sad-sack work detail.

Shitter-burners used foo gas as an accelerant: jellied jet fuel was abundant. Burning feces gave off a black, acrid shit-storm: foo-poo.

On Nancy, we sent desultory patrols, minded our manners, and caught a few day-lit Zs. We were lucky to get four hours a night in the boonies. Every man was alert for half the night. Even off guard, we were too nervous to fall asleep for hours after twilight. Often, the whole company went on alert ninety minutes before daybreak, when NVA liked to attack, thus neutralizing our air and artillery advantages.

Good times on Nancy! Soon enough, our stay stopped being comfy, in-country rest and recreation. The battalion CO ordered Delta Company's CO to investigate a clearing to the west. Aerial reconnaissance said fresh graves. We'd count bodies. Long ago, Delta Company had decided that counting bodies was a poor way to gauge war progress, no matter how much General Westmoreland admired our growing piles of corpses. We didn't yet know how the new boss, General Creighton Abrams, felt about counts. Later, we learned that Defense Secretary Robert McNamara, M.B.A., ex–Ford Motor Company executive, was losing faith in the importance of the rate at which our piles of their skulls* grew relative to their piles of our skulls. But the numbers still assured President Johnson's

* After World War II battles in Pacific hellholes like Iwo Jima, Okinawa, and Tarawa, Paul Fussell wrote that Marines and Army infantrymen had retrieved putrefying Japanese skulls and had washed, bleached, and packed them into duffel bags. Back home, the skulls became lurid souvenirs that had more cachet than German lugers or Iron Crosses. When *Harper's Magazine* published Fussell's essay, "Thank God for the Atomic Bomb," outraged Marines protested what they claimed were his "macabre fictions."

Then came a counterrevolution. Harper's was deluged with Kodachromes: four-color evidence that empty brain casements had indeed been collectibles. In recreation rooms from Levittown to Orange County, glistening white brainpans were shown propped up beside bowling trophies, bear skins, and antlers. So it goes, as former World War II POW Kurt Vonnegut would say.

restive nation that we were, ahem, "winning." The CO picked my platoon. Bored as always, I assigned myself to lead a squad. I'd rather move than sit. Bring entrenching tools, the CO said. If intelligence is right, you'll dig. We took our time, in no hurry. We'd smelled death. We hoped not to find anything as noxious as the rotting water buffalo we'd chanced upon earlier. The stench carried a kilometer and didn't improve on proximity.

We arrived at a clearing where vegetation had been shredded by a blizzard of shells. Scruffy patches of trampled dirt nearby looked like crude graves. We shoveled. It was a hundred degrees. Fetid air was sour. A foot down, the stink was horrid. We took off our T-shirts and covered our noses and mouths with grimy, wet cotton. Impossibly, the vileness increased anyway. Could something once human smell so foul? Three feet down, pay dirt: torn, slimy, putrid skeletons; the bodies of four North Vietnamese who'd been massacred by artillery. Strings of moldy flesh hung to their shattered bones. Red-starred belt buckles and remnants of dark green cloth revealed they were, or had been, NVA soldiers.

Specialist Noble (as I will call him) was a devout Seventh-day Adventist, an able soldier who grumbled only mildly when our work made him defile the sabbath. However, one hour of mortuary duty did something to this decent man that months of combat had failed to do. He went nuts. He stabbed a noisome skull with a bayonet: now he was Specialist Ghoul. He held his prize aloft. Grinning, he was a character from an eerie fifties comic book, *Tales from the Crypt*. The undone grunt returned to the base, brandishing his grisly trophy.* He'd snapped. Abracadabra didn't bring him back. Four kills landed on our slain-bad-guy pile.

That night, an explosion inside Nancy's perimeter marked the onset of a sad new phase in our glum, dumb war. Enlisted men across Vietnam were enjoying themselves less each passing day, virtually an impossible change, since we started with disgust, and abomination wasn't far from that on the loathing scale. Black Panthers hadn't infiltrated infantry units, but power handshakes with multiple dappings (each dap was a jazz riff, a handshake with soul) were spreading from rear bases into the jungles. On the front lines, our misery was too well shared among black, brown, white, and red men for racial grudges to fester. We had the same unprejudiced bugs, the same mortal worries. Ours was a class struggle, not a racial clash: our enlisted peasants revolted against the most obtuse members of the privileged officer class.

An enlisted engineer apparently wanted to eliminate the proximate source of his woes, his company commander. At the time, self-pitying followers struck surreptitiously at their lousy leaders by fragging them. After midnight, a fragmentation grenade rolled under the captain's cot in the enclosure housing engineer officers. Equally put-upon ground-pounders couldn't understand how lucky REMFs, rear-echelon motherfuckers who got to sleep in cots, walk on wood floors, take showers, and eat hot chow *every day,* could get so upset with a dipshit leader. Somebody should send these jerks to Vietnam, we agreed. In the boonies, bad officers were dispatched directly. Sometimes, an errant bullet struck an incompetent fool amid a firefight. Problem solved. Next?

The day after the captain was blown up, our mortar pit went *blam*! No thump of a mortar round leaving its tube. Just: *blam*! Three mortar platoon members writhe in brutal sunlight. Medics scramble. *Whaaaaa?*

For several days, a private in Robert McNamara's give-a-shit, breathe-and-you're-in Army had played the same grotesque joke. He pulled the pin of a hand grenade, making a distinctive ping, and rolled the grenade toward his mates. The first time he pulled this depraved stunt, his mates scattered, terrified. Nothing happened. He laughed. Before tossing his little present, he'd pulled out the detonator cylinder, rendering the grenade harmless. When his buddies regrouped, the dope showed them that the metal ball was hollow, harmless. Ha ha ha! His goggle-eyed mates pummeled him: "Never again, Bozo!" He played the same trick the next day; this time, his mates beat him harder. The third day he pulled his idiotic stunt, his mates flinched, sighed, muttered, and kept eating. They wouldn't fall for the lame gag again; but this time, he'd forgotten to pull the rod.

Prone and trembling on the pit's rim, men didn't look hurt. American grenades don't render flesh as gruesomely as do artillery, claymore mines, or tumbling AK-47 bullets. Each fragmentation grenade expels six hundred tiny wire splinters. If a grenade lands on you, flechettes can rip off your arm. More likely, if it lands close, they'll kill slowly by driving deep into viscera, causing internal bleeding. A grenade is diabolical because it doesn't kill outright: it requires uninjured men to help victims, demobilizing whole units. The wounded men moaned. One died en route to Chu Lai, another died in the MASH unit, fratricides, plain and simple. The third and fourth guys didn't return.

So it went again and again. If they didn't kill us, we killed one another. Friendly fire, accidents, and stupidity caused a third of U.S. casualties. Collateral damage, we call it now when ordnance falls where it shouldn't and hits unintended victims. "FF": shorthand, a sterile euphemism, for slaughter and gore.

"What should we do with this dumb cluck?" Our new CO, a proper captain, thank goodness, posed a rhetorical question. "I'll court-martial him," the CO said, "unless you have a better punishment."

After ten weeks in country, by default, I was the tenured company officer, not its most senior. I had status as a counselor, not a decision maker. The perp was just a kid, and a dope. He sat forlorn, dull eyes glazed, alone with self-centered, incoherent thoughts. His life would never be the same, I hoped, nor should it be.

Don't court-martial him, I said. You send him to Long Binh Prison, he goes on trial, we send witnesses, lose manpower. The court finds him guilty. He goes to Fort Leavenworth and serves ten years for manslaughter. He's in Kansas! We aren't. He has a toilet; we don't. (We have the runs in the bushes.) He can exercise and watch TV, if he behaves. Then he gets a dishonorable discharge. B.F.D. He's free.

No, keep him here. Make him live with us. Every cherry will hear his pathetic story the day he jumps off the chopper. Give him the worst duty you can think of—walking point, carrying the base plate. Serves him right. Make him burn our shitters when we're lucky enough to have them. Maybe he'll get shot. Maybe he'll die. Who cares? That works for me.

My solution appealed to the CO. After all, one military punishment was closed to us: we couldn't send him to Vietnam.

6.

What Crawls on Its Belly and Blows Us All Up?

Late the next night, guys in the bunker on our left, to the north, heard noises. Radio-whispering, they said that tin cans hanging on concertina wire were tinkling. The night was windless. What to do?

These men weren't our sharpest bayonets. "Their shit is weak," Doc Froemming said, dismissing alarums. "They're flaky."

Moreover, they might have taken a bottle into the bunker. I'd seen one of them furtively heft what looked like a fifth. I should have investigated, but ignored the non–Government Issue container. Looking the other way was a mistake. However, I was swigging some contraband, too. Emulating Jimmy Capps's North Carolina kin, who sent him mountain moonshine in detergent bottles, Kit's kindly Grammy had emptied a plastic shampoo container, refilled it with eight ounces of Scotch, and mailed it to me. I could stand one solitary, soapy gulp per night (one part White Rain to ten parts Dewars), but I didn't feel like throwing stones at my neighbors. After all, we were in the rear. Other men had drunk their ration, two warm, watered-down GI beers. What the hell. We baked inside an airless smokehouse as big as Indochina. Our nerves were frazzled, parboiled. Anyway, things heard in the pitchy night proved inconsequential in the morning. "I got movement," a fraidy-cat would whisper. Sometimes rabbits got under the wires. Dislocated from the nearby village, dogs or pigs scurried about, too small to set off mines but big enough to rattle cans. Nonetheless, our muddled brains stayed wary.

Nothing happened. We told ourselves that there'd been no noise. We stood down at midnight, starting regular shifts, getting three hours of sleep in quick slices. One man was alert in every hole. Others slept. In a base camp, three or four men shared watch, not a solitary, exhausted SOB who wanted to kill you each time you awakened him (as you wanted to kill him).

At 2:00 A.M. or so, *crump, crump, crump, crump, crump.** Incoming mortar shells. Four, five tubes. One barrage rolled into another.

When an artillery shell drops nearby, it's a truck crash—BALOOOM!—huge, apocalyptic; but the NVA had no artillery: some consolation. Occasionally, our own howitzers misfired. Friendly fire is as deadly as enemy fire. Howitzer shells come unseen. Sixteen-inch shells from the battleship *New Jersey,* a ton apiece, rumble like an elevated locomotive before striking far away. A battleship barrage is a fifty-car freight train passing over an iron bridge. Mortar rounds are different.

They don't whistle, for one thing. *Ssshheeww . . . thud!*

* Years after I returned to the Land of the Big Post Exchange—you candy-ass REMFs call it "America"—backfires would make me panic, seek cover. At the gala opening of Disney World's Epcot Center, a boondoggle for media executives and their families, a colossal fireworks display rendered me a knee-walking, hollow-chested, backflashing cipher. People around me, especially kids, cheered in awe, bepixillated and Disnified forever. Not me. I thought I was going to die. Again.

Mortar shells fall straight down on you before you hear them, except you can detect the vacuuming *thunk* a round makes as it starts its arc up, before coming down, toward you. It's not that big a deal, you tell yourself . . . until it is.

Mortar shells explode all around us. We're singletons, pairs, trios. Fuck the company. Fuck the Army. Fuck the world. Under attack, your zone of comprehension shrinks to the envelope provided by your precious thin skin. If you make an effort, you may consider the hides of the men closest to you: inextricably, your well-being is interconnected. Anyone you can't see is of no consequence.

Before night had fallen, I'd sent our newest guys to contrive a listening post (LP) below our line across from a bend in the river, where attack was most likely to come. PFCs Cumbry and Hartry, both new guys, both African American, passed their last night on earth hearing the lulling sound of a slow-rolling river lapping a few meters away. Shells blew off their legs. Bleeding to death, they passed their last moments in acute agony. After dawn, when our mop-up squad reached them, they were long gone. (Specialist Noble came to my post in midmorning, carrying a dismembered leg. He asked: "Should I stick this in its own body bag, sir? The thing is, neither of those guys has legs. I don't rightly know who this one belongs to. They're both black guys. Hartry was lighter, but I can't tell from the color. What's left is all bruised and bloody."

This predicament would befall me an eternity from now, merciful hours after the ghastly night. Right now. Now, the LP was of no use: nonfunctional, bypassed. We fixed on our plight. Shadowy bad guys skittered around. Specters had voices. Un-American chatter behind us! Excited Vietnamese voices: enemies to the rear, enemies everywhere. Rounds landed in the plantation. Was this when the shell landed on poor FNGs Cumbry and Hartry?

When the attack began, I was taking a leak, sleepily sprinkling a stubby tea plant a few meters from our hole. Fortuitously, I wasn't in a bunker, unlike almost all the other Americans. Before the mortars started falling, a unit of North Vietnamese sappers had infiltrated our lines. The guys who'd heard movement proved to be right. Dead right. The sole uninjured survivor in our neighboring bunker would be bonkers the next morning: babbling, lost. We dusted him off with bleeding men, though he was unscratched. For his sake, I hope that Specialist B. was only temporarily nuts. Flipped-out and gibbering, he was of no use.

The attacks were aimed at 1st Platoon, us, our overextended line. The river and village drew strategic arrows through our tired force. Deftly, gingerly, sappers—demolition experts—cut our booby traps and crept beneath the C-ration cans. Loaded with pebbles, a couple jangled. When the barrage lifted, the sappers rose on cue and pelted our bunkers with dynamite. How many? Fifty? A hundred? No way of knowing. Enough. Too many.

Sappers use diabolically simple plans whose success depends on surprise and grim willpower. The NVA's elite forces were scrappy counterparts to our Special Forces and SEALs. We duck and hide, a sensible reaction to a mortar attack. However, sappers want us to fear only mortars. As we cower, hugging the hard earth, they toss satchel charges inside our sandbagged bunkers. Small, square blocks of TNT daze or kill men squatting in packed earthen enclosures, making havoc in our dirt boxes. A bunker roughly five feet deep, eight feet long, and four feet wide makes a fine coffin. Charges kill with concussive force. When a charge goes off inside a bunker, and you're in that claustrophobic space, concussion turns your brain to mush. You cook, instant mental oatmeal. Your skull cracks from internal pressure. You hemorrhage from your ears and nose, your lungs fill, and you gurgle to death.

We think we're taking more mortars. Each blast is too loud

for discrimination. When an explosion is a hundred meters away, too far to hurt, it's too close. Your teeth rattle. You can't think. When something blows up mere feet from your tender corpus, the sensation is indescribable.*

Leaning over, presenting a small target, then hunkering over, scurrying, I try to detect a pattern, a rhythm that might tell me whether it's safer to stay in the open or seek shelter. I seek an omen. Anything. Please. Standing in a cacophony I feel more than hear—in my chest, feet, fingertips, guts, scalp, and bones—I'm dazed, transfixed. I might be standing on a barge afloat on the East River on Independence Day. A devilish orchestra with no strings, winds, or brass is playing an infernal, atonal Stravinsky concerto in a minor key. All we hear is the percussion section. Timpani, bass drums, cymbals, snares, and god-awful feedback swallow us, whole. No New York Philharmonic, it's Lucifer's music.

Shells land on a ragged line along our defensive barrier. (Fake Hollywood battles create more fire and light but less noise than reality. Military ordnance produces modest, fleeting balls of fire and some smoke. Mainly, they strew dirt, making tiny volcanoes. *Private Ryan* got this right.) As special effects go, modern munitions disappoint. Getting caught in a mortar barrage, however, is like holding fireworks in your hands,

* As they made their way down the Trail, North Vietnamese soldiers regularly came under lethal storms called Rolling Thunder—B-52 strikes that flattened whole acres at once. How did North Vietnamese soldiers stay sane—if they survived the humongous bombs? Imagine the brain-boggling, spirit-numbing, lung-sucking sensation of earth erupting around, under, and inside your sweet body. Massive bombs drive into the ground, ignite, and overturn tons of dirt, trees, and plants, pulverizing ground, vegetation, and flesh, creating a miasma, a bloody red-green mist of human tissue and chlorophyll. For cubic acres around the point of impact, oxygen is sucked away. Everything alive is torched.

In *The Sorrow of War,* Bao Dinh, a North Vietnamese veteran, described the aftermath of a B-52 strike. Bombs produced a hideous storm, "a rain of arms and legs."

pockets, and between your gnashing teeth. You don't see: you feel.

Something loops toward the bunker I'd vacated. In the strobelike half-light, it looks like a big dog treat. Satchel charges* are dynamite blocks tightly wrapped in a bamboo casing—a charge weighs about a pound. Tracing the charge's faint arc backwards, I throw a grenade where I think they might be, *whammo,* and race to our bunker.

They throw another charge. *Wham.* Me, too. *Wham.* Back atcha, Giap. Another one from them. *Wham.* This charge goes off beside our bunker.

At the moment of impact, Doc Froemming is peering over the bunker's lip. Debris and pebbles blow into his eyes. We're all stunned. The charge blows out my right eardrum and dazes the other two men huddling inside. An engineer "filler" from the construction company, one of the men beefing up our emaciated infantry line, is reduced to a quivering homunculus. Even rock-steady Jimmy Capps is stunned. Then the big North Carolinian gets up and fires his M-60 at the peninsula across the river. Firing at sappers behind us would imperil our rear echelon. Instinctively, we hope to repel a potential ground attack that might penetrate holes in our lines made by the sappers. Jimmy crams a new clip into the chamber, chomps a chaw of tobacco, and keeps going.

Doc, blind, yells over the radio: "Help us! We're being overrun!" Yet the satchel charges aren't coming anymore. At least one of my grenades found its target. Perhaps all three worked cumulatively. Who knows? I have a good arm, yet I wasn't aiming or throwing far, just guessing and getting lucky.

* They weren't sturdy leather suitcases, literal "satchels," a term dating to bags that limeys—no, wrong, limeys are British sailors: I mean Tommies—heaved into Jerry's machine gun nests in the First World War. (And vice versa.)

Aping Capps, I aim my snub-nosed AR-15 at the isthmus across the river. My rifle jams. The notoriously weak magazine spring fails even though I'd loaded it with only sixteen rounds, four less than its supposed maximum, as a precaution. A round lodges between clip and chamber, turning the automatic weapon into a flimsy club. I pick up an M-79 grenade launcher and pump ten, fifteen, twenty rounds into the peninsula that Capps is lighting with tracers. The giant shotgun propels a shell that's roughly three times the size of a 12-gauge slug. Moreover, each slug is an explosive grenade.

Overhead, white phosphorus stars drop earthward, dangling from parachutes. In the strange light their man-made firmament creates, my grenade arcs up. I can see it! I lose it as it loops down. *Crash!* There! Shells explode satisfyingly, but we can't see anybody. The sappers came from our front but exited on our west flank, we learn later.

Puff the Magic Dragon, a twin-engine C-47, circles overhead, firing stupendous cannons, thrilling us, but doing little else. At daybreak, three sapper bodies lie twenty meters behind our hole. They aren't torn like their shattered comrades we'd disinterred in the boonies. Like our forlorn mortar men, these slender kids are riddled with tiny wounds. Each steel chink, roughly a quarter-inch in size, penetrates body cavities, doing little visible carnage, but lethal nonetheless.

Because I'd sounded cooler on the radio than I was, our battalion commander put me in for a Silver Star. Doc Froemming had been my contrast gainer. Of course, his eyes peppered, bleeding, Doc had reason to be scared. The colonel is glad the sappers are dead, dead, deader than doornails. Our bad night might have been worse. His citation won't be crisp enough, however, and he'll omit the clichés required for high awards, like "above and beyond the call of duty" and "with reckless disregard for his personal safety." My prize will be downgraded to a Bronze Star with V device. I pretend not to care, but a Silver Star is a real medal in a time of gross award inflation.

Medals are strangely compelling swatches of cloth and metal. Many good Germans died happily after the Kaiser, and then Hitler, pinned Iron Crosses* to their loden coats. George Washington and Queen Victoria knew the mystical powers of cheap ribbons. Napoleon proved that soldiers who pretend to disdain pretty baubles nonetheless fight recklessly for them (and to avoid disapproval from *les autres Poilus de la Guerre*).

My busted eardrum qualified me for my second, or third, Purple Heart. I never got the actual medal, just the authorization in my paperwork. So many men were being wounded—three hundred thousand—that medals never reached us. But what about our dead enemies, young men whose deaths made my medal possible? Do I feel some sort of eternal connection to them, there for the grace of God, et cetera? Hell, no. I've never cared what the sappers' surviving families thought, either, except when feigning empathy, crying crocodile tears, trying to simulate someone with normal feelings. Returning to the States, I brought a souvenir from a Conex container back on LZ Jane, another gouged hill, our brigade base camp. I carried

* In World War I, German soldier Ernst Jünger spent four years on the western front battling the British, whom he admired, and the French, whom he did not. He won the Iron Cross but prized a simpler honor. In *Storm of Steel,* Jünger describes his last, worst wound: "I amused myself once during the monotonous hours on my back by counting the number of times I'd been hit. I found, in all, fourteen times: six by rifle bullets, once by a shrapnel bullet, three times by bomb splinters, once by shell splinter, and twice by splinters of rifle bullets. Counting the ins and outs, this made precisely twenty punctures, so that I might confidently . . . take my place in every warlike circle. Certainly I could assert my claim to belong to one order, at least: that of the gold wound-stripes . . . the gold was only yellow-lacquered metal. Yet I must confess I had it sewn on my coat with pleasure, for if doctors and professors, for all their correctness, do not look askance upon the stamp of an official title, why should a soldier refuse a visible sign of his gallantry?"

a green NVA pith helmet. Its owner had delicately carved his name into the leather liner with exquisite dexterity and incongruous tenderness: he'd etched a tiny palm tree, too.*

Our fire base lost fifty-four men that night, news reports say. I remember fewer casualties. Odd: usually memory exaggerates, seldom does it minimize. One of our dead men was a guitarist with an ironic turn of mind. Hours before the attack, he'd serenaded us with a ditty by Country Joe and the Fish:

Well, it's one, two, three
What're we fighting for?
Don't ask me I don't give a damn . . .

Day broke lethargically. The sun rose grudgingly, a leaden yellow balloon. Usually, it popped up like a helium-filled clown, dazzling us with its instant fire. What was left of our insomniac platoon patrolled, finding dozens of NVA bodies and blood trails. We gingerly investigated the village through which we thought the attack had been staged, and threw grenades in suspicious-looking bomb shelters. We found no enemies: not even a bloody bandage.

Terrified villagers caught between combatants had fled their huts. Some ran west. They said that retreating sappers had carried away perhaps sixty casualties. Three companies of NVA infantry were staged around the village, they said, awaiting a signal—whistles and bugles?—that our line had been

* I treasured that pitiful helmet more than my medals, the two I got, and several that never came, including a Vietnamese Cross of Gallantry and an Air Medal. A Mayflower moving man stole the helmet in 1983. Our belongings, heading from Texas to Massachusetts, were stuck in transit. That hot summer, the trailer holding our belongings was parked in Tennessee. As Kit, Cassie, and I cooled our heels on the Jersey Shore and other places, our canned goods cooked and exploded. Nonperishable stuff (like the helmet and a South Vietnamese flag that I'd retrieved from a desolate ville near My Lai) disappeared.

May that plundering moving-man dick rot in Nashville: die, you thieving cracker bastard, you ghoul.

breached. That signal might have started a massacre. We held the base.

In a few days, Delta Company would go elsewhere, always elsewhere. Motion is fundamental to Army tactics. Generals avoid making stationary targets of their forces. They take initiative. Armies move. In Vietnam, movement was a fetish. Hyperactivity suits me just fine, but because of our ceaseless disruptions the bulk of our army never knew more than a handful of the people we putatively defended, nor did we speak their language. We moved among them like wolf packs.

OPTIMAL EFFICIENCY: TWO, MAYBE THREE MONTHS IN COMBAT

In the wake of world war, military historians like General S.L.A. Marshall, whose initials, "Slam," gave him America's second-best fighting-writing acronym, began thinking about infantrymen. Previously, megathinkers concentrated on commanders. Historians surveyed the grand sweep of battle, looking down from the general's high ground and the admiral's bridge. Grunts in trenches and sailors below decks were inconsequential. In the second half of the twentieth century, Fernand Braudel's seminal work examined ordinary people. Military researchers sifted through after-action reports and read postconflict psychological assessments. They discovered that combat soldiers were at their most effective from two to four months after they started fighting. For the first month, a cherry doesn't know what he's doing. Time passes. He gathers confidence. His comrades begin to trust him. He trusts them. They weave themselves into a protective network. Metal flies, buddies bleed, and in time, carapaces that once protected them from considering their own mortality begin to crack. Under fire, not-quite-new soldiers slide into funks. After several months of combat, a grunt wants to survive. He's reluctant to take risks. Paradoxically, soldiers who go numb, trying to risk nothing, risk everything. Combat infantrymen who survived 240 days (or more) in a battle zone had a fifty-fifty shot at developing full-blown neurosis—also called combat fatigue, shell shock, and the heebie-jeebies. Today we call it post-traumatic stress, or a sane reaction to an insane situation.

After a year of shooting and being shot at, a combat soldier is toast. He's done.

7.

Big Blond Grunts and Little Brown Kids

In late August, Delta Company spent a week near the coast. We swam butt-naked in the sparkling China Sea. Nice duty. At night, we guarded a bridge; in daylight, we patrolled. As bridges go, ours wasn't much. However, most of the country's commercial traffic crept like ants along Highway One, a shriveled artery that stretched the four-hundred-mile length of the fraught, fidgety, bifurcated nation. Therefore, watching bridges like this dinky, rusted one was sound if tiresome duty. The iron span crossed the same languid waterway that flowed by FB Nancy. Two lanes merged on the bridge's rusting girders. The bridge's disintegrating boards supported a whimsical vehicular hodgepodge, a squawking, third-world mobile feast, ingenuity propelled by desperation: Citroëns, Simcas, and Renaults, microcars, motorcycles and scooters, oxcarts, exotic wheeled and foot traffic. Lambretta scooter passengers held chicken crates. Feathers flew. Cacophonous traffic streamed, beeped, squeaked, chirped, and squealed. Impossibly, Honda cycles bore two people and a driver. Three-wheeled trucks were crammed with geese, ducks, and pigs. Minibuses overflowed. Water buffalo lumbered, dragging carts. Old women cantered unsteadily, cloth strips tied around their foreheads supporting their loads. Americans drove jeeps and armored personnel carriers. Vietnamese soldiers rode in trucks.

Years of sabotage pocked the packed earth and broken asphalt surface with a zillion potholes. Highway One, such as it was, was vital to the Vietnamese economy, such as it was. An occasional mine was buried under the road. "Highway One" sounds, well, streamlined, but looking at it didn't remind you of an interstate highway. You conjured seventeenth-century Russian goat tracks.

During the fifties, main-force Viet Minh battalions had ambushed French armored cavalry on this disconsolate road. The French called this stretch La Rue Sans Joie, "the Street Without Joy." Thirty-some years after the Frogs skedaddled, Delta Company defended a bridge on the joyless road. A detachment of South Vietnamese soldiers was encamped in concrete forts on both sides of the bridge. These curious structures dated to the French era. Defenders gazed through narrow horizontal slits in round watchtowers. Inside these ugly taupe pillboxes, lookouts peered suspiciously at the surrounding river, road, and paddies. To the east, low dunes hid the South China Sea.

Inside, duty was good, I guess, if you weren't claustrophobic and if you didn't mind rats, mold, and centipedes. At least you weren't slogging through rice paddies, setting off booby traps, inviting ambush. Squatting in concrete dungeons,* you demanded that the enemy think before attacking.

*These pillboxes were miniature versions of the massive turrets that lined the grandiose Maginot Line. After World War I, to deter the Germans, L'Ancienne Régime de la France sank steel and concrete battleships into the rich earth of their eastern flank. From Belgium south, every few miles, a fort hunkered, connected to neighboring forts by tunnels. Long before the Vietnamese learned to

Our Indochinese-Gallic forts were stationary targets that attracted rockets and mortars at random intervals. Americans stayed clear. We preferred being drenched and getting foot fungus. Our bunkers were well-sandbagged sinkholes. Personally, I was glad not to be in a gloomy, mildewed tomb. We roving cowboys preferred GI fighting holes, even if they leaked like sieves. We gotta move. We could hop out and scatter. Bunkers weren't sanctuaries anyway, we'd learned. At least we didn't have to dig new holes every night, nor did we awaken with reddish-brown grime ground into our fatigues. We did fret that timid SVN troopers would forget we were on their side.

Our company line stretched up the river, encircling our 105mm howitzer battery. We defended Red Legged artillerymen. They defended us. Symbiosis. Interlocking fire. Reassuringly, in the event of a ground attack, they would fire decapitating canisters. Our modern cannons delimbed assailants, much as in the Civil War cannoneers wearing the Zouaves' red pantaloons fired vicious grapeshot.

Company headquarters was an abandoned Buddhist temple missing half its roof tiles. The captain (our third CO in seventy days, and a real live captain at last) sat below the altar near an old pyre of burnt joss sticks. With luck, especially if a monsoon swept by, we'd stay here awhile.

On our first night, our men saw movement near the village abutting our southern flank. The enemy used darkness as cover, so a curfew was in force. All activity between dusk and dawn

---

burrow from their Gallic overseers, Frenchmen used their coal-mining skills to produce engineering feats in Europe. Smaller casements armed with machine guns and pocket artillery pieces were sprinkled between the big ones. Landlocked dreadnoughts offered false confidence. France had created a beached version of the Spanish Armada. Although Panzers forced only a single French bunker to surrender (after its ventilation system failed), the Maginot Line failed to slow the Blitzkrieg. In 1940, German tanks trundled around the forts, rolled through unfortified Belgium (no fair!), and destroyed the French army piecemeal: bloody Huns.

was suspicious. Firing on movement, interdicting it, was okay. Sixty-second bursts of automatic fire, expending a couple of clips of ammo per man in glorious "magic minutes," soothed us but accomplished little besides expending cordite and littering the ground with spent cartridges. Meanwhile, our flashing muzzles had revealed our positions. Our fire warned our enemies, if any were out there, but didn't presage a serious tussle because no one fired back.

Our second evening beside the river, a gaggle of old men cautiously walked to our southern bunker waving handkerchiefs. They spoke our common patois, an amalgam of pidgin French, broken English, and Vietnamese. *Où est votre* commander? *Merci beaucoup!* America number one, *mais oui*? Spec Four Spider Randolph brought the duffers to my position. They bowed. I lacked Eastern manners, but I bowed stiffly, afraid my men would snicker at my affectation. The elders wore wispy beards and flip-flops, Ho Chi Minh sandals made from worn-out tires perhaps blown out during the motorized trek along the eponymous Trail. Bare feet were common, fine for traipsing in paddy muck or along dusty dirt roads.

"Come," they asked me. "*Allez avec nous. Di di.* Please. Be guest. *Parlez.* Okay?" They pointed to their village, fifty or sixty huts smooshed together. Sgt. Rico Cololucci was away on R&R. Our new platoon sergeant, Butch Dexter, a cheerful, thickset E-6, had been transferred to our chronically under-strength, shot-up outfit. Sun had bleached Butch's brush-cut hair white. Mine, too, had reverted to a sunburned facsimile of my towheaded boyhood self. We could have been poster boys for Aryan Youth after a Bavarian summer, circa September 1937. Every one of us was tanned. When Spider Randolph, a light-skinned African American, removed his T-shirt, he, too, revealed a deep tan line. His contrasting flesh tones amused our rednecks no end. "Lookit! Spider's been using Man-Tan," they cackled.

These skinny old villagers were so frail and careworn I

didn't think anything bad could befall us. After months in this tempestuous fever ward, this would be the first time I'd place myself at the mercy of Annamese natives, so I was nervous. Fewer than a hundred and fifty meters separated us from their village. The sun was falling fast, as it does in the tropics. The sky was rosy. Twilight was a wham, bam, thank-you-ma'am affair. As we approached the village, children ran from pinkish-hued huts and tagged behind their elders, who, too, had taken on a benign pastel cast. The kids looked at us shyly. Americans usually passed their village on clanking tanks, armored personnel carriers, or truck beds. Mechanized, implacable, we were robotic blurs, Caucasian/Negro/Hispanic blurs. When we dismounted, we were wary, and we discouraged kids from loitering near our lines. When bold enough to approach, Vietnamese kids begged for handouts or tried to sell us their sisters: "She number one bang, bang, GI! You see! Only six hundred piasters! Five dollah!" Ten-year-olds and their parents liked menthol cigarettes. Kids and wizened seniors alike puffed as if each drag might be their last, as indeed it might be. These exchanges didn't build international amity. We were too close, too big, too different, too much. We were exotic, dangerous zoo creatures.

These kids drew closer, drawing courage from one another, giggling. Would we bite? Yell? Shoot? When we didn't bare our teeth, show our talons, uncoil our tails, or fire, they came closer.

One bold youngster touched my arm and ran back to his friends. He survived. Another kid touched Sarge and lingered. A mob swarmed us, many small hands touching us at once. Softly stroking our Caucasian arms, their little mitts pawed gently. They tittered and cooed. *Oooooohhh. Hee hee heee. Ahhhhhhhh*. Delicately, their fingertips caressed our strange skin, calming us. They marveled at blond hairs set off by tans in high relief. I'm not hairy, but compared to the Vietnamese, I was a yeti. The hair of the Vietnamese was duochromatic. The children's hair was jet-black, and their elders' hair was gray. Save for coarse white whiskers of the oldest men, the Vietnamese had no body hair.

Tiny women, hair pulled into tight pigtails, looked sixteen or ninety, their skin ranging in hue from beige to bronze. Pale-skinned city women wore elegant long-sleeved, ankle-high dresses, *ao dai*s, and carried parasols to thwart sunshine, but rice farmers spent hours daily in a broiler, wearing heat-absorbing black pajama suits and thatched hats. Old women chewed betel nuts and smiled through mahogany-stained teeth. We were peculiar, hairy, and discolored. Even in what were to us high states of melanin, to them we were hirsute albinos.

Shooing the children away, the elders urged us to sit. We did, awkwardly, reluctantly. A Vietnamese peasant's home lacks divans and sofas. Elders squatted on their haunches and expected us to do the same. A typical American, even slenderized by combat, intestinal worms, C-rations, and fatigue is bulky and gristly with honking big calves, thighs, and glutei maximi. Squatting is hard. But when in Annam, do as the Annamese do: we lowered our substantial butts over our booted heels, and soon, the pain penetrated from legs to spine. Squatting requires both effort and balance.

We were rewarded for imitating them: four-ounce glasses of clear, strong rice whisky, one apiece. I'm guessing over 100 proof. We hadn't sipped hard stuff for weeks, just an infrequent 3.2% beer. Our tolerance was low. Stimulated, parched, our thirst came alive. The potent home brew hit hard. Fun. Offered another, we accepted greedily. Once we were properly softened up, relaxing, here was their entreaty, the gibbering polyglot translated by a twelve-year-old boy:

Not shoot us, please.
Especially at night.
Sometimes we go to fields, we make waste.
We fertilize paddies.

Still your friends.
We not harm you.
Don't shoot us.
Please.

We live in straw houses.
You shoot, you kill us.
So please.
We are not Viet Cong.
We loyal to South Vietnam.

Villagers throughout Vietnam contended with constantly changing American "defenders." Every week or so, a new trigger-happy American unit replaced the old guard. Anxious newcomers fired at phantoms. A few times, American bullets hit their huts. People had been hurt. Would we restrain ourselves? They poured our third glasses of whisky and drank with us. We warmed into boozy brotherhood. By now, every kid in the village had touched our weird skin and caressed our too-light hairs many times. We were just tame blond orangutans. Harmless gerbils crawled up our arms. Rice whisky seeped into our toes, fingers, and noses. We might have been back home, if our nieces and nephews had been more interested in us than in TV. We were drunk, soothed, and happy.

I said: Of course we will not shoot you. You are our friends, right? (I sought assurance.) Yes, they said, smiling. Tipsily, woozily, we offered thanks and farewells and reeled back to our line, looking back a few times just in case our new friends wanted to shoot us as we weaved home. A worse fear:

would our men mistake us for bad guys? Loudly, we slurred our passwords. Whew. Safe.

That crepuscular hour in that nameless village was the best time we'd spent in that forsaken land, Sarge agreed. The next day, the heavens opened. It rained for three days. Paddies flooded impressively, preparing winter rice. Our howitzers were almost underwater. We didn't shoot anyone for days. No proper attack could be mounted in a monsoon. Sopping, we were becalmed.

In 1971, a year before all remaining hundred thousand American ground forces finally left, the ARVN made an ambitious foray into Laos. An operation called Lam Son 719 was supported by fifteen American armored and infantry battalions. They spearheaded a path through Khe Sanh and northern South Vietnam. By congressional fiat, conventional U.S. forces couldn't enter Laos, Cambodia, Burma, North Vietnam, or China. Several ARVN divisions, including elite forces, crossed the border and interdicted NVA supply lines at the hub of Ho's trails.

ARVN Marines and Rangers held their ground in Laos for several days until the NVA rallied, routing them. Losses on both sides were roughly equal, but NVA soldiers had repelled the attack. Retreating in disarray, the ARVN ceded a huge chunk of Laotian and Vietnamese territory.

The American Military History Encyclopedia says that the Lam Son disaster further sullied the tainted notion of Vietnamization. American and SVN forces lost seven hundred helicopters. Seven hundred! One hundred were completely destroyed, the rest badly damaged. This wasn't just writing on the wall: it was etched in boulders visible from outer space that read ARVN LOSES.

8.

Two Sergeants—One Heroic, the Elder Not So Much

SERGEANT LIFELESS

An older guy, a gen-you-wine Army veteran, joined Stacked Deck in July. He was a lifer, as NCOs with retirement in mind were called—as if they'd sentenced themselves to the military version of San Quentin. This grizzled sergeant stopped by our unit for a couple of days on his way from Fort Knox to our rear echelon, traveling fast, fueled by prodigious incompetence. Drill Sgt. Useless was destined for a battalion supply job. Under duress, he developed sleeping sickness. When bullets whizzed, this ex–drill instructor, this pretend hard-ass, became a stone-cold narcoleptic, snoring, mouth open, falling into a coma. He fell asleep behind a burly banyan tree.

If Yossarian had learned how to sleep while his bomber flew into Axis flak, he might have resented World War II less. Anyway, a war zone is no place for a wrinkled thirty-five-year-old Kentuckian. Youth ruled in Nam as in few other wars except perhaps the Civil War, in which twenty-three-year-old boys like George Custer could become generals. But fortunately, Sergeant Useless Narcoleptic was gone.

RECKLESS, RARE RICO

As day broke the morning after the sapper attack, nineteen-year-old buck-sergeant Rico Collolucci led what was left of our enfeebled unit to repel attackers who might be lurking nearby. Rico had been acting 1st Platoon leader when I arrived. There was no better platoon sergeant of any age. A skinny kid from Boston, Rico emitted energy like helium leaking from a balloon. His voice squeaked. He wisecracked, fidgeted, and fussed, always in motion. He made me look calm by contrast, an effect I seldom achieve.

Slogging along dispiritedly behind the wire that had done such a crappy job of protecting us, we checked enemy bodies* to make sure they weren't playing possum, ready to spring up and frag us. Even our reddest-necked crackers and boys from the block knew the dead men were teenagers with untroubled, unlined faces: kids wearing scanty loincloths so that flapping cloth wouldn't tangle on wires. Their cheeks, foreheads, and bodies were daubed with charcoal to keep moonlight from reflecting. Retreating, the survivors dragged wounded men by tugging on bamboo straps that had been wrapped around their ankles before the attack. Blood spoors were everywhere.

Bamboo-cased satchel charges hung from the waistbands of the sappers I'd killed. They'd hoped to kill us, *di di mau* up the hill, wipe out the company command post, and attack the

* Occidentals have trouble telling Asian ages. Sometimes we fail to differentiate their sexes, too. We're Americanocentric. We knew black, white, Hispanic, and Native American. Asians looked very young or impossibly old. Koreans didn't look like Vietnamese: we could tell ROKs from ARVNs. Our Korean allies were bigger, for one thing, with broader cheekbones, and they were meaner, too.

battalion commander's hole farther back. In our bastardized Vietnamese, *di di mau* meant skedaddle, *cwoc a dau* meant "I'll kill you" (mispronounced as "I crocodile you"), *dink au dau* meant "you not right in head." "My sister beaucoup virgin!"—that you get without translation.

I couldn't understand Rico, who spoke impenetrable Bostonian. Platoon sergeants were supposed to be grizzled NCOs, E-4s or E-5s, lifers like Sleepy, the DI, men in their thirties at least. Rico was a year and a half removed from high school in Boston's Italian North End. Fuzzy-cheeked enlisted men called me "Old Man" without irony. They called him "Rico," not "Sarge."

Our enemies were tough, elusive, and all around. We touched one another with fire nearly every day: ambushes, mines, grenades, mortar, flare-ups, big rumbles. When we were lucky, we found them. Metal flew. People bled. In these random firefights, Rico demonstrated a gift. As shots sounded, Rico materialized, alighting like Warren Zevon's spectral Headless Thompson Gunner, his weapon blazing, rallying troops. He had an uncanny instinct for plugging holes. Don't misunderstand: Rico wasn't a calm machine or a methodical Terminator. As bullets zinged, he was a twitching mess trapped in his own myth. We expected him to act heroically: he was obligated. When people were getting hurt, his eyes widened but his body did the job. When it counted, he quelled his demons and soldiered on. We loved him.

No one faces death fearlessly. Fear accumulates as rapidly as a checking account empties after you lose your job. What you do with that fear is what counts. Rico was the Man. He led a counterattack on our eastern flank. I took the rest of the platoon south, slowly. Rico charged like a halfback. Chief's juju was a phantasm. Rico's karma worked. Somehow, he survived a year in the field. He was too fidgety to make a proper target.

9.

Shamming: Happy, Kinda Safe

After the sapper attack, I was medevaced to China Beach Navy Hospital. My new wound, a legitimate sham, was negligible. Hearing? Who needs two ears? I was gimpy, one-eared, and off-kilter like my old man. Inside the White Elephant, a naval officers' club in nearby Da Nang, were popcorn, beer, movies, and security. My inner ear and head buzzed and hummed: a low, staticky cranial speaker drowned out speech. Yet no pain! Badly injured men (Doc Froemming, the ground-up Spec Four, and Sergeant Schaefer, I hope) had been triaged to a Navy hospital ship, then to Japan, and home. We never heard from them. Grunts are lousy correspondents and we were always moving. A letter Kit sent me in July followed me from the Cav, to the hospital in Qui Nhon, back to the Cav, to China Beach, back to the Cav, to Advisory School, then to the wrong advisory team, and back to school, reaching the right team after I'd come home. It caught up to me in March 1969, at the Fort Dix officers' BOQ, six months after Kit had sent it.

My second reunion with clean sheets in six weeks! After

being strafed, ambushed, overrun, shelled, and wounded two and a half times, my second hospital stay was splendor indeed: showers, hot meals, fans. Bliss. Moreover, the cure for a perforated eardrum is laughably painless. An ear, nose, and throat specialist unraveled one of my fresh, hygienic Marlboros, emptied the tobacco, cut a small patch from the cigarette paper, and stuck the square over the torn membrane. He said: Cool it for a week. Well: all right! I was ambulatory. Aside from skin infections and a fungus covering my face, I was a shammer.

That was a grand week, except for the second afternoon. I was replenishing my depleted supply of Zs when a commotion awakened me. In the ward's far corner, an EM was ranting. "Motherfuckers!" he said. "Get back, you bastards!" Brandishing a big black pistol, the kid, whose cherubic face, wispy mustache, and pale complexion signified desk jockey, cook, bottle washer, held nurses at bay.

Weapons were banned in hospitals. How'd he smuggle this one in? A mystery. This kid had a mouth, a grudge, and a substance abuse problem. But combat had inured me to danger. This moron was sitting on clean cotton sheets for which he should have been thanking his stars, bars, and stripes. He made no sense. "Get away, bitch! I'll kill you," he told a supplicating nurse.

Someone walked up to the young man and calmly requested his pistol. Just like that, the kid shut up and handed over the pistol, butt end first, as you'd do on a target practice range. Unarmed, the kid bawled that no one understood him. He'd seen bad shit out there, he said. It had fucked him up. (Decades later, Zevon sang two spooky songs about the bad shit that had fucked him up. This kid was no pop singer, however.)

When the ward was quiet, a nurse thanked me for disarming the young man. Me? No. No way. Couldn't prove it by me. This out-of-body experience was no more connected to my festering, sunburned, hard-of-hearing self than it was to Saint Peter, Captain Kangaroo, Senator John Stennis, or George Custer's moldering corpse. After the kid was taken to the brig, I returned to my bed and fell asleep. When I awoke, I remembered the kid's terrible reign, but not how he'd been disarmed, nor by whom.

The nurse retold the story twice, thanking me. In her third telling, the incident came back: *bam*. I shook. How incredibly foolish! What a crazy jerk I'd become. I was another Rico—a wild-eyed would-be martyr, just asking for it, somehow surviving despite myself.

10.

Instead of Bursting Hearts with Bullets, Something New: Winning Minds

After humping the boonies with the crack First Cavalry Division, I was dispatched to language school to become an adviser. I had no choice. To prevent crafty field commanders from ridding themselves of duds and losers, general staff orders delineated a narrow Reduction in Force. Junior officers who'd been commissioned between May 15 and July 1 (that included me) were ordered to leave their American infantry units in order to attend Advisory School near Saigon. It was a military version of an *n*th name sample.

The idea was that by sensitizing young infantry leaders to Vietnamese mores, then integrating ourselves into Vietnamese units, we'd embody the new strategy to win the mulish minds of the people, pretending to let the "good" Vietnamese run their own damned war instead of exterminating them all higgledy-piggledy. After two weeks of instruction in language and culture—plenty!—I became an adviser to a South Vietnamese Regional Force Company in Binh Son District, Quang Ngai Province, I Corps. Sadly, Vietnamese food, music, and history were lost on me. I preferred Skippy peanut butter, Smucker's grape jam, and Wonder Bread to *nuoc mam,** fish, and rice.

I'd had sufficient opportunities to bang-bang mama-san, thanks, from which I learned that the nation's prostitutes weren't enamored of American manhood, perhaps because we gave them cash pittances and gonorrhea. They reciprocated by giving VD back to us. (Tag!) Reluctantly treating me for the venereal aftermath of a trip to a nearby combination tire repair shop, restaurant, and brothel (one-stop shopping), a Baptist doctor lectured me. Captain Brimstone said: Set a better example for your men.

My men? My problem had resulted from a ten-dollar present from my counterpart. I was winning hearts, minds, and body parts one STD at a time. Everyone who'd been with me that day had outranked me.

Our team advised 140 of the least-best soldiers in Asia. The Regional Force Company we helped was polyglot, partly comprised of men from Saigon. In the village-oriented countryside, these soldiers might have come from the moon. City soldiers had no connection to our rural hicks. They sneered at peasant farmers or were terrified by them. The most urbane RFs were quicker to shoot than nervous Americans were, which was plenty fast. RFs saw ambushes behind every paddy berm and hedgerow.

One October morning, our RF Company, Sergeant Thomas,

* To Vietnamese people, *nuoc mam,* pronounced "nook ma'am," is as sacred as Tabasco sauce is to Louisianans and soy sauce is to Japanese. To make it yourself, visit Alabama's Redneck Riviera in July on an especially hot day. Catch fish. Cut off the heads. Eat the fish. Toss the heads onto the beach. Let the remnants putrefy. When papa-san says "It's time!" a week later, scrape the crud together. Pour it into bottles. You're good. Sprinkle the juice on anything whose flavor you wish to extinguish. Beware. It makes chili peppers seem weak.

and I left the compound before dawn. Our mission was to search a string of enemy-controlled villages called the An Diems, colored pink on the district maps, meaning: Beware. It was surpassingly strange to be walking quietly through the town of Binh Son before daybreak like real soldiers. Rifles were at the ready, though safeties had been clicked on to prevent accidents. We passed down narrow alleys. Homes pressed tightly against bamboo fences demarcating each property. Inside the cramped hootches, families stirred. Women started their cooking fires for breakfast. Just a single kilometer west of our base camp, we passed from An Diem One across a rice paddy en route to An Diem Two, walking slowly, nervously. Our point element halted. They'd seen something suspicious in the predawn half-light.

And the lead squad fired on full automatic. We rushed forward to inspect our quarry: a middle-aged woman, shot several times, already dead. She'd broken curfew that morning, perhaps to get an early jump on hoeing her family plot. Like everyone in this torrid land, she wore black cotton pajamas, a uniform only by default. Going outside before sunrise had mortally endangered her. Our twitchy RFs thought she might be VC or NVA. Perhaps she'd carried supplies or messages. Women fought with the Communists, and fought well. Yet there were no weapons, papers, or maps near her lifeless body. She was alone. Her hands and bare feet were callused, soiled by simple toil.

That afternoon, a sniper shot at us as we approached An Diem Three. Our nervous premature firing had spoiled the only advantage we had: surprise. Now everyone in all the An Diems knew that a company of South Vietnamese soldiers was headed their way.

Pop. Wait a minute. *Pop*. Wait another minute or two. One man with a rifle was firing one badly aimed shot at a time at us, *ping, pow*. No pattern to his fire. No effect, either. He was harassing us. But the RF Company commander, a Roman Catholic captain who had no relatives or ancestors from Binh Son, and no combat experience either, was angry. He asked me to call in jets or artillery.

He shouted at his block-headed counterpart (me) to act now, fast, to bring pain, to make the earth erupt in that wonderful way Americans could. His twisted logic replicated that of an American officer down in the Mekong Delta, who'd said, "We had to destroy the village to save it." Nine words encapsulated our tactics.

But this was one sniper who was trying to get us to shoot back to give away our positions. And he was inside the same village we were. The rifleman hadn't hit anyone: not close. I said no. I wouldn't take half-baked orders from a man who looked sixteen and weighed 110 pounds. But as night fell, worrying, I asked the howitzer battery at Fire Base Bayonet to send a white phosphorus flare so we could see bad guys. A shell exploded. A willy peter round burned, brilliantly, fluttering down on a cute parachute.

The flare landed two hundred meters from our position atop a thatched hut's roof, setting ablaze a home that housed ten people, two dozen chickens, some pigs, and a few ducks. Outside, there was a water buffalo, tethered to a stake. The hootch burned down in a few minutes. No An Diem Volunteer Fire Company put out the blaze. The family that had lived inside these stick walls for generations helplessly cried and ran around the conflagration in circles, drawing buckets from the well. The buffalo survived. Not the hootch. I'd exercised restraint and good judgment, I thought. Disenfranchised villagers didn't know that. Mine was a Pyrrhic victory.

The night passed. The sniper was silent. We camped atop the hillock at the center of An Diem Three, awaiting first light. At daybreak, we were brewing coffee.

BALLOOOWEEE!! a gigantic explosion on the road below. A

155mm howitzer shell? Perhaps. Clods, chunks, and bits of stuff rained on us, an ugly storm. A deep, smoking crater obliterated the town's main thoroughfare. Torsos and body parts—seconds ago, whole boys and girls—were strewn about the hole and driven deep within it. Six kids had been killed instantly. Six survivors were badly torn and bleeding. Had unfortunate children been setting a booby trap for us? One they'd mishandled? Or was this a Commie mine meant to hit us as we moved west that the kids had stumbled upon? Each explanation was equally plausible. Were these kids guilty perps or unlucky innocents? Who knew? It didn't matter. They were shattered, harmless.

I visited their grieving parents, said I was sorry in English, as if they knew what I said—but I was sad, and that they understood. I called a dust-off and directed the medevac chopper to a small field near the crater.

A boy of eleven or twelve tugged at my sleeve. "Go away, kid," I said. Staff Sergeant Thomas, my buddy, my aide, popped a smoke grenade. I directed the pilots. We ignored the little bugger, who grew more insistent. Okay. What?

He pulled me to a clump of stumpy bushes and pointed at a claymore mine. The business side of the repurposed U.S. mine aimed its ball-bearing load where I'd been standing mere moments ago. Claymores send six hundred pellets in a quarter-moon arc. Propelled by plastic explosives, detonated by a trip wire or remote control, its steel hailstorm destroys life in a swath twenty-five meters away.

Gingerly, I traced the firing cord. It snaked along a hedgerow to a bunker with a slit lookout, an easy-off trapdoor, and a sod roof. The slit overlooked the path that ran from the village to the point where I'd been standing. Perhaps two traps, the big one in the road and this little one, had been designed to go off together as we moved west. Perhaps NVA would join the ambush. We might have been blown to bits if we'd embarked on our mission at first light.

Perhaps the RF captain was right to be frightened. I hugged the kid, who half-smiled and pulled from my embrace. He'd taken a risk. Somebody from the village could snitch to bad guys about what he'd done. This strange land offered both citizens and soldiers many ways to die.

11.

Our Personal Charm Offensive

Lieutenant Tom Warden, Sergeant Thomas, and I pocket-a-pocketed down Highway One in late October. Not that hot: only 90, 92. Our target was Quang Ngai, twenty kilometers south. A hundred thousand Vietnamese and a few American missionaries lived in the ramshackle provincial headquarters twenty-five klicks south, which boasted a hospital and an American PX stocked with Skippy peanut butter, Smucker's jam, Martini and Rossi's sweet vermouth, and plenty of beer for Sergeant Sullivan, our medic. The road was laced with quadrillions of potholes, and the vulnerable bridges, guarded by jumpy Vietnamese, were traversed by the customary parade including American armored personnel carriers, convoys, and tanks. The provincial capital, 250 miles north of the Mekong, was light-years from Saigon.

We approached a jerry-rigged pontoon bridge under a blown iron bridge. Civilians with a hundred years to finish were doing the repairs. Sergeant Thomas and I wove through the procession: buffalo carts; teeny trucks loaded with rice, vegetables, squawking birds, and squealing pigs; Honda, Kawasaki, and Yamaha cycles; teensy Simcas and Renaults. At the temporary one-way bridge, an old dude was pushing his aged Citroën crammed with produce, furniture, and chicken crates strapped to the roof. As he pushed, an American military policeman screamed at him and threatened him. South Vietnamese policemen watched. The engine had overheated, but the geezer hoped to get the jam-packed car down the ramp and up the far side.

Gravity didn't help. The old man and his passenger (grandson? nephew?) shoved uphill. Wielding a *choggie* stick, the MP spurred them on: "*Di di mau!*" ("Move, now!")—"*Allez vous!*"—"Merde!"—and "Fuck you!" Viet policemen looked on silently.

The MP screamed again, slowly.* Each sarcastic syllable belonged on an entrenching tool.

"Move, mother . . . fucker! Move . . . or . . . I'll . . . shove . . . your . . . sad-ass shit . . . auto . . . mobile . . . into the fucking creek! Ya mother-fucking bastard! *Di di mau, maintenant! Allez vous! Mange le merde!*"

The old man verged on infarction. Sergeant Thomas, two American truck drivers, and I pushed him across the bridge and up the ramp. The MP said: "I should have made you shove that bastard's crap-mobile into the river. American convoys need this bridge. Dumb fuck is gonna get his heap started again and pull the same stunt on the next busted bridge."

Sometimes, winning hearts and minds is hard.

* When foreigners don't understand, Americans yell louder. Getting nowhere, the MP began beating on the bonnet of the aged Citroën with his *choggie* stick, a relic from the Korean War. *Choggie* means "hurry up." The burled rods, carved from hard wood, were part cudgel, part riding crop, part transportation system. At the business end, this MP's tool featured a fist and an upraised middle finger. Asian peasants toted longer sticks that lacked fuck-you flourishes.

LITTLE SEOUL

The major gave Lieutenant Warden, Sergeant Thomas, and me another special assignment. He asked us to accompany a squad of Regional Forces and check out some fresh, worrisome intelligence: that our enemies were stashing supplies in an abandoned Republic of Korea fortress not far from our district base. The major told us to patrol the perimeter of the ROK's former base, a concrete pile beside the An Diem villages. Take a look-see inside, too, the major added.

Lt. Tom Warden (not his real name) was senior to me, like every ROTC graduate who matriculated in college in the early sixties, and therefore he was again in command. Born in England, raised in the States, Warden regularly reminded us that Great Britain had given America everything, starting with language, culture, and law. Moreover, Britain's empirical achievements were superior to our parvenus, our mish-mash, walloping Indians, pirates, and Spaniards. Before becoming an adviser, like the rest of us, Warden had served with an American infantry unit fighting VC and NVA. He'd learned that no Vietnamese, uniformed or not, is trustworthy.

This brand-new advisory effort brought American infantrymen deeper into a culture that had repulsed us. In our new roles, suspicious, paranoid, we took over pretty much while pretending not to do so. Unsettled, we were surrounded by men who lacked the esprit de corps, training, language skills, and fighting spirit of the most dispirited American units. It wasn't fun to be reassigned from, say, the 82nd Airborne Division or the Big Red One to baby-sit a bunch of fraidy-cats. Hence, we were twitchy. Defensive-minded, infamously tough, the South Koreans defended their base with great brutality against all comers and were more feared than their allies, the Aussies, Kiwis, and Americans. ROKs had buried mines and booby traps in a diabolical defensive system, adding claymores, grenades, toe-poppers, ball-busters, and an occasional 105mm howitzer shell, plus foo-gas (buried barrels of napalm).

As we approached the ROK base, Warden asked our RFs to round up a dozen villagers. He said in broken Vietnamese and loud English that the villagers would walk point and clear the area for our soldiers, Americans and South Vietnamese alike. The thing was, the villagers weren't Korean. The ROKs hadn't taken them into their confidence. Instead, local folks had avoided the base, and they hated the ROKs, who were famously brutal, especially to unarmed civilians. Somehow, though, Warden believed that all Asians (never mind nationalities) could determine where the mines were, perhaps by luck, by cunning, or by stepping on them. Anyway, the villagers shouldn't have let the Commies get so close. Sure, the mine layers weren't Commies but our own departed allies, who had plunked themselves amid the villagers, but hey, we were in a war. When spoken under stress, tonal languages like Vietnamese become shrill. Mama-san and papa-san wailed in protest. Our mine sweepers were getting on in years, and none too fearsome in appearance.

"Move on," Warden said.

They moaned in protest.

"Move," he repeated. "*Di di!*" I argued ineffectually. This isn't fair, not right. We're supposed to be helping these people, not using them to do our most dangerous jobs. Warden ignored me and held his rifle more menacingly, not pointing straight at them, not yet, but they got the message.

Inching at a snail's pace, inspecting every step, the villagers proved to be flawless mine sweepers. Perhaps living for decades in a war zone where Japanese, French, Viet Minh, South Vietnamese, North Vietnamese, and American troops—not just Koreans—had deployed mines had somehow sensitized Annamese to telltale signs that we clumsy Americans didn't see.

Maybe Warden wasn't cruel. Maybe he knew things. *Naah.*

We didn't find any AK-47s, no rice: nothing. The old ROK base was taboo ground, as feared and shunned by the Communists as their brutal Korean enemies had been.

THE MASSACRE AT BINH HOA

In 2008, by accident, I discovered that My Lai wasn't the only unspeakable tragedy that had taken place in our tiny but sanguinary bit of Asia. Retaliating for Communist attacks that had been launched on their base camp from nearby villages, South Korean marines had slaughtered five hundred South Vietnamese. They perpetrated this particular massacre in a village called Binh Hoa in 1967.

That atrocity's perpetrators had lived in the same camp that we were going to search little more than a year later, in the fall of '68. Warden's decision to deploy elderly villagers as mine sweepers was a savage irony, but he didn't know that both sides had brutalized these villagers, sometimes at once. None of us knew anything about Binh Hoa. It was like living in Yonkers in 2002 and not knowing that the World Trade Center had been leveled. Binh Hoa vanished from the ground and from subsequent maps. We knew nothing about My Lai, either, but there was a difference. My Lai wasn't in our district; Binh Hoa was. Indeed, it was close to its heart. Today, you'll find little history of Binh Hoa except in raggedy online reports posted by amateur historians who tried to visit the remains of the village, seeking truth, a quest that proved fruitless. The new government of Unified Vietnam was uninterested. Asian-on-Asian violence didn't match the widely accepted consensus about the war's narrative. Americans, even many Americans agreed, had been the war's bad guys. Who cared about Korean troops one way or another?

After fighting a war for survival from 1950 to '53, one ended only by a shaky, oft-tested armistice, with new threats and probes coming almost daily from the North, ROKs were brutally efficient troops. They had trained in the shadow of their own DMZ, the 38th Parallel that divided their peninsula into free and unfree. The Korean press wasn't eager to investigate rumors about Binh Hoa. The victorious unified Vietnamese government saw no advantage in exhuming the sad story. Unlike Americans, who wish to atone for our mistakes by paying respects and contributing a little money to the My Lai monument, few, if any, Korean tourists or veterans would come to visit a Binh Hoa memorial, the government of Vietnam surmised.

12.

Gunny: Lifer Gyrene

"I don't suppose you want to visit my Marines, wouldja, sir?"

The gunnery sergeant's question followed an ancient military tradition. An NCO pretends to ask a favor, subtly telling a junior officer what to do, by saying "sir." Junior officers become senior officers by heeding subtle questions from NCOs. Feigning deference, NCOs make higher-ranking men do their bidding.

We'd just met, the Gunny and me. He'd ridden into Binh Son in a beaten-up jeep whose armor was a layer of sandbags carelessly dropped on the midget vehicle's floor back in the Chu Lai motor pool. These bedraggled, flattened bags offered no more protection than mosquito nets against mortars. Marines get crappy equipment . . . and they like it. Stiff-necked, self-denying pride is the Marine Corps mystique: doing more with less. (Semper freaking Fi.) In the child-sized backseat was a scratched PRC-25 radio, along with a tumble of loose grenades and marking flares. Visiting his far-flung Combined Action Program (CAP) teams, the Gunny relied on chutzpah, not armaments.

He added, sotto voce, "No Army officer on this concrete pile has ever ridden shotgun, so probably you won't either."

The rest of our advisory team backed off. This wasn't Gunny's first invitation. He grinned, hard, as if he might bite. Okay: I was bored. Soldiers face many enemies: real ones, yes. Just as pernicious are shallow thresholds for boredom. As combat risks go, boredom is a close second to steel. The tedious humdrum that lasted forever between invigorating skirmishes drew us closer to our enemies. Gunny also played on the ageless tension between the Corps—the few, the brave, gimme a break, the proud—and ordinary Army grunts. The Corps believes it owns the true, oaken Military Cross. Therefore, I was going with him for sure. I was no FNG. "Where we headed, Gunny?"

"Over there, Lieutenant," he said, pointing east toward the placid China Sea. He didn't act surprised that I'd accepted. "Folks need to see me. Uh—see us."

I asked for permission to tag along. The major agreed, happy that someone in his chicken-shit outfit was taking initiative for a change. (He thought the trip was my idea: I didn't disabuse him.) I hopped aboard. The Gunny drove into Indian Country on an unpaved oxcart path, driving several kilometers on a market road connecting villages to Binh Son. A squad of Marines at the CAP team were happy to see Gunny. We chatted, then took the same rutted oxcart path back to Highway One, checking every clump for ambushes, looking for mines.

Taking a path at a certain time, finding yourself unhurt at journey's end, you take hope. Your sense of durability may be misplaced, as you may learn. Actually, you won't learn anything. Delusion is a soldier's friend. Feeling secure on lucky roads, crossing at a steady pace, you fall into a trap, a mistake that General Ulysses Grant never made. Retracing your steps, looping your own loop, you endanger yourself. To be sure, in motorized vehicles, you have little choice. You can take the road, or ruin a peasant's rice field, or stay home. Armored units chose the agricultural route. Why did peasants hate us? Drive a forty-ton tracked vehicle over your neighbor's garden to find out why American military might doesn't always earn the respect of property owners. Even a jeep can set off rage.

Every few days, the Gunny or his company commander, never together, drove into our district base camp, seeking their dopey Army buddy. The Gunny and I, or the CO and I, would visit a couple of combined action squads dotting the district. Combined Action teams consisted of a squad of American Marines and perhaps thirty Vietnamese militiamen: tiny semi-American atolls afloat in a stormy red sea.

We traveled in late morning. Routines soothe, but by repeating comforting little trips over and again, driving on the same ground, you create a pattern of unimaginative behavior that's discernible to people who mean you ill. Two or three days out of every week, Gunny picked me up at about 10:30 A.M., and we drove east on the same market path to visit the same CAP bases. At 5 mph, our jeep's open top created a modest breeze. We'd drop the windscreen as if riding a chopped-down woody on the California coast, two carefree dudes on a surfin' safari. The Gunny didn't look like a beach bum, Beach Boy, or Jan or Dean, however. He looked like a fire hydrant, but with head stubble and a grand mustache. The country was too dangerous to be driven at first light or dusk, and impossible at night.

The second time Gunny dared me to join him, bored, as always, I acceded again. The third time, too. And so on. We drove through a fraught landscape populated by misleadingly delicate-looking people. When we got as far as the coast, infrequently, we saw beautiful white sand in the distance. Going and coming, we passed a thousand little paddies, Rice Krispies squares, irrigated in dry seasons and flooded in wet ones. On the far, western side of Highway One, lowlands rose gently into brushy hills, jumbling into wild, thick foliage and mountains. An impenetrable maze unimagined even by Tolkien in Middle Earth gave way (on maps, at least) to the highlands of Laos and Cambodia. To anyone on foot, they were indistinguishable.

When the Gunny and I drove west, as we did on one excursion in late October, we saw fewer people, but didn't feel less frightened, or I should say, I didn't feel less frightened: Gunny didn't let on. By the time we reached the CAP team west of the An Diems, rain was falling. The sky darkened. Tropical rain fell in globules as big as plump baby fists, soaking us in seconds. We raised the canvas top but we were already drenched and chilled. Reaching the ridge above the village, jarheads and Popular Forces appeared, mildewed, groady. During the day, they patrolled. At night, every other man stayed awake until dawn, night after night, when PFs got up to till their paddies. Despite the Marines' exhaustion, they were happy to see the Gunny, and by extension, his Army buddy. Gyrenes saluted: surprise! Most Marines show only contempt for doggies of any rank. Nobody salutes in the boonies, either. Someone watching through binoculars has a prime target. But the Gunny had shared his aura with me as if I might know what I was doing.

"Why don't we chopper in a hot meal, Gunny?" I asked, touched by the welcome. "Good for morale."

As a warlord, junior grade, I could make a helicopter bring in Thermadors—ten-gallon containers filled with hot food or cold ice cream—instead of C-rations and rice for a change. I could bring fire, earthquake, thunderstorms: you name it, I could produce it, magically. A quick radio call: *Voici!* America's gifts and demons would fall from the heavens.

Amused, the Gunny said: "You gotta be kidding, sir. No way! These guys love this shit. They're Marines."

The Gunny wanted my Army's powers of destruction, not its largesse or munificence. Mostly, we drove east. Up, down, around the Batagnan Peninsula to the east—that wasn't pro-American territory. Near the China Sea, rice paddies were more productive than in the foothills, yet scarier and far more crowded. More people: more bad guys.*

We talked to mask nerves. In a land that lacked nice work, jarheads, I realized, had the worst jobs. The Gunny and the captain wove their jeeps over bad roads, alone, each of them. Riding together would have been like flying both the president and vice president on Air Force One. If their shared jeep blew up, the company's chain of command was destroyed, too, and there would be no Speaker of the House waiting back in Chu Lai to take over the Combined Action company.

Enemies and peasants wearing pajamas and conical hats looked alike. Every bump in the road could be a buried shell. Every clump of brush could hide an enemy squad. On their lonely treks, the Marines were susceptible to ambushes, booby traps, snipers, and command-detonated mines. The Gunny and the CO admitted no fear, an institutional failing—or virtue—of the Corps. By contrast, Army doggies have no compunction about whining. Marines are taught to shut up and accept destiny from Parris Island on. Instead of bitching, Marines gobble secret jarhead speed. Gunny personified the Crotch. (This scrofulous variant of "the Corps" stands for "Uncle Sam's Moldy Crotch.") Gunny's luxuriant handlebar mustache was flecked with gray and its ends twisted buoyantly in an affectation that only a Marine who worked in the boondocks could sport. His octagonal campaign cap (with matte black eagle-anchor-and-globe) topped sunburned sidewalls.

* Tim O'Brien wrote about the peninsula in *Going After Cacciato* and *The Things They Carried*. Tracy Kidder's *My Detachment* was set in a fire base called Bayonet, north of the An Diems to our west.

Usually, Gunny boomed. From his shiny boots up to his tidy head, Gunny was pure command. His rank—gunnery sergeant—is unique to the Crotch. The Gunny was a reservist who'd chosen to return to active duty. Fourteen boring years of customs work had driven him bats. He'd risen through the ranks to become a supervisor, a GS-12. But customs routine lacked surprise: all Mickey Mouse, no blood or guts. His team searched travelers' bags for contraband. Once in a while, his crew found something. Now and then, Gunny arrested a smuggler. Rarely, an accused suspect resisted arrest: good! Gunny loved physical stuff. He yearned for the adrenaline surges from fighting on the Korean Peninsula. Old soldiers forget their pains but remember thrilling brushes with death. They're here: ipso facto, they know not death. Nonimmortal warriors are now in heaven, and teach the living no lessons.

The Gunny saw harsh duty as the Corps held off North Koreans and Chinese while the U.S. retreated from the Yalu River. Equipment malfunctioned. Machine oil froze into sludge. Nothing worked. Americans bled to death in subzero weather. Prisoners were brainwashed. The First Cavalry didn't distinguish itself in that war, which contributed to the tensions between my old unit and the Corps. Our predecessors had skedaddled. Sneering at our oversized shoulder patches, Korean Marine vets said: "The black band is the Yalu you never crossed. You never rode that horse, either. Yellow? That's your backbone."

Adding his customs and Marine Corps duties together, the Gunny had accumulated eighteen years of service, so he could retire at half-pay in two years and start a new life before hitting forty. In twelve more years, he could retire or get a new job and double-dip. Not bad. But the Gunny was too antsy for prudent retirement planning. He thought about the squared-away, gung-ho, cocky kids passing through Camp Pendleton. Gunny was falling farther behind his brothers. After earning two gold combat stripes in Korea, he wanted a third. Each stripe represented six months of fighting, but meant nothing to most of the people who'd see them. As we jounced, Gunny told me his plans.

I had no postwar ambitions. I wanted to finish one lousy tour, intact. In the jeep, we wondered if our shared idiocy—itching for action, ignoring consequences—was genetic or behavioral. Why do sensible people avoid harm, but guys like us seek danger? We were restless, impatient sumbitches: our pants, consumed by fire ants and termites. Gunny's pants were permanently ablaze. So were mine.

The Army's Americal Division overlapped our advisory group's territory. Fat lot of good that did us. In 1968, its area of operations, or AO, stretched from Chu Lai down through the fearful Batagnan Peninsula to Quang Ngai, and swallowed villages called the My Lais. The Americal was a crappy division, the worst American unit to serve in Vietnam: led by lousy officers named Calley and Medina, among others, the Americal lacked experience, training, and gumption. Several of its underachieving commanders were relieved of duty in the field. The division was deactivated in 1972. What we didn't know in 1968—me, the Gunny, the major, Warden—could, and eventually did, fill books. For example, we didn't know that the citizens of our unassuming, impoverished province had seen the best and worst of Americans. The Americal Division had slaughtered hundreds of civilians willy-nilly. On the other hand, after local doctors fled, we treated their sick. Marines worked compassionately with poor peasants, turning them into warriors. They really won hearts and minds while exposing themselves to mortal danger. Army advisers were less stellar, but we, too, were forces for good.

One fact not in our possession: we didn't know that our district was the birthplace of the Marines' enlightened CAP program. In *The Village,* a memoir, Marine Bing West wrote that General Walt had tried to Vietnamize the war starting in

1965, choosing a Binh Son village called Binh Nghia a few klicks north of our headquarters for the experiment. An Americal platoon commanded by Lieutenant William Calley had paid a calamitous visit to the My Lais in spring '68. We didn't know about the atrocity until Sy Hersh took a look-see.

We knew yesterday and today, and had some hope for tomorrow, but that was it. After a few silent minutes, I asked the Gunny: "What about that good hot chow?"

"Sir, like I said: they don't need hot chow, or mail. They don't need fancy rifles or atom bombs. They're Marines!"

The Gunny's answer, a mantra, grew on me. The Gunny didn't want help from anyone in the pantywaist U.S. Army. Marines are self-sufficient. The Gunny wanted my personal wisecracking company, insufficiently Marine-ish though it was, but nothing else. Gunny admitted he feared dying alone, or worse, being wounded and taken prisoner. His Marines and their Popular Force partners, scrawny even by Viet standards, worked together like gangbusters. Despite their dearth of materiel and training, the PFs had one big thing going for them: they fought for their villages, families, ancestral graves, and crops, against an increasingly foreign enemy from the North. Meanwhile, our Army machine voraciously (if inefficiently) chewed up the VC.

Marine platoons lived with their allies, teaching them fighting skills while drawing on impeccable PF intelligence gathering. Together, they were a formidable team, unless a main force unit attacked. No reinforced platoon can resist a company, much less a battalion. That's General Custer stuff. Such carnage happened less often than it should have, though, thanks to Marine grit. You cannot understand how it depresses me to admit it.

BAC SI

The wooden base of the building's long porch across from District Headquarters said NHA THUONG—hospital. "*Nha thuong*" didn't mean clean sheets or sterile operating rooms. It promised nothing that Westerners expect from hospitals, not cleanliness, competence, or even much care for that matter. It said maybe there's a doctor (*bac si*) here. Maybe not. Take your chances. Are you better off inside than on the earthen floor of your hut? Not for us to say. Your call.

Happily, Bac Si existed. Plump, cheerful, hard-working, and most important, here. Smarter doctors threatened by the Viet Cong fled elsewhere. Bac Si trained his nurses, who worked in a dingy, ill-supplied, unsanitary, understaffed, overcrowded, but revered *nha thuong*. Sick, wounded people came to Bac Si. His nurses cadged supplies from Americans—antibiotics, bandages, sera, scalpels, needles, sutures. Unless Binh Son's villagers had the fortune to start bleeding within view of Americans (who'd fly them to Chu Lai), Bac Si was all they had. He turned over critically wounded patients to us, but his wards were thick with people and flies. It was hot despite open unscreened windows, yet not as stinky as you'd think. As hard-hearted as GIs can be under fire, or threatened by fire, we atoned for our sins with medical compassion. We fixed our victims, swabbed their infections, stitched their cuts, and smeared them with Bacitracin.

Bac Si brought his worst cases to our little aid station. When called upon, our medic, Sergeant Sullivan, E-7, triaged. One morning, three people arrived on the Bac Si's three-wheeled Lambretta "ambulance": an old man, a younger woman, and a kid, each in tough shape with multiple fragmentation wounds. The morning had been quiet, but hot enough to make our brains squishy soft. Gunny and I were drinking beer while I posted multicolored overlays on the district map.

Colors indicated the current assessment of the control

our ARVN and CAP forces enjoyed over the countryside. Blue splotches were friendly places. You hardly needed a weapon to walk there. Kids there were nice. Light blue zones were sympathetic to South Vietnamese forces and us, but were more treacherous than darker blues. White areas, contested, belonged to us in daytime and anybody dumb enough to sit on them at night. You could shoot in white zones with a halfway decent reason. Pink zones leaned VC. Red zones were just that. You could shoot without seeking permission, though it was not a right but a privilege we could lose if we kept hitting civilians. To the west, the Batagnan Peninsula was so crimson that no one from the district ventured there without help from the Americal Division. Marines would do, too, but Marines were in scarce supply.

Cutting and pasting acetate overlays to the maps was important work. Visiting dignitaries liked visual briefings as much as they disliked going into the field. Colored maps replaced body counts as measures of Allied success. A good SITREP—situation report—was blue spilling into white areas, and shrinking pink. A negative SITREP was widening pink and red zones. As I worked, happy to be using the creative talent that had made me the art director of the high school yearbook (and painter of Christmas and Thanksgiving murals on Fort Dix mess hall windows), Gunny explained why Marines were superior to doggies. He knew it infuriated me, but like all jarheads, he enjoyed getting under thin doggy skin.

Outside, a Lambretta wheezed, coughed, and cut Gunny off. We went to the LZ to take a look-see. A child and an old man lay on canvas litters. A woman sat in the passenger seat. The old guy's withered, lacerated body trickled with blood running down his gray-brown skin, clotted folded wrinkles. He mumbled. The woman was silent. The child was perfectly still. There was a swollen contusion where its face should have been, and it was dwarfed by a plasma bottle.

"*Min,* Bac Si?" we asked, Westerners, ratiocinators, forensic detectives. He stopped fooling with the IV, turned, greeted us amiably, and nodded.

"VC *min?*"

He grinned but shrugged. Who knew? What difference did it make? We wanted someone to blame. He was a fix-it guy. Of course it didn't matter. After Sully patched them up, we called a dust-off. The Gunny and I went back inside the shade where air was stirred by electric fans. I stuck up more acetates, colors to come. Gunny continued his lecture. Marines were volunteers: that was the difference.

For once, I ignored him, letting the argument drop, not pointing out that now even the moldy, proud Crotch was drafting people. We popped another Budweiser. Lunchtime was close.

13.

Mom Saves My Life

On November 8, 1968, I went home on emergency leave. My mom had died on November 4, the day Richard Nixon was elected. Because of her last selfless act, I joined my family in mourning in Delaware: falling-down Dad, disabled sister, and teenage brother. Mom, sixty-one, was younger than I am today. Helen Mae Jamison Nylen died from renal collapse, a complication of diabetes, as had her mother and two aunts. Technically, Mom died in a hospital in Wilmington, Delaware, but you can't tell me that on some metaphysical level, she didn't die for me in Vietnam.

Back in Delaware, Kit and my family pleaded with me not to return. It took a week to persuade me to seek reassignment. Then I embraced the idea, and groveled for reassignment at the Pentagon. In my favor: my mom was dead; dad, brain damaged; sister, cerebral palsied; brother, in high school; fiancée, had demanded her parents lose every game of canasta for months. After two and a half wounds, a third would get me out of combat or kill me. Against? Mine was a personal problem.

The chaplain should solve it, the majors I begged said. Not them. The day before I was scheduled to go back overseas, however, I was compassionately reassigned to Fort Dix, New Jersey, and spent every weekend in Delaware, thank the heavenly Bee Jesus.

In mid-December, Tom Warden wrote. Good news: the Ruff Puffs, led by our intrepid advisers, had repelled an attack on District Headquarters. An enemy company had tried to crawl through our garbage dump. Rattling through unkempt garbage piles, scattering rusting cans, the clatter gave them away. My colleagues had slaughtered them. Warden's letter enclosed macabre pictures, dozens of corpses intermingled with debris from the nasty dump and stacks of captured weapons. He sent bad news, too: a week after I'd left, a command-detonated mine had blasted the CAP's CO and his shattered jeep into the hereafter. Two weeks later, Warden said, the Gunny and his jeep were obliterated, too. Gunny was driving to a CAP team we'd visited together that was under siege. A buried howitzer shell tore through his floorboards as if they were made of cardboard. Sandbags on the floor didn't do any good. Gunny knew they wouldn't. If Mom hadn't died, chances are that I'd have been riding with one or the other of these crazy, brave men when they were blown up, not writing about them. As it happens, both died fast, a blessing, I guess, but they died alone as they'd feared.

I'd forgotten their names. Back then, I didn't work with many Marines, so our ranks sufficed to identify us: we were the Lieutenant (me), the Gunny, and the CO.

In 2006, seeking clues about my Marine buddies online, I found a 1969 yearbook for the 1st CAG based in Chu Lai. Incongruously, the black-and-white album looks like a digitized version of an ordinary U.S. high school annual featuring cheerful young men, mostly teenagers. However, stateside students who aren't available for photographs were at band practice, math club, or wrestling matches. The guys omitted from these pictures had been zipped into body bags (if bodies could be found) and shipped home. As I see them now at the remove of decades, a queasy, unreal aura looms over their grins. The yearbook mentions no casualties. No one had died, or will die. Each squad is fully staffed. Sometimes, smiling Marines pose with happy villagers and their kids. There are no combat scenes, no blood. These kids, brown, white, and black, are having a swell time in the sunshine.

A roster reveals that 1st CAG men killed in action included "Rainey, Thomas, Lt., of the First CACO; CO; died on November 11, 1968." When I didn't ride with Gunny, Rainey was my alternative mate. Gunnery Sergeant Alfred Frazier McCants died on November 29, 1968, with CAP Team 1-3-1. McCants, thirty-six, was killed by "multiple fragmentation wounds." Between their names two hundred men intervene on the Vietnam Memorial. I could have been slain alongside one or the other. They'd been my brothers. But much of what I remembered about them was wrong. For one thing, though he never mentioned them, Gunny had three more Purple Hearts than me. He wasn't a Southern Californian as I'd thought. Before going on active duty, McCants was a customs and immigration officer—I was right about that—but he worked far from Camp Pendleton, in sunless Buffalo.

IN REMEMBRANCE OF THIS HEROIC UNITED STATES MARINE CORPS SERVICEMAN WHOSE NAME SHALL LIVE FOREVER—SIX AWARDS OF THE PURPLE HEART MEDAL—ALFRED FRAZIER McCANTS: GUNNERY SERGEANT

WORKING ON THE PEACE BRIDGE BETWEEN THE U.S. AND CANADA, HE VOLUNTEERED FOR SERVICE IN VIETNAM IN SEPTEMBER 1968 . . . KILLED IN ACTION ON 29 NOVEMBER 1968.

GUNNERY SERGEANT McCANTS SERVED IN THE KOREAN WAR, RECEIVING FOUR AWARDS OF THE PURPLE HEART.

Posted by: CLAY MARSTON

Posted for: ALFRED FRAZIER McCANTS:

You were the best, bravest Marine I met in the Corps. You were as loyal to your young Marine charges as we could hope. I remember you as my friend and mentor. You died coming to help my men. I told you not to try, it was too dangerous, but you did. I'm forever grateful.

God bless you, my friend.
Posted by RICHARD J. BREAGY

CASUALTIES

For Americans, 1968 was the war's most murderous year. The infantry company I left to help Marines and Ruff Puffs regional forces win civilian hearts and minds (instead of blowing them to kingdom come) suffered disproportionately. After nine fatalities in 1966 and seven in 1967, twenty Delta men would die in '69, eleven in '70, and one in '71. During my pitifully brief time with Delta, ten men died, including three from 1st Platoon:

SGT. RONALD MYRON CLOUD, 23, Ponemah, Minnesota
PFC. OTIS CUMBRY, 20, Detroit, Michigan
PFC. JOHN EDWARD HARTRY, 19, Kemp, Texas

In addition to the myths about his tracking skills, among the misconceptions I'd held about Chief White Cloud, aka Ronald M. Cloud, was that he was a southwestern Indian who should have liked this tempestuous, broiling climate. In fact, Cloud was an Ojibwa from Ponemah, a slender isthmus jutting between Upper and Lower Red Lakes near Canada. His tribe was closer to Winnipeg than Minneapolis, nearer Ottawa than Pueblo. The Red Lakes ice over in winter. No Hopi, Navajo, Paiute, or Pima, Ronald Myron Cloud was a freaking Minnesotan. He'd have been more at home in wintry Ashfield than Vietnam. Before white men came, his ancestors lived quietly: fishing, hunting, picking berries, growing maize and wild rice, and making maple sugar. They built birch *wiigiwaams* and huddled in *pau waus*. They fought defensively, unlike warlike Cherokee, Cheyenne, Pawnee, and Sioux. In other words, Chief Cloud was no better suited to walking point than I was. Less so: my ancestors were stone-cold killers.

Sorry, man.

14.

Mom: Farmer's Daughter Turned Flapper; Dad: Squarehead Turned Bomb Maker, Fall Guy

In a way, thinking about my life as an unusually difficult experience in American toughness is laughable given the stark circumstances my parents' and grandparents' generations faced. My folks were born in 1907: most Americans still farmed. Helen Mae Jamison rode a plow mule from the family's ten-acre farm to school in Peach Bottom in southeastern Pennsylvania. Instead of indoor plumbing, her parents' brood of twelve kids had a well pump and an outhouse. After Grandpa Howard Jamison's first wife gave out, leaving him a widower with two sons, he remarried. Bearing ten children, his second wife, Helen's mom, plumb wore out, too, as they said in the Fox Valley. One of Mom's brothers died of lockjaw. Farm life was hard, and medical care was spotty. The antecedents of the twelve Jamison kids were Scots-Irish, Welsh, and English, simmering in a Presbyterian cauldron. Aunt Gyla told me she scarcely saw their father, who was either working in the fields, walking to a Nottingham factory job, or sleeping.

At fifteen, Helen Jamison, a sparkling student, was senior

class valedictorian. A year later, she left Millersville Normal School and Teachers College when the farmhouse burned down and headed for the nearest city, Wilmington, Delaware. She worked in DuPont's ad department. In 1928, an ad job, even industrial advertising, was glamorous for a farmer's daughter. She sent home a chunk of her pay to help with the mortgage. Bright, pretty, and eager to shuck her countrified ways, Helen ran with a fast crowd. Her metamorphosis was swift. New friends were flappers with spit curls, silk stockings, and short skirts, and playboys who drove spiffy automobiles. In Wilmington, she heard live jazz, drank fancy cocktails and cheap gin in speakeasies, smoked cigarettes, rode streetcars, saw moving pictures, and bought her first radio. City life was grand, she thought.

On a warm summer night in 1930, Helen was riding with her swain, a dashing DuPont scion, in a flivver with the top down. After hitting a few speakeasies, the couple were on their way to another clandestine saloon. The car veered off the road, overturned, and tossed her out. The car rolled over. The windscreen nearly severed her leg. Operations patched her femur together: perhaps she got special care because of her grand smile. After three months in the hospital, limping, she met a sober-sided young man at work. Bertil Nylen, the dark-haired son of Swedish immigrants, put himself through Middlebury College by operating a loom. Witty, shy Bert was a big change from the rich swells who'd proven unreliable. Helen was gimpy, but she was more fun than Old Midd's future schoolmarms.

Helen introduced Bert, whose parents were faithful teetotalers, to highballs. In turn, he swept her away to Charleston, West Virginia, the first of eighteen cities in which they'd live. Susanne Marie Nylen was born in Munster, Indiana. A congenital brain affliction in the birth canal produced athetoid spasticity. She'd go rigid or shake uncontrollably. For crippled kids (as they were called in that unaffected age, before they became "handicapped," "disabled," "physically challenged," and "differently abled") there were no social services. Sue took her first uncertain steps in heavy metal leg braces at age eight. In 1941, our brother, Tom, was stillborn. I was the first surviving son. After John was born in 1949, Mom bled for days and had an emergency hysterectomy.

In 1951, Granddad Jamison was painting his old truck on a warmish February day. He lost his balance, fell off the car roof, cracked his head on the frozen ground, and died.

In 1959, Dad fell down and fractured his skull, and his promising career came to an abrupt, painful end. (See a theme here? Our family falls down . . . a lot.) At fifty-two, Dad was a pensioner. The Nylens and Jamisons were lucky, just not good-lucky.

MY DAD: SQUAREHEAD

Before he fell, Bertil Carl Nylen shared lessons in our La Grange Park, Illinois, den. We'd tune in a boxing match and he would drown out the commentary with monologues, variants of "Horatio Alger: Swede, Ascendant." Growing up in a busy mill town, as a six-year-old, Bert took a steamship to Stockholm with his mother and his aunt. Relearning English, Bert decided that he was American. Hyphenated terms weren't common: in street argot, Bert was a Squarehead, a Svenski, who grew up with Micks, Guineas, Frogs, Norskis, Wops, Krauts, Kikes, Hunkies, and Polacks. White Protestants weren't WASPs. They were Yankees. Eventually, Bert would come to refer to himself as a Connecticut Yankee, but he was joking: no Yankee he, except by birthplace.

As Willie Pep, Carmen Basilio, and Rocky Marciano pummeled their opponents, Dad meant to buck me up, I guess: I was a brittle thing. Yet his boasts were as detached from me as Sugar Ray Robinson's TKOs, runs by Crazy Legs Hirsch, and

Norm Van Brocklin's passes. Bert played catcher without a mask. He couldn't afford one. Foul tips busted his nose twice. Knotty bumps were proof. He played schoolboy baseball, basketball, track, and football. As center on Middlebury's football team, he played offense and defense. Everyone did. His undermanned team held Dartmouth to a scoreless tie in a snowy scrimmage at Hanover. Dad recounted the great Sam Guarnaccia's exploits as if he were reciting *The Odyssey*. The Indians' center rebroke Bert's nose, but he stayed in the game.

DAD, WORKING

To earn tuition, Bert was a piece-rate weaver. The faster he ran his heavy silk loom, the more he made. At school, Bert and a fraternity brother ran a pants-pressing service. Nonetheless, his savings ran out after junior year. To earn his keep, he missed graduating with his friends in the Class of 1929, emerged into the Depression in 1930, and abandoned his goal of becoming a landscape architect. He became a junior DuPont executive. Landing a job with a big, prestigious company as unemployment soon reached 25 percent would do fine.

Graduating in an age when most grown men abandoned games and went to seed, Bert played industrial-league basketball. For years, he trotted around at night on dimly lit crummy courts whose obstacles included thinly padded posts spaced at odd intervals and opponents who grabbed his trunks. He quit as an old man of thirty. During deflation, wages and prices sank. His pay was reduced twice. He went where the company bade him go. He rose through the ranks, taking every transfer offered him. Each move meant a bigger job and more pay. In those days, executives accepted vagabond lives. Paradoxically, family security depended on the breadwinner's restlessness. He and Mom moved nineteen times in thirty-five years, a vagabond life that was harder on her than on him. He had a fraternity of DuPont executive mates. Mom had solo chores: finding new houses, moving from old ones, making new friends, and raising her crippled child. During the war, they moved to Birmingham. At the Alabama Ordnance Works, Bert supervised the manufacture of high explosives. DuPont was good at blow-up stuff. Gunpowder was its first product: half of the Union's gunpowder in the Civil War came from DuPont. Thatched roofs atop stonewalled workplaces were designed to blow off in accidents. (Accidents were plentiful. Expedient design allowed survivors to get back fast to the Powder Mills by the Brandywine River.) Dynamite and smokeless powder came next.

During Dad's time, The Company, as it was known in Delaware, invented nonexplosives including neoprene, the first synthetic rubber; nylon (1935); Lucite; and Teflon. After the war, DuPont made Mylar, Dacron, Orlon, Lycra, and Tyvek; in the 1960s, Nomex, Qiana, Corfam, Corian, and Kevlar. The company's slogan was "Better things for better living . . . through chemistry." That wasn't ironic. In the fifties, chemicals were *good* . . . before LSD arrived, without DuPont's help, and "chemistry" took on meanings unimaginable to Eleuthère and Pierre S. du Pont.

MAKING THE BOMB

In the winter of '43–'44, Mom, Dad, and Sue moved to a city that didn't exist a year before. In thirty dizzying days, abracadabra, three thousand bewildered farmers and families were ousted from what became Oak Ridge, Tennessee, exiled from three villages scattered over 56,000 Smoky Mountain acres. Why? No one said. "Crops were still in the fields, and hay was fresh in the barns," Jay Searcy wrote decades after his family arrived in 1943. "Agents swarmed the countryside like ants, pounded on doors, and citing the War Powers Act, informed owners that the government was taking their land and buildings. They had 30 days to evacuate. The price—an average of $56 an acre—was not negotiable."

The atomic bomb and I were born sixteen months apart. I beat Little Boy out of the chute. There wasn't much for a couple to do in the supersecret neocity but make babies.

Around the top-secret compound, Skidmore, Owings, and Merrill designed a pretty town for seventy thousand, a heavily patrolled city that sprang up, offering grocery stores but not many groceries. There was a Firestone dealership, but few tires. Food and gas were rationed. There were movies. At night, the most secret part of the mysterious enclosure emitted an eerie yellow-orange glow. Work went on around the clock. At its fevered working peak, Oak Ridge drew as much electricity as the island of Manhattan. Dad couldn't tell Mom anything about his job. Thousands of wives were cloistered, as ignorant as the male spouses of working women. Anyone lacking a need to know knew nothing. Major General Leslie Groves chose Oak Ridge, Tennessee, Los Alamos, New Mexico, and Hanford, Washington, for inaccessibility. Oak Ridge didn't appear on U.S. maps for years after Nagasaki and Hiroshima were eradicated. Until then, the place was called by aliases like the Clinton Works and the Manhattan Project. Despite its somber mission, Oak Ridge was a precursor of Levittown.

Dad ran the process that separated plutonium from uranium. His crew made radioactive tubes stored in the nuclear pile, nerve-racking drudgery. He loved his part-time assignment, guiding visitors, including Oppenheimer, Fermi, and military brass. Dad's gift of gab entertained geniuses who'd enabled the incredible, awful invention as he showed them what happened and where. Late one summer night, sirens sounded in the sequestered inner fortress, the Pile. Guards found ten physicists drunk and splashing in the reactor moat. Miraculously, no one was burned. Dad admired superscientists but disdained their peculiarities. They thought few mundane, practical thoughts. An industrial engineer, Dad thought their choice of swimming hole bespoke their madness. Assembled from all over the country, townspeople included physicists, mathematicians, and chemists; servants such as laborers, cooks, and bottle-washers; and managers from chemical companies like DuPont, Eastman, and Union Carbide.

Trapped in a muddy compound fifty miles from Knoxville, women gossiped, listened to Walter Winchell, went to movies, read censored news, and raised families. Were they lucky enough to get outside the fences—say, taking a bus elsewhere—they wouldn't meet anyone who hadn't been born in the Smokies, much less random spies. Still, security was paramount. Every fourth person in Oak Ridge was a U.S. government spy. People who asked too many questions were exiled. Atomic scientists who escaped from the Nazis said that the Germans had begun to work on atomic energy long before Americans met under Chicago's Stagg Field. Subsequently, historians like Richard Rhodes have disputed whether the Germans had made significant nuclear progress by war's end, but back then, no one knew for certain. It seemed best to err on the side of paranoia.

For Searcy, Oak Ridge was an idyll: new playgrounds, schools, a fine hospital, and no crime or booze, though not nearly enough cigarettes. While their families lived in prefabricated houses made from modular Cemesto sheets—bonded cement and asbestos, no kidding—dads worked with radioactivity in a brave new world. Everything was deadly, including their new, apparently antiseptic homes.

When he wasn't managing the men who made the innards that would power the bomb that leveled Hiroshima (Hanford made Fat Man, Nagasaki's flattener), Bert helped Helen raise Sue. Neighbors and friends patterned Sue's spastic limbs in arduous routines that stimulated her muscles. No pretty baby I. Mom said I provided contrast for a beautiful girl in the bed next to hers. Visitors cooed over the pink baby until my caterwauling interfered. "Your baby is nice, too," they told Mom. Ha. I was a colicky, red-faced gnome.

Even after the bombs fell, ending the war, little about the Manhattan Project was clear even to Oak Ridge's inhabitants. According to Jay Searcy, "Grass-roots America never quite understood what they did beneath the yellow glare of light in those distant, windowless plants in the '40s. 'Everything has changed,' Albert Einstein said after the atomic bomb detonated above Hiroshima, 'except the thinking of the people.' "

AFTER THE BOMB DROPPED

Our family moved back to Wilmington. Bert made nonradioactive chemicals and started a nonprofit organization for handicapped kids, dunning bosses for donations, and was my Cub Scout master. Men of that era prepared their own taxes, changed car oil, mowed the yard, and fixed things. Years later, after his catastrophic fall, his skull smashed, doped on barbiturates to ward off seizures, Dad glued wooden cannons onto the decks of sailing ship models. With no memos to dictate, rapt, his tongue licked his lips, but his eyes were glazed. Thereafter, Bert was three-quarters of the man he'd been. He'd outlive his wife, take care of his daughter, worry about his sons, and putter for thirty-six more years. Depriving him of complex reasoning skills, his fall cost him his job, banter, and small talk. Yet his pension paid bills and my tuition. He had more falls. After the first crash, his left ear constantly roared. Before DuPont let him go, he fell in an icy parking lot. After his second fall, the company man no longer had a company to admire or curse. This fall left him with a misshapen ankle and a permanent limp like his late wife's. He studied to be a Realtor and got a license, but this, too, was beyond him. It was in his early eighties, after transient ischemic attacks, that Dad fixed a dent in his five-year-old Oldsmobile with a ball peen hammer and epoxy. The result was Frankensteinian.

At eighty-six, Dad was still an independent coot. The ceiling leaked. Teetering and yawing, he fixed roof shingles and troubled to clean the gutters. John asked: please come down. John threatened to call the cops. Dad finished at his own pace. Into his eighty-eighth year, he plumbed, electrified, sawed, and hammered. Nels Nylen had set a tireless example without modern necessities like duct tape or Bondo.

Two weeks before his eighty-ninth birthday, taking out the trash on an icy day, Bert broke his hip. He began recovering, aspirated food, got pneumonia, and told me he'd had enough. His longtime doctor doped him on morphine. He died.

15.

Me, Back in the Land of the Giganormous PX

Intact, more or less, I was delighted to breath smoggy autumnal mid-Atlantic all-American air. I wasn't crippled or irreparably traumatized. My vision was unimpaired; hearing, slightly affected. Smell, touch, taste: fine. No gripes. Yet as we filed back one by one to the Promised Land that inflamed our dreams, the sumptuous Eden overflowing with stuff somehow wasn't as nice as we'd hoped.

During my final lax, desultory tour at Fort Dix, New Jersey, my tan faded, my hair grew, and I put on weight. Bones stopped showing. After spates of mortal fear, bad food, bacteria, fungus, facial mold, heat, and sleeplessness, I walked, talked, smoked, and watched news on the tube, simulating a regular person. But when a car backfired in the parking lot by the BOQ, I hit the floor. I didn't need to shred a Marlboro on completion, but did anyway: force of habit. For fun, I zipped a new 125cc Yamaha dirt bike through Fort Dix's sandy trails—until the throttle jammed and I flew over the handlebars and bonked my knee.

Had you seen me, you wouldn't have noticed perceptible derangement. I thought I passed for normal. Yet I was an easy mark. Salesmen saw my latent military bearing: sucker! I paid sixty dollars at the Cherry Hill Shopping Mall for a leather jacket two sizes too small. On Ransom Street in Philadelphia, I paid three hundred dollars for an engagement ring with a flaw visible even to my untrained eye. My sidewall hairdo said: here's a moron! Kit pretended not to notice the coal chunk. We GIs left home singly, joined our units as individual replacements, and then came back solitary souls. No parades. That was okay. We didn't talk. We wanted normal lives, whatever that meant, but we'd changed, and normality was elusive. Walking away from the pine barrens of the Fort Dix Physical Combat Proficiency Testing Facility, I toyed with the idea of staying in: a captain, commanding a company. Naaah. I was adrift, twenty-five, and damaged goods. Notwithstanding my clean-cut, newly married status, I was unemployable. The gruesomeness of the fighting became known. War support waned.

I applied for work at ad agencies, publishing houses, and newspapers, offering an amorphous English major, a lousy GPA, and no skills beyond setting up interlocking machine guns and firing-and-moving. I could speak sentences that sounded like Vietnamese . . . but if you were Vietnamese, they meant nothing. My search was fruitless. The business world decided I wasn't suited for executive work. I applied to sell insurance on consignment. In other words, the deal would be: if you sell a policy, we'll pay you a commission. Until then, you're on your own. Unfortunately, the personality test said: he's too aggressive. Did you know you could be too tough and angry to sell life insurance? I sure didn't.

With no job to distract me, I set about recording my war to understand myself. Catharsis is good, right? Confronting my experiences, I'd lay them to rest. I applied to business school. Kit's job paid the rent and bought groceries, and the GI Bill paid my tuition to the Wharton School at the University of Pennsylvania.

Reading, studying, remembering, I became a half-assed war protester, until Vietnam Veterans Against the War creeped me out. Testifying to Congress on TV, John Kerry looked sincere, but long-haired guys in faded fatigues guiltily confessing to atrocities seemed phony to me, acting out LSD-enhanced lies. Decades before recovered memory syndrome was debunked, scruffy vets' testimony about rape and torture presaged spurious allegations by "victims of child abuse." The VVAW was a bunch of narcissistic losers, I thought unkindly. Still, when I wasn't fretting about our futile war, I marched: twice. After the invasion of Cambodia came the Moratorium March: young capitalists at business schools raised money to run an ad in *The Wall Street Journal.* (That'll show 'em!) Four guys in fatigue jackets begging from a folding table in Wharton's Dietrich Hall raised five thousand dollars. In a quiet lecture hall, I asked a hundred students who were about to take their calculus final to contribute, too. Not a good venue: half of my targets were Air Force and Navy veterans. Their war was radically cleaner than mine. They booed me. Back in the hall, Nobel-winning economist Laurence Klein gave us a check for $1,000.

In the fall of 1970, Assistant Dean Scott Lederman and I drove to Manhattan to protest, confronting counterprotesters in Wall Street. Construction workers in hard hats strolled from the World Trade Center site to taunt our motley band of dancing hippies, Yippies, and Quakers. I was mortified to find myself on the same side of the barricades as tie-dyed anarchists and Weathermen. Although their rage made them ugly, the guys in hard hats were more my type than the hippy-dippy, spaced-out, loony New Agers on our side of the blue wooden fences.

I tugged Scott away, and quietly we drove back to Philly. I felt ashamed, both for going and for dropping out. I marched no more, though I kept my Che-style revolutionary mustache, an enduring war souvenir, which fell out in 2006 and '07 along with every other hair on my body.

16.

After the War, a Job, Finally; What's Scarier than War?

Psychologists say that our deepest phobia is fear of heights. Few people suffer from classic vertigo, but no one wants to fall, especially from up high. Number two on the fear list is public speaking. Big, bad butterflies bedevil even actors and politicians. Victims of stage fright go mute or gibber senselessly. I've done both. According to Jerry Seinfeld, "The average person at a funeral would rather be in the casket than doing the eulogy." Yet sooner or later, even shy folks will be asked to say something sometime. When the call comes, our voices will shake, our papers will tremble, and our throats will dry up as we wheeze, stammer, and screech. We confront speak-o-phobia in school, church, and business.

My first real job was at *Look* magazine. Inexplicably, *Look* hired me to be an ad salesman. I'd never sold anything in my life except a dozen lightbulbs in a Boy Scout drive, but I'd read a *Harvard Business Review* article on salesmanship that stipulated that good salespeople were both empathetic—they could pretend to listen—and aggressive. That was me, I said. I got two job offers, and decided to go to New York City to sell ads for *Look* instead of Kansas City to be a Folgers Coffee assistant brand manager.

Sales work required me to be on stage, albeit a small, metaphoric stage, usually performing for one impassive witness at a time. However, most media decisions are made by consensus, so I'd address small groups, too. These audiences wouldn't be doting relatives at school assemblies, wishing me well. They'd be suspicious *buyers,* wary of our sly, manic ilk, oily members of the sales nation. Like my predecessors, the Music Man, the Fuller Brush Man, and poor Willy Loman, I'd learn to speak or die trying. Really die: remember poor old man Rodale? He croaked on *The Dick Cavett Show* . . . while recommending that everyone live a healthy, organic life, as he did. Oops. Stress is a killer.

Sure, at the Ordnance School, I'd taught soldier-instructors how to overcome their anxieties about teaching. I confronted ingrained military anti-intellectualism that daunts even battle-hardened NCOs. Before learning how to kill people, few servicemen considered acting or teaching. Soldiers love to yell, but screaming isn't public speaking. Moreover, soldiers think diction and grammar are for sissies.*

Yet I'd called in air strikes and artillery as coolly as if ordering pizza. After the attack on Nancy, our battalion CO fell for my act of feigning self-control on the radio. Had I killed a hundred sappers and saved every one of my men, but stammered on the horn: no medal.

Combat experience should have helped me in business, huh? Unlike grunts, few of my new glad-handing comrades had

* Field Sergeant Joseph Tomayo addressing my Basic Training company on the day we graduated: "Listen up, you miserable scumbags. The men who filled that nasty Trojan rubber with jism and stuck it on my doorknob are *lower than whale shit*! Giddown and gimme thirty push-ups, you worthless shit-heads! Don't care if you're in dress greens. Knock 'em out now!"

bled on the job, so I had an edge in carnage delivered and received. Business and combat are linked by the grim prospect of failure, number three on the phobia list. In offices and foxholes, we often act as we do in order not to embarrass ourselves. My new job meant constant contact with my worst fear. Speaking to blank-faced people had unnerved me since the sixth grade. I nattered or clammed up. Over time, I'd learned that writing short scripts reduced my tiny terrors. Before I called on one of my junior salesman's cat-and-dog accounts, unwanted by senior salesmen, I wrote my lines in longhand and rehearsed. My first target: a Puppy Palace ad account buyer. No kidding. Her goal was to decide which medium would sell the most caged kitties, puppies, and birdies. My goal was to get her to think of *Look* as the right medium for dispensing pet litters to the masses. I believed it was. My conviction was an asset.

On my first phone call, my aim wasn't to persuade, but to avoid humiliation. Gathering my wits, twitching, I dialed. A secretary answered. Her boss was in a meeting: a reprieve! The next day, my customer picked up the phone herself. Curtains up! Klieg lights! Sweat! Shake! Quiver! I read my stilted palaver, including a quip I'd plotted out the day before, word for word.

She didn't hang up. She asked me a question. I panicked and hung up. Spontaneity? Beyond me. I had a problem. Making cold calls, even before insinuating myself into a buyer's office, I had to *converse,* unrehearsed. I've never had a problem chatting. Banter comes as easily to me as breathing. If glibness were gold, I'd be a billionaire. This was different. Talking for salary plus commissions is stressful. At the time, my boss, *Look*'s New York ad manager, required three sales calls a day, in person. He pretended not to notice that his forty-man platoon was a beaten, sad-sack unit. After years of chilly kiss-offs, our oldest pros had Post Traumatic Sales Disorder.

Look's weaknesses began with semi-fraudulent subscription sales efforts. Our circulation department hired college kids who went door to door, selling weekly plans like their kissing cousins, encyclopedia salesmen. Targets lived anywhere parents wanted their kids to succeed, in trailer parks, tenements, and working-class developments. Salesmen touted *Look*'s low-cost education: only thirty-seven cents a week, and the world is yours. Customers lacked math skills, and didn't know that was twenty bucks a year. This scam, perfected by our own John Suhler, Sr., produced an inflated circulation whose goal was to equal the huge audiences of network TV prime-time shows. It was two-thirds brilliant. Every magazine mastodon copied us. Also, yeah, okay, those snooty bastards at Time-Life were brutal competitors, too, but *Life* only briefly outlived *Look*. We both outlived the brontosaur that was *Collier's* and the stegosaur of *The Saturday Evening Post*. Then we, too, plunged into the tar pit.

When *Look*'s space peddlers should have been hustling, instead we felt sorry for ourselves, called our bookies, bought coffee for each other on Cowles's expense accounts, or nodded off at movie matinees. We bought one another lunches at restaurants that didn't charge too much: not La Grenouille and the Four Seasons, nor Hamburger Heaven and the Blarney Stone. Little French bistros in the West Side were perfect havens.

Personally, though, I was so callow that I didn't know that most of my comrades were AWOL. I was still striving to make one daily phone call. In March, after weeks on the job, except when a pitying senior guy took me along on a rare call of his own to show me how it was done, I had yet to meet a potential buyer. What had I learned? If you wanted to avoid a rude "no," you called an old friend who'd eaten your free lunches for decades. Sometimes he'd be in the rag trade down in the Thirties on Fashion Avenue. Or he'd be a superannuated Benton & Bowles media buyer. You'd chat and leave, dignity in hand, with no sale.

In the spring of '71—thank the sweet be-Jesus—I got my patter down and entered actual offices. Hey, I charmed! I could do this! On my third trip to the U.S. headquarters of British Leyland Motors, the ad manager lent me a Triumph 6. Kit and I drove to Cape Cod for the weekend. Returning the car, raving about it—it hadn't broken down—I made a sale: one fat four-color full-page ad that would run in October '71 for $50,000, four times my salary. Woo hoo!

However, *Look* magazine closed forever on a bright fall morning in October, weeks before the ad ran. Department by department, our elegant owner, Gardner "Mike" Cowles, and his CEO (whose name I forget and can't be retrieved on the Internet—a warning to all dominating, world-conquering CEOs), as well as *Look*'s publisher, Tom Shepard, told us that the magazine was "suspending publication" after suffering millions of dollars in losses for several years. The troika assured us we'd get severance checks: a week's pay for every year of service. Ergo, I'd get a week's pay for my seven months, roughly $275, next month's rent and groceries. Kit was working for Pepsico, so we wouldn't starve.

First, the editors and the art department got the bad news. After our turn on the gallows, at 10:30 A.M. the veteran peddlers repaired to local saloons where no one looked askance at pre-luncheon tippling. The magazine's youngest salesmen helped our sniffling creative friends drink a ten-gallon coffee urn of Bloody Marys—cheaper than drowning our woes at Goodale's. The instant Irish wake was a gift from Pat Carbine. She'd left *Look* in 1970 to cofound *Ms.* magazine with Gloria Steinem. Special-interest magazines like *Ms.* were replacing mass magazines, as this gift made clear. Commiserating, we sipped tomato vodka. Jerry Schachter, *Look*'s top sportswriter, asked an editor: Who are the three strangers?

"Salesmen," she said. "They work with us. Well, they *did*."

Schachter was instantly angry, spittle-flecking mad. "You

guys," he said. "Guys on the business staff. You killed this magazine!"

We had no defense. Our careers were over before they'd started, we were woozy, and we revered editors. He was probably right, and we didn't like confrontation—anger doesn't sell—so we agreed with him. Jerry calmed down, drank another Bloody, and turned his ire toward Mel Grayson, "that conservative bastard." Mel, our promotion chief, wrote our ads, supervising lead ad writer Joe Heller—ever heard of him?—and wrote polemics that Tom Shepard delivered to the ad community. These compensatory talks were meant to offset the perception in our polarized land that *Look* was antiwar, pro-ecology, pro-love, lefty, and too liberal. (Unlike . . . um . . . lefty-liberal antiwar *Life* magazine?) Since *Look* was indeed all these things, Tom's oratory might have been disingenuous, yet ours was a snazzy-looking, brilliantly designed, flashily art-directed family magazine, too. Sure, we covered civil rights and the war in Vietnam, handsomely, poignantly. Sure, our San Francisco office was gaga over Frisbees, Esalen, good dope, Love-Ins, and the Dead. Everyone was sick of the war.

Why not us, too? However, *Look* management was desperate. Ad dollars were hard to come by. Big TV shows like *All in the Family* reached more than thirty million viewers a week. Our inflated circulation was a quarter as big. Even adding pass-along readers browsing in beauty salons and dentists' offices, we weren't close.

Mel pinned the nation's problems on Ralph Nader and liberal media—but not, say . . . well . . . *Look*? Before we went verklempt, then kaput, Mel ended his schizophrenia by decamping for Spiro Agnew's speechwriting team. He joined Pat Buchanan, Mel Gold, and William Safire, alliterating speeches that denigrated the nation's nattering nabobs for Nixon's Nixon, Spiro Agnew, the nation's nasty new numbnuts naysayer.

After the Bloodies ran out, in the early afternoon, we sobered up and commuted home. Watching the evening news, we paid unconscious tribute to the medium that had killed us. On Channel Seven, New York's ABC station, Harry Reasoner said: "*Look* magazine died today." He paused. Our final cover, a gorgeous shot of the White House with white columns, green lawns, and blue sky, appeared on the screen. Harry continued: "*Look* never was much good anyway." Weeks later, guitarist Duane Allman's death in a motorcycle crash would be a sadder story than the end of our big, sweet, sometimes great picture magazine. Duane didn't get dissed by a bitter old TV fatwad, either. When I awoke the next day, hung over, I had no place to go and no income. Never again would I see my only city friends in our jaunty birthday-cake building, 488 Madison Avenue. I applied for unemployment insurance, as elder salesmen (even Yalies) recommended.

17.

The Third Newsmagazine . . . No . . . Make That Number Four!

After *Look* expired, I took six job interviews in ten days, each a sales call, cubed. If psychologists were to include "interview" on their phobia lists, I think it'd be our worst fear. When a self-salesman is pricked, does he not bleed? Self-pityingly? Blushing and sweating? *U.S. News & World Report* hired me anyway. My new boss, Charlie Taney, liked former infantry officers (like himself), especially with irreverent mustaches (like his). I chose the wobbly third newsmagazine over *Glamour.* Yes, *U.S. News* was dour. The pay wasn't great, either, but it was a newsmagazine, a weekly that played in the magazine industry's top tier, albeit clumsily. I was a snob. *U.S. News* covers featured . . . type. We weren't alone: *Reader's Digest* was all type, too. Visual dullness didn't prevent DeWitt and Lila Wallace from reaching nearly twenty million subscribers.

Graphics? Well, yes, eventually, *U.S. News* offered art: dollar signs, dingbats, and sometimes little snapshots. People! Flags! Red, white, and blue! No color photos, though: ours was a *serious* magazine. Let *Time* and *Newsweek* put Cher on the cover in the same week. Fine! Soft news—not us. We did hard news: monetary policy, interviews with Senator John Stennis and the postmaster general. When our minimalist redesign hit newsstands in 1972, the new cover featured three headlines (down from five) and a small color photo. Milton Glaser, you ain't seen nothing yet! Drab as we were, we were a newsmagazine, by God, hanging a rung beneath the tippy-top of the periodical jungle gym. We had two million subscribers. As an employee, like my peers, I held a small piece of *U.S. News,* the company—a cozy, weird place.

SNOOZERS GATHER

In 1973, unaware of how tough our jobs would soon become, *U.S. News* salesmen met in Washington. Three times yearly, we got pep-talked, feted, and harangued. We came from ad sales posts in New York, Detroit, Chicago, Cleveland, Dallas, and Los Angeles. Manhattanites rode Art Deco elevators in 45 Rockefeller Center. We touched no buttons. Operators with cotton gloves punched the numbers so we needn't soil our fingers.

Captain Eddie Rickenbacker's offices were across the hall from ours. The World War I flying ace, retired from Eastern Airlines, which he'd founded, wobbled on rickety legs, but he'd outlived racing car crashes, dogfights, and airline battles. After a 1942 plane crash in the Pacific, his crew drifted in a life raft for twenty-four days, injured, sunburned, and dehydrated. Food ran out. On the eighth day, a seagull landed on Rickenbacker's head. He killed it. The survivors set aside meat for fish bait and drank the blood. Everyone lived. Was this a tough guy, or what? When I saw the Captain entering the elevator to visit his bank across Fifty-first Street, I'd trot back to my window to see if the bandy-legged coot would make it again. Capt. Eddie didn't deign to look at onrushing traffic. Cabs and trucks skirted him anyway. He was blessed.

Born before gasoline engines, the Captain lived to run fleets of jets and see men land on the moon. Not everything in the modern age was sleekly streamlined, however. Calculators were born as big as the desks they squatted on. IBM mainframe computers did mysterious things with payrolls and mailing lists. The clatter of the Telex machine said: Don't worry! I'm on it! However, its clackety-clack ceased before the end of the decade, like the telegraph, the tom-tom, and smoke signals before it.

D.L.

In D.C., we U.S. Snoozers gathered in the Shoreham Sheraton, a blompy brick hotel connected to an apartment complex wherein dwelled David Lawrence, the octogenarian founder of two long-merged magazines called *World Report* and *U.S. News*. Known by his Telex signature, D.L. lived in a condo with his prized possession, a private Teletype machine. He didn't need a yacht or fancy car. In those days, rich news junkies craved only a newswire to the AP, UPI, and Reuters. The old man had already given his company to his employees, an unthinkably generous gift for a tailor's son who'd succeeded by working hard, embracing conservative principles, and truckling to powerful pols.

On May 15, 1972, associate publisher Walter Marek welcomed us to the city in which the best of the North (hospitality) met the best of the South (climate). In soupy, self-important Washington, that line wasn't so comical on the sixth hearing. W.M. got away with cornball stuff because he'd once walked on water. In World War II, he'd saved a ship equally endangered by an Atlantic storm and a nutty skipper. A junior officer named Herman Wouk with whom he served wrote *The Caine Mutiny,* featuring an idealistic, naïve junior officer named "Steve Maryk." In the movie, Van Johnson played Maryk. (Him again!)

Actually, until it petered out to mild applause, Walter's good-humored ramble was a highlight of those tedious sessions. Worst parts were séances with senior editors preceded by ninety-minute drink-a-thons. At the cocktail reception, senior salesmen advised: do as we do. Drink heavily to fortify for the tribulations ahead. Our female promotion staff pretended we were witty. We preened, tippling as if doomed. Each forum with The Editors—average age, sixty-eight; median disposition, crotchety, conservative, and argumentative—would remind us how little we knew. Editors, old *Wall Street Journal,* UPI, and AP hands, pontificated, ignoring pushy questions from tipsy salesmen. Wise men on the dais wore dark woolen striped suits, white shirts, and rep ties. Our togs, by contrast, were hip, we imagined.

Some of us wore the latest style, plastic duds predating today's breathable microfibers, wide-lapeled polyester suits. Jumbo ties featured colorful paisley patterns. We worked for a conservative magazine, but some of us had joined the Peacock Revolution. Our Ohio manager, Paul Brunst, wore the regalia the nation called "Full Cleveland": cream-colored suit with flared trousers and a back-belted jacket, plus a plaid ocher-colored ultrawide tie and tan Corfam slip-ons. Later, Paul's outfit would be impregnable armor.

Before D.L. introduced his editorial panel, his custom was to share the latest news with us, fifteen minutes of ditherings spewed from the Telex. (Picture D.L. as Daniel Schorr without the youthful vitality or wit.) This day, however, our frail benefactor provided breaking news. Alabama governor George Corley Wallace, Jr., the churlish third-party presidential candidate, had been shot in a Maryland shopping center. D.L. (who was called "the Walking Cadaver" behind his back) held the stage: ". . . and then the alleged shooter, Mr. Arthur Bremer, was tackled by police." Wire service protocol then updated major stories with new facts as they came in, providing subscribers with accounts that were as fresh as possible and ready for publication. These reports weren't supposed to be read aloud, however. Only an obsessed newshound could follow every mind-numbing change. D.L. was that bloodhound.

Every three minutes, a minion brought a new skein of ticker tape. In monotonous catechism, D.L. read the same story, repeatedly. Peddlers grew restive. Our bloodstreams had reached peak alcohol content some time ago and were now falling dangerously. D.L. held forth for thirty or forty minutes. The panel that followed would last for two hours, we knew. Hearing a Möbius taped loop about the attempted assassination of a segregationist governor, needing spirits, we were all civil rights workers, even our reddest-necks. We wanted Governor Wallace and D.L. dead.

A white knight appeared! Gene Williamson, our promotion director, lurched from behind the dark velvet curtain, moving unsteadily. Perhaps he'd been at another bar before arriving at the Shoreham. He tottered toward the Talking Cadaver, thrusting his arms before him like Frankenstein's monster. D.L. droned on, heedless. Twenty feet, fifteen, ten feet separated them. Gene staggered relentlessly. We watched enrapt for D.L.'s storied life to end dramatically.

Whoosh! A polyester flash emerged behind Gene and D.L. Gene was two uncertain steps away from strangling the great man when Paul Brunst slammed him to the floor. No Cleveland Brown, not even the great Jim Brown, could have done it better. Gene went down like a sack of yams.

Oblivious, D.L. continued as Paul dragged Williamson's semiconscious body from the stage by the heels. The editorial panel discussion, a stupefying anticlimax, was mercifully truncated. Meeting over revivifying cocktails, we thought that Paul had done a noble thing, though some of us were unhappy that Gene hadn't gotten to drag off his droning quarry. Gene's intentions were altruistic if murderous. D.L. died a few months later, at age eighty-five, in his Shoreham apartment, not in front of velvet curtains at the unsteady hands of an ungrateful employee.

18.

Tough Bosses

1) BILL

In the mid-seventies, a couple of years after D.L.'s near-death incident, my big boss at *U.S. News* was a new guy, Bill Dunn. He'd been a Marine in the Big One, and he walked with legs splayed, ready for danger. His bulldog nose had been squashed across his broad Irish American face. When he rolled up his sleeves, loosened his tie, and roamed the halls seeking malingerers, he resembled Lou Grant, Mary Tyler Moore's pretend boss. Alternatively, J. Edgar Hoover might have been Bill's face-sake, but we knew Bill's snout had been flattened legitimately. The longtime FBI director's concave honker only looked as if it had been mashed in a fight. A childhood boil, not a punch, made the overachieving cross-dresser's nose look that way. Hoover was less butch than he seemed.

By contrast, Bill Dunn was tougher than he looked. He worked for *McCall's* magazine after getting out of college, selling ads to ad agencies and their clients. The fifties and sixties were the Mesozoic Age for big print beasts, happy, lush times.

Multimillion-circulation dinosaurs like *McCall's* gallumphed across Madison Avenue, fat and prosperous. But then network TV landed, *ka-boom*.

Meteor? What meteor? Oh . . . that.

Bill had won his first executive job by taking an unusual step up the corporate ladder. After a hard day of schmoozing in the Chicago Merchandise Mart, doing symbolic trade-show battle with competing "seven sister" magazines like *Woman's Day* and *Better Homes & Gardens, McCall's* guys hunkered in a saloon in the bowels of the cavernous building. Far from home, they'd tie one on and tell tales like the traveling salesmen they were. They thirstily knocked back martinis, manhattans, and scotches.

Bill's boss was an Ivy Leaguer. Many ad salesmen then were second-rate graduates of first-rate schools. These men—always men until the mid-seventies—may not have been the brightest graduates of Yale, Cornell, or Williams, but they feasted atop the marketing food chain by pushing intangible space and time for magazines and TV networks. Snobs said ad salesmen were just high-end empty suits who were too dumb to be doctors, lawyers, or even stockbrokers. They weren't bright enough to write or edit. They weren't rich trust-fund heirs. They were still saying that when JFK Jr. started a magazine called *George* decades later. (Young Mr. Kennedy passed the New York bar exam only on his third try before he decided to pursue a career in publishing.)

In the saloon, drinks one and two slid down their hatches, crashing into empty stomachs like 100-proof depth charges. Faces turned red and the volume rose. Preposterous tales of sales conquests, dirty jokes, and random chitchat turned idly to school ties. School ties weren't metaphors back then. Colorful silk swatches were emblems of dear almae matres: Harvard, crimson; Princeton, orange and black; red and blue for Penn; Dartmouth, green; Cornell, red; brown for Brown; Yale, blue;

Columbia, baby blue; and purple for the little Ivies, Williams and Amherst.

Unlike his Brooks Brothers– and J. Press–wearing peers, Bill wasn't an Ivy Leaguer. After he got home from the Pacific, the GI Bill enabled Bill to attend the University of Massachusetts. Hence, Bill was wearing a generic Zoo-Mass maroon and white striped tie. Bill's boss looked down on Bill, both literally and figuratively. Somewhere between drinks three and six, his boss, a big guy with inches and pounds on Bill, as well as a diploma superior to Bill's crummy state-school sheepskin, suggested that Bill's academic pedigree wasn't up to snuff.

"Isn't UMass a big ole aggie school, Bill? Out in the sticks? Its students Irish dopes from Boston and Holyoke?" Bill was a smart, short-tempered kid from South Lee, Massachusetts. He clocked his boss square in his big fat pink chin. Although the guy was big and Bill was on his payroll, he went down, *boom*.

Word of Bill's audacity reached *McCall's* publishing headquarters. Ad director Steve Bowen, a Holy Cross grad, resented snotty WASPs, too. Bowen decided his Manhattan sales team needed Bill's fighting spirit. In order to beat the other women's magazines in bare-knuckled ad wars, Bowen promoted Bill, who believed sales work was thinly veiled combat. He was Old School. Old Public School: chalkboards, linoleum floors, knees to the groin, mumblety-peg knives driven into the ground next to your rival's Keds sneakers, and flying fists. Bill called me "Bobby." No one but my late mom and Kit called me Bobby unless they wanted to get my easily gettable goat. Bill gave everyone nicknames. He owned their goats. Decades before Dubya exercised the power of nicknaming in the White House, Bill understood it was better to grant than to receive a familiar name.

Most of my colleagues were older than Bill, who was in his early fifties. More than half of *U.S. News*'s sales staff had been pilots in World War II. They'd served in the RAF, Canadian Air Force, U.S. Army Air, and U.S. Navy Air. They'd fought Jerry and Tojo. They'd shot Fokkers and Zeros. They were predators: salesmen are besuited warriors, closers, killers. To Bill, who'd been a Marine flight mechanic in the Pacific, sixty-year-old Charlie stayed Charlie, irreducibly, and Finnish American Arne, fifty-eight, was also safe, his diminutive Christian name an unalterable unisyllable. But sixty-year-old Philip became Philsie, sixty-year-old Edward was Eddie, porky forty-eight-year-old George shrank to Georgie (but was spared Porgie).

Bill was never Billy. He called my best boss, New York ad manager Charlie Taney, "Charles." Bill owned nicknames or ignored them, so Charlie got an upgrade. Charlie was good to me. Liberal and compassionate, Charlie hated his ancestor. Chief Justice Roger Brooke Taney had decided the Dred Scott case, upholding slaveholder rights. Working for a conservative newsmagazine, Charlie feared he was fulfilling a jinxed family legacy. He gave me good accounts and nurtured me. He "mentored" me, a term I'm reluctant to use. Though Charlie thought *U.S. News* was a reactionary old rag, he depended on it to send his nine kids to college.

Selling ads to companies of dubious virtue bothered Charlie. Ads for tobacco and liquor companies like Philip Morris and Seagram's comprised nearly half of all newsmagazines' lineage. Toiling for a magazine he didn't respect, pandering to purveyors of nicotine, minks, and booze, ate Charlie up. Chunks of his ulcerated stomach were surgically removed. Yet he celebrated his fiftieth wedding anniversary, hit eighty, and died slightly rich years after Mortimer Zuckerman bought *U.S. News* for its priceless Rock Creek property.

In my seventh and final year at *U.S. News*, Bill Dunn needed bypass surgery. Before departing for a brief rest before his ordeal, he promoted me and moved me into a spectacular office next to his. Side by side. We overlooked the Rockefeller

Center skating rink and the golden statue of Prometheus twenty-three stories down.

Bill stopped smoking . . . overnight . . . going from fifty daily cigarettes to zero. Before Bill told us he was facing surgery, I'd set up a sales call with one of his powerful friends. Bill ignored his angina to call on Lorillard's CEO, the leader of Earth's third-biggest tobacco company. In Lorillard's posh 666 Fifth Avenue offices, Bill apologized. He was sorry for getting heart disease and sorrier for giving up his beloved Kents. In the best sales call ever, Bill turned a dire prognosis into money. Bill regretted that he was no longer man enough to puff his friend's fine cigarettes. He promised that we'd attract as many readers to Lorillard brands as we could, though our average reader was roughly Bill's age.

I chimed in, suggesting that we'd find more covers for Lorillard. Our ad schedule jumped from twenty-six pages to thirty-nine. Thirteen additional four-color pages in one year meant six hundred thousand bucks, net. Thanks to us, aging *U.S. News* readers would enjoy more blandishments leading to emphysema, cancer, and heart disease. (Don't worry: I'll get mine.) Then Bill left Jimmy, his deputy, in charge and departed for his operation.

As Bill recuperated in the hospital, I repaid his trust by taking a job with a hot little magazine in Austin, Texas. Two days after Bill's operation, I told Jim my news: I was leaving for *Texas Monthly*. Blanching, he said: "Tell Bill. I can't. He'll kill me." Bill had promoted me. I repaid his kindness by deserting him. Jimmy was right. It was a matter of honor. I had to be the one to break the news. Ruefully, I trudged to the hospital, expecting Bill to make me suffer, to remind me that I was leaving a major magazine. (We have our illusions.) I'd leave a new office overlooking golden Prometheus, the skating rink, the Christmas tree, and the world's ad capital for a dinky magazine in the boondocks.

Post-op, doubtless, tubes were running from Bill's portals. When I got to the hospital room, I stood in line: one of Bill's unemployed friends was seeking his advice. Waiting, I grew warm though it was late December. I dribbled flop sweat like a dying comic. Even in normal circumstances I perspire, but these beads became rivulets, discoloring my starched dress shirt. Bill's chest had been cracked, his clotted arteries had been reamed, and his circulatory system rerouted. What had I been thinking? I'd change my mind. Stay.

"Now what do you have on your bright young mind, Bobby, me boyo?" Bill rasped, grinning through the pain, affecting the brogue of his ancestors. After seven years as the magazine's youngest space peddler, at thirty-three, I was still the team's tyro. I blurted my news. His eyes beetled: "You sure?" he asked.

"Yeah—well—yes," I stammered.

"Well, then," he said, "we'll miss you. You're making a mistake, but that happens. Good luck. You'll do well. Stay in touch, kid." Thank goodness for morphine drips.

2) TEXAS THE HARD WAY WITH MICHAEL R. LEVY

Mike Levy was, is, three years younger than me. He will always be richer than I am: roughly twenty million bucks wealthier, at least, after he sold *Texas Monthly* to Emmis Communications in 1998. Mike introduced himself as "mikelevypublisherof texasmonthly" in one breath, until, unthinkably, he retired in August 2008.

In 1982 at a management retreat in a resort on Lake Travis, senior managers for *Texas Monthly* and *California* magazine listened to expensive gobbledygook from Dallas management consultants about company organization. Out of the azure Texas sky, Mike appointed me president of *Texas Monthly*, flabbergasting everyone, mostly me. A day later, after my surprised peers complained that Mike had destroyed our symmetrical ranks, Mike dis-appointed me.

Mike looked old on purpose: he dressed in white shirts, dress shoes, rep ties, and blue suits in order to be trusted. Before he launched the magazine, Mike met with a job candidate during a thunderstorm in Houston. The men parted in a violent downpour. Mike got confused. He couldn't tell the overflowing sidewalk from the adjacent motel pool. Slipping into the deep end, thinking fast, Mike hurled his satchel crammed with precious business plans back to his job candidate, who caught it. Safe!

As the first issue of *Texas Monthly* was being printed in 1973, founding editor Bill Broyles (later editor of *California* and *Newsweek*, and screenwriter for a dozen movies including *Apollo 13*) confessed to Mike: "I don't know what I'm doing." His sole magazine job was stringing for *The Economist*. He was only twenty-eight! Mike said: "I'm twenty-six, Bill. My magazine experience is selling ads to cemeteries for *Philadelphia* magazine."

My arrival had touched off rebel yells from native staffers who thought my hiring was another sign that *Texas Monthly* was being Yankified. I was from Manhattan: ipso facto, a jerk: no U.T. burnt-orange yellow-dog Texan I. At about the same time, Bill Broyles hired Californian James Fallows (Fallows later became editor in chief of *U.S. News*). He also hired Nicolas Lemann from *Washington Monthly* (today, dean of the Columbia Journalism School and a contributor to *The New Yorker*) and Joseph Nocera, also from *Washington Monthly* (now a columnist at *The New York Times*). Yankees were all over the place. In my first Texas sales presentations to agencies in Dallas and Fort Worth, I didn't help myself by adopting a spurious drawl. Transplanted New Yorkers and Detroiters working for Texas ad agencies knew a smarmy accent when they heard it. They, too, had been outsiders, Northerners, but they'd stopped pretending. They mocked my mushmouthed faux Southwestern delivery. Can't say I blame them. I didn't like that guy, either. I rationalized that I'd been born in Tennessee, like Davy Crockett, who died at the Alamo, forever Texan. Recalling my phony efforts to pass, I blush.

Soon after arriving, I instituted a big ad-rate hike disproportionately affecting our Texas sellers (not national salespeople in California, Detroit, Chicago, and New York). I faced an insurrection. Rebellious Texans confronted me at the home of lead mutineer Lee Petty, a San Antonian who loved the Lone Star State more than life itself. After I'd arrived, Lee had tried to Texify me, outfitting me with cowboy boots, which hurt, bad, and a custom-fitted Manny Gammadge high-roller hat. Thing never fit right: my head is colossal.

Lee resented my indecisive non-Texandom. I didn't know Texas Commerce Bank from Austin Savings, Southwest Airlines from Braniff, or Roche Bobois from Dillard's. I'd never been to South Padre Island, the Piney Woods, or Marfa. Why didn't I pack my carpetbags and go home? Why? Well, I was here, now, as were Cassie and Kit. We loved Austin at first sight. Cassie sang "Da Yerro Rose of Texas" in Montessori school: "She wants no udder ferras, she rubs no one but me . . ." They couldn't run me off. For some reason, maybe because they were less confrontational, saleswomen tolerated my slipshod efforts to pass for a Lone Star Statesman. I stayed, resolved to do better, work harder, fly and drive farther. In 1979, the first year of American Airlines' Advantage program, I flew a hundred thousand miles, earning free tickets to Hawaii. We stayed at the Hotel Hana Maui: no TVs or in-room phones, a Polynesian respite. Two days after we'd settled in, the concierge woke me at 6:00 A.M. to go to the lodge's office phone. Urgent! Mike was upset. Neiman Marcus was throwing a party, and he hadn't been invited. I had to do something! I went back to bed. After a day I spent bodysurfing on a black sand beach, Mike's party invitation arrived in Austin. Phew.

Back in Texas, I began firing people. I'd be a hard-ass boss if never a proper Texan. A burly guy, Mike is hairy everywhere but his pate. In Houston's Hobby Airport in 1979, a congressman tried to charm him, pointing out their bond. "Mike, I see our hairlines are receding in the same way," the congressman said. "Dunno about you, sir," Mike snorted, "but mine already done receded."

Mike labored demonically in his sunny corner office for twelve, fourteen, sometimes eighteen hours weekdays, plus several hours on Saturday and Sunday. He saw the southeastern Austin panorama, a sky view of the best city in America. He'd graciously ceded westerly Hill Country views to the editors. From our side of the sixteenth floor, he could watch the city's biggest fire station in action. After his magazine, his wife, Becky, and daughters, Rachel, Mara, and Tobin, Mike loved firemen and EMTs best. Hearing sirens, he'd learn where the trucks were headed on the emergency scanner and get there first.

Mike walked hurriedly, bouncing off sidewalks and bumping into people, especially when agitated. Driving his late-model Impala ("You can have any company car you want, Bob, as long as it's a Chevy"), Mike had two speeds: too fast and not fast enough. He drove with pedal to the metal, accelerating madly or braking abruptly. Mike had a pilot's license—a frightening fact—but the prepsters at Dallas's St. Mark's had taught him that he was neither an athlete nor an Episcopalian. Mike retaliated by protesting mandatory chapel, seeking religious freedom in a Christian school. (He won.) He enlisted in the Marine Corps. Drill instructors gave Mike a bad back that was still problematic long after his medical discharge. Every other week, Mike spent hours lying on his office carpet to stop spasming.

A devoted son, Mike was polite, courtly, Southern, a St. Mark's old boy despite himself. Bill Broyles and I were three years Mike's senior and combat veterans, but a scolding from Mike humbled us. He had a dark side: he was cruel to mail boys, assistants, and secretaries, and anyone else who let him bully them. He wanted people to show moxie, I learned after months of terrorizing.

He said: "You can fight back!" He admired people who withstood his fire. Mike Levy is a force of nature. I'm lucky to know him, although writing about him means I'll get an angry phone call and a cease-and-desist letter.

3) DAN OKRENT

I met Dan at *Texas Monthly,* where he was a consultant, telling the editors how to publish books. Before long we became business partners, starting a magazine of our own.

Technically, Dan was never my boss. I was his elder and CEO of *New England Monthly*. He was president and editor in chief. Partners. Equals. Before starting, we agreed that we'd rule separate realms: I'd run the business side; Dan, creative affairs. However, Dan's ferocious intelligence and quick wit put him in control of any subject or situation he chose to master. He knew every writer in the world, could do six-digit calculations in his head, and had a wickedly sarcastic mouth on him. He knew jazz, history, baseball, politics, government, and classical music. More important, he was fearless.

During *Texas Monthly* management meetings, for fun, Dan drew the U.S. map state by state, starting from the Midwest and working outward to the coasts. He didn't fill a simple outline, east to west, in the conventional way. Dan preferred being challenged. He drew his national jigsaw piece by piece. Discussion stopped as Dan puzzled over Indiana, Nebraska, Wyoming, West Virginia, and Utah.

After *NEM,* at Time Inc., he helped run *Life* magazine as a Gulf War weekly, then took over the monthly *Life,* and then Pathfinder, the abortive Time Inc. online enterprise, and nearly *Sports Illustrated,* too, losing a "bake-off" to an insider. In 2006, Dan turned down a chance to run the world's most venerable newsmagazine: nearly been there, nearly done that. Dan became *The New York Times*'s first public editor. He appears in documentaries and an occasional movie, but mostly he writes meaty books.

In 1984, to declare his editorial independence from powerful people, his premiere column in *New England Monthly* trashed . . . our landlords. Nice! In reconstructing the dead old brick Brassworks building that now housed our first offices, Dan complained, our landlords had used tax breaks, political connections, and seedy gummint deals. Co-landlord Gerard Doherty had invested $33,000 in our little magazine. He and his real estate partner, Herb Berezin, gave us a deal: four dollars a square foot. Dan pissed on them. You can't buy me, Gerard, Dan implied.

As publisher, I dealt with investors and landlords. Our first issue initiated an internecine war with the men who controlled our heat and rent. When a million leftover sand granules that had scoured the wooden attic floor above our own floor began sifting into our computers, stalling our $30,000 typesetting machine, Herb ignored my complaints.

That summer, during a raucous senior management meeting, I screwed up a spreadsheet, again. Frustrated by my stubborn refusal to admit the mistake that all nine managers could see, Dan threw a chair and stomped from the room. I could be a bonehead. He could be a pill. He didn't suffer dopes. (A couple of years later, a fancy IQ testing company asked him to take a genius exam. Dan posted the results on his office door. They stayed there for a year. He says it wasn't that long, but witnesses saw the color printout of his cerebrum.) The only one of his cranial quadrants that wasn't "genius" was the lobe for "empathy."

In 1989, after years of trying to get out of his job that had started to bore him soon after our first issue, efforts that I thwarted by holding his chubby feet to the fire, Dan finally quit. As we drove from Connecticut to New Hampshire during his last month on the job, I told him whom I'd picked to succeed him. Dan was appalled. He'd made his own selection, but I was adamant. He threatened to jump from the car. However, the company Jetta was going 70 mph. Dan couldn't open the door, sparing him and allowing him to appear in *Sweet and Lowdown* and *The Hoax*. Dan slowly disentangled himself from *NEM*, and I continued to pretend I was an entrepreneur.*

4) KEITH

Keith Drake was my last boss. Our magazine had been bought by the Canadian company Telemedia. I was a lousy underling. I don't like orders. Authorities annoy me. I bridle at policemen,

* From a 1987 article for *Folio* magazine, "Meeting the Entrepreneurial Challenge Is Tough When You're Allergic to Fear," by Robert Nylen, Publisher, *New England Monthly:*

"Before I started *New England Monthly,* I hadn't started anything, not even a lemonade stand. I've been a car washer (and dryer), a plastic grinder, a GI, a space salesman, and a writer. I was an associate publisher, code for sales-manager-with-a-nice-office. I never ran anything except a mangy rifle platoon, and didn't yearn to be my own boss until my thirties.

"So I'm an entrepreneur only if you define the job as small businessman with the soul of a car washer and the vanity of Charles de Gaulle . . . True entrepreneurs invent truly brand-new things. Henry Luce, for instance, invented the first newsmagazine, the first good business magazine, and the first sportsweekly. There was only one Luce, one Condé Nast, one Harold Ross. The rest of us imitate."

drill instructors, bosses, Bill, Mike, and especially Dad. Like Bill, though, Keith just plain scared me. A big, ruddy British bear, his unnaturally blue eyes inappropriately tinged by periwinkle were cut from glacial Nordic stalagmites. He didn't blink. His bottomless stare emerged from a northern European gene pool of marauders: Vikings, Picts, Gaels, Saxons, Angles, and Franks. When the descendant of ravening Norsemen stares at you through unfluttering lids, you tug your forelock, bow, and fall prostrate. Keith stared like Steve Forbes or Ross Perot (without messianic political theories).

Am I dating myself? Very well. Imagine that you're a raw singer who's fallen under Simon Cowell's pitiless gaze. Stress makes you go off-key, forget your lyrics, and wail. Like Simon C., Keith seemed to be most comfortable when others felt acute pain. Immobile and Buddha-like, he sat through silences. Personally, conversation lulls disturb me. I natter. Keith let me speak as if he were preparing to pillory, draw, and quarter me, then chew my bones. At home in his pale skin, he apparently had malevolent designs on mine. People warned me before our first meeting: be afraid. Keith, the company's COO, was the bad cop to CEO John Van de Kamer's good cop. Keith didn't work at intimidation: no strain. He was impassive, as some powerful people are. Had I babbled in tongues, he probably wouldn't have been surprised.

So I spoke. I'm loquacious—prolix—even when I'm not nervous. Under pressure, I talk. That's good for a salesperson. Buyers like to be entertained, but I'm an information donor, an information hemophiliac.

Keith asked me how we were faring. His international company was integrating our five-year-old magazine into its American subsidiary, led ostensibly by, um, me, consisting of three magazines. We were a cog in a big Canadian machine with dozens of French and English magazines and scores of radio stations. Our U.S. subsidiary had started a new magazine, *Eating Well,* and was reviving *Harrowsmith,* a respected but money-losing magazine devoted to celebrating rural living.

At the time, James Lawrence, who'd created *Harrowsmith* and founded *Eating Well,* and I didn't agree about how to integrate our operations. I wanted to bull ahead. James didn't want to fire his people. Plus, Dan was about to leave.

Instead of telling the frank truth, I talked about what we did right, filibustering—minutiae about circulation, ad sales, competition: bullshit. "What are you doing wrong, Bob?" Keith asked. He wasn't hostile. He sounded like a camp counselor. He wanted to help, but he was a Viking who'd impale me when his mood changed. Keith was English by birth and Canadian by citizenship. He'd come to Ontario in the tag end of World War II, learning to fly a Spitfire on the flat farmlands in Ontario. He'd kill Nazis, or be killed, before the war ended.

I froze. What are your weaknesses? Your mistakes? Who answers such questions? Try asking a U.S. president what policy error he most regrets. Request that a headmaster discuss his feelings about children as sexual objects. At what age is it okay to fondle the bunnies, sir? This exercise was the oral equivalent of a foible-seeking questionnaire from the human resources director. However, Keith wasn't an HR flunkie with a psych major and a mean streak. He was a freaking executioner.

Instead of an innocuous cop-out, like "My staff says I work too hard," I said, "Maybe Dan and I are too tough." It was half a joke and half a lie. Dan was the magazine's creator, brain, and soul. I was the spleen. In 1986, Dan suggested that we trade jobs. Frustrated by our business torpor, bored, his Hail-Mary scheme was to become the publisher, and I'd be the creative guy. He needed a challenge. I dilly-dallied for a month before saying no. My nerve failed me.

If I'd agreed, he'd be getting interrogated. "Too tough" was safe, I thought. Dealing with a world-class hard-ass, venturing onto hardpan seemed risk-free.

"Have you thought about changin'?" Keith asked in his north-country accent, clippin' gerund endin's.

Well. Um. No? "Maybe you should." Rather than compliment my moxie, he implied that being overmoxied was trouble. But I'd been kidding! Sure, Dan could be cruel to fools, but not sweet little me. Although I'd fired people, even in groups (including, soon, a group that included my beloved wife, who was our ad services manager), my tough-guy pose was pure BS. I was a Nice Guy! Mike Levy had said so when he hired me. ("You're a nice guy, Bob!") Sure, I'd killed people and ended a few careers with my blunt hatchet, but mine was a little white lie. Mercifully, Keith took a break.

LIEUTENANT EXPLODING PARACHUTE, MEET CANDIDATE UPSIDE DOWN

Over drinks and dinner, we trod common war-torn ground. Keith's war story was a doozy. In late 1944 and early 1945, plenty of dying was still going on in Europe. The Luftwaffe desperately protected the fatherland from Allied bombers. Dispatched to Ontario for RAF fighter training, Keith was a kid who'd just turned twenty. Upon graduating in late spring, he'd be shot down too, he feared.

"Planes were fallin' like snow," Keith explained. "Jerry had Messerschmitts. He had flak. He was savin' nothin'. I was goin' to my grave. Had no choice, though. At least Canada was far away from the tight rationin' and the V-bombs hittin' London. I was goin' on my first solo, just months from goin' back to England to do my worst to the enemy.

"My trainer was taxiin' down the runway. I was alone for the first time. It was a long runway. A little headwind, which you want. I picked up speed. Then, smack! Can't see a thing. Not airborne. Hit the brakes. Cut the engine. Tried to pop the canopy, but I couldn't see.

"The inside of the cockpit was all white, all silk. Turns out I'd popped my parachute. An accident. Delicate things, parachutes. Material enough to keep dozens of girls in stockin's for years. Takes hours to fold and pack each one. I brought the chute back to the riggers, nice ladies. Asked them to fold it as well as they had the first time. They kidded me: 'Don't do it again, young man.'

"On my next go, rollin' down the runway, pickin' up speed, anxious—somehow—I did it again. In one's desire not to make *this* mistake, one's mind works against itself sometimes. This time I knew what was wrong. This time the parachute riggers weren't happy to see me.

" 'The record is two,' they said. 'You tied it.'

"I set a new record with my next go. Three blown chutes, and still no solo."

He succeeded on his fourth try. Keith smiled wanly at me over his Scotch. No boss had ever shared such a revelation with me. Was this a lesson about perseverance, an implicit lesson? His candor encouraged me. I told him my Upside Down story. There: we tied for self-abasement. Today, I know that if I'd actually had to fly a fighter on my own, something I'd dreamed about doing before meeting Keith, I might have deployed my own parachute ten times, given a chance. Plus crashed my plane.

There we were, Keith and I, admitting that neither of us was as tough as we pretended to be. That exchange was balm for me. We all behave like frightened rabbits sometimes, Keith implied. The important thing: push through; don't try to quell fear. (Can't be done.) Keith's lesson was tacit. He let me work out the moral on my own. The best learning is absorbed straight into the bloodstream.

Maybe toughness is an illusion, a chimera. What looks like a hard stick of dynamite turns out instead to be a ripe metaphorical sausage, stuffed with odd ingredients: some theater, bluster, lots of bravado, and a dash of mystery meat. It's ground up and laced with flop sweat, but it's just cheap bologna.

19.

Starting Up, Cringing; Raising Money; Danger on the Roof

After I'd angrily quit my Texas job—Mike Levy sent one offensive memo too many—Dan Okrent and I leaped into the start-up abyss. We had needs, not safety gear: no parachutes or bungee cords. For two months before Kit and I bought our Ashfield house, we lived out of suitcases, nervously waiting for our investment broker to finish raising money for the launch of *New England Monthly.* We bounced from Austin to Delaware to Avalon, New Jersey, to Philadelphia, to a rented house in Worthington, Massachusetts.

We were ambivalent about retreating under pressure. We loved Austin's warm, friendly vitality. Smart folks, we know, peopled New England, but they spent half of the year hunkering inside in sweaters, flannels, and long johns. In Austin, you don running shorts in January and can swim in Barton Creek every day of the year, hot or cold.

Yet *New England Monthly* was wildly successful with media mavens and critics. Dan won awards. Big-footed reporters wrote laudatory articles about us in the *Times,* the

Globe, Ad Age, and *Adweek*. We were on Boston TV. Cameras liked Dan. So did readers. We were smug, yet diffident. We were anxious, but good copy. We boasted, but made fun of ourselves. We were bound for glory. We attracted 120,000 subscribers. Wowser. In 1986, director Frank Collins asked us to talk to his Radcliffe Publishing Course students. Each summer, eighty semi-rich new college graduates attended a six-week course on Harvard's drowsy campus. (Later, the program moved to Columbia University.) Kids paid big bucks to earn certificates with no academic value. However, employers treasured kids with Radcliffe's sheepskins. Telling our picaresque stories, we were heroes, then goats, humble, vain, funny, silly, and serious. When Dan described our trip to Scotland to court investors, I heard it afresh. His tale was so hideously cringe-making that I'd repressed it until Dan sent me twitching back to April 1983. I had entrepreneurial PTSD. When he finished, I was dazed.

MEMO TO WOULD-BE PUBLISHERS: SQUELCH PHOTOS OF YOUR EDITOR IN LEOTARDS

A fund-raising excursion to Boston in March 1983 swerved into a ditch when our prospect looked at Dan and said: "I know you!" He didn't know why. Me, he knew not. Puzzled, the money guy ignored our pitch. "Aha!" he said, and abruptly left, returning with the current *Esquire* magazine in hand.

Dan and I sighed. The jig was up. Our prospect turned to a first-person account bylined "Daniel Okrent." A color photo showed the author in dance couture, his gut bulging over the elastic band of his tights, a cigarette dangling from his unshaven gob as he executed a balletic move. The article explained that Dan's former boss, Bob Gottlieb, a bookish éminence grise, had acculturated him by introducing him to opera and ballet. The VC gave us nothing but needles. We were learning the hard way. We were young! Well, youngish—Dan was thirty-four and

I was thirty-eight. We were impulsive, but for once, our impatience was going to be an asset. "Risk-taker" sounded better than "reckless, impetuous fool." As Chairman Mao said, the road to yes begins with a thousand nos.

GREAT BRITAIN

After test runs in the States, Dan and I went to the British Isles with our investment broker, Hobby Abshier, and two of his associates. Hobby had good contacts overseas. Some of his Gulf Coast oil fields and South American mines had come in for Kleinwort Benson, Gartmore, and Touche Remnant. British investment bankers trusted Hobby. So did we. "I'm just a beggar shaking a tin can at folks," Hobby said, chuckling. His blue blazer rode up his neck over a perma-pressed shirt. His tie stopped short of his belt. His gray slacks were stay-pressed, too. No fashion plate, by golly, Hobby was persistent, supersmart, and had the courage of our convictions.

We'd raise a third of our funds in the U.K., he'd promised. Nonetheless, our European jaunt began more somberly than our hideous first American excursion. Centuries ago, English financiers had made fortunes in the Colonies from the Hudson's Bay and East India companies. Duping natives was easy, they found, and fooling their own colonists was no harder. In the home of our erstwhile oppressors, our plans to differentiate Vermont's communards, upper-class Bostonians, and Cambodian immigrants were, well, pointless.

We started with jet-lagged meetings in the City, London's financial district. The next morning, we took British Airways to Scotland. Our first target was a Glasgow pension fund, with a solemn mahogany-paneled boardroom. Here we were, ill at ease, trying to talk thrifty men who managed railroad employees' widows' and orphans' pension funds into dropping thousands of pounds into a speculative venture based in—where again?—ah, yes: New England. "That's in the state of Boston, is it not?"

A business, I should add, being started by a Swedish Scots Welsh Irish Delawarean and a Jewish American Detroiter. What were we thinking? Delaware and Michigan aren't New England. Our sins against geography were worse than my failure to be Texan. Tenured Texans date their ancestry back a paltry five generations. Proper Yankees count twelve generations to the Mayflower. The Scots weren't skeptical, however. They offered no criticism. They were baffled, nice, and asked no questions. In Scotland, Thailand, or Sugarland, Texas, no questions means no sale. A good salesman prefers argument to silence. Polite silence means: Get out. Now. Please. Leave no leave-behinds.

Counting rejections in the States, we were 0-for-17. Glumly, we rode British Rail across southern Scotland. Why were we here? What were we doing? Could Edinburgh be as bad? Impossible. Edinburgh is Scotland's intellectual center: church spires, castle turrets, grand relics of empire; new buildings were rising, too. Arriving in the elegant Athens of the North Country, we said: They'll get it! The Enlightenment sparkled here. Adam Smith shone his economic light from Old Town. The city had produced David Hume, Charles Darwin, Sir Walter Scott, Robert Louis Stevenson, Sir Arthur Conan Doyle, Sir Sean Connery, Tony Blair, Gordon Brown, and J. K. Rowling. (Our kinda peeps.)

We checked into the grand old Caledonian Hotel, teeming with workers, symbols of Britain's resurgent economy. While our rooms were being renovated, over lunch, we pitched a hopelessly junior banker from a Scottish investment bank. We were Dan; Hobby; Tim Wright, a Scottish investment broker; a Texan who worked for Hobby; and me. There was one of him, a nervous young man both shy and outnumbered. Perhaps he felt out of his depth. (Little did he know how far over our heads we were swimming. Dan and I were so far submerged in Loch Ness the monster couldn't find us.) The kid swigged two Scottish tranquilizers. As his single malts dived home, he unwound. After his third Scotch, he began telling stories. A fourth, then, for the sidewalk? Why not? Departing, he cheerily promised to give our documents to someone who could make a decision.

The firm had apparently sent the mail clerk on a lark. We were dead men walking. We glumly strode from the Caledonian to a Georgian square lined by regal town houses, residences being converted into offices. Mike Morgan greeted us at the door of his brand-new one-man investing fund. A block of Gaelic gristle, Morgan was Braveheart in a blue suit, not blue face paint. Chippendale chairs were shoved against the wall and covered with sheets protecting them from plaster, dust, and paint. Morgan's fund had a million pounds to invest. Even in Scotland, that wasn't much. Consequently, he was determined to make no mistakes. Mr. Morgan had read our prospectus, paying sharp attention to detail.

He interrupted my spiel, challenged my numbers, and pointed to a math mistake. I'd altered the spreadsheet late in the prospectus printing process, splicing ten rows of new numbers atop hundreds of old ones. Recalculating the bottom line, I'd failed to alter sums on right-hand columns. Therefore, the numbers didn't tie out. Financial people expect numbers to add up left, right, and down. I stammered. Morgan said we were up to no good. Bad math was one thing, but our plan was clear: we meant to cheat him! My voice quavered. I wheedled, stuttered, and waffled. Hobby's voice was naturally high-pitched, Texas-twangy. Hearing me going crybaby, Hobby bleated, a calf in barbed wire.

Although Dan is the most self-confident person in the universe, he, too, went down. He'd be the guy in the red sweater in Ken Burns's PBS specials. His baritone sounds as godlike as that guy who did all the movie trailers: "In a world gone mad . . ." Dan had already *invented Rotisserie Baseball*! But Dan caught a case of doubt from Hobby, who was disheartened by my audible fear.

As that awful meeting dissolved one sweat bead at a time, I was as scared as if we were taking incoming. Fear of failure fuels business and battle, but *actual* failure—being humiliated before your peers—is devastating. When your ego shatters, it doesn't matter that your skin is intact. Morgan ripped out our spinal cords. We slithered from his office. We knew how poor bloody Wogs had felt facing Royal Scots or the Black Watch. Salespeople learn how to protect themselves from rejection by accumulating a callus overlaid by rationalization. It's not me they don't like, but my cruddy product. Me? I'm fine. But when your bright *idea* is rejected, my friend, then you, your best self, are being personally rebuffed. Calluses don't lessen the excoriation. The membrane between your pet project and your persona is too thin.

We oozed and slimed along, invertebrates, trying to rally for the day's most important meeting to come, our last stop. The next brownstone was bigger than Morgan's not insubstantial building. Its partners managed more money. We were climbing its imposing steps when an elegantly dressed man burst from within, spring-loaded, to bar our entry to his sanctum sanctorum.

"Timothy, Timothy!" The tall, pinstriped gentleman addressed Tim Wright, our Scottish escort and protector. "Been trying to reach you all day, Timothy! Left messages! Didn't know where to reach you here. Wanted to give you fair warning. But you were traveling. Teddibly sorry, Timothy, old man: teddibly. But you see . . . we're just not interested.

"Now, seeing that you're here . . . would you like to come in for some tea?"

Our entourage demurred. Hobby and Tim hopped into a

cab and took off for London. Dan and I trudged desultorily to the Caledonian. Rain began falling. Soon our clothes were as sodden as our drowned souls. Back at the hotel, we couldn't get into our rooms: construction. We flipped a coin to see who'd get to call home. Dan won. Seeking commiseration from sweet Becky Okrent, Dan reached the family's answering machine. Dan spent ten pounds we didn't have just to hear himself say he wasn't in. That night, we drank single malts. If you'd told me before our trip that a glowering Scotsman could frighten me as much as a Kalashnikov, I'd have jeered. But when your family future depends upon skeptics who not only fail to share your vision, but think you're a criminal—that's the business equivalent of bullets.

The next day in London, we rejoined Tim Wright and Hobby. Six months earlier, Tim's doctor had warned him that his esophagus would disintegrate if he continued drinking. From that moment until the night of Morgan's assault, Tim hadn't touched a dram. Then he drank a whole wagonload of whisky. That morning, his pallor betrayed his hard fall from the wagon. Our Scottish day had been so awful that Tim had dived headfirst into a bathtub of Scotch on his return to London. He shook. We were all hung over except for abstemious Hobby: once again, imperturbably optimistic.

"Okay, boys," he said at our next stop. "Tell 'em about your newspaper." We had no hope. Our prospects dire, our spirits subterranean, we undersold. Spent, beaten, we seemed calm, self-assured, not defeated. Dan was droll and compelling. A tall, red-haired gentleman from Kleinwort Benson (named Neill Young, no fooling) became our champion. Neill liked what he heard. "We'll invest four hundred thousand dollars," he said. He called two banking friends, greasing our skids. Go figure.

In three meetings that lovely day: whammo, gold, a million

bucks. Elapsed time: three English hours, total. Hobby raised the rest of the money in the States. When Hobby finally put $3.25 million in our bank, the Nylens' nomadic summer ended.

NEW ENGLAND

The Nylens bought a two-hundred-year-old colonial house in a small town in the Berkshire foothills after reneging on two purchases before the money landed. After blithe, sunny Texas, where the temperature in September seldom falls below 70 degrees, we settled in a place where the thermometer seldom climbs over 70 in September, and falls like a pointy icicle. Overnight, it seemed, it was 1986, and the Reagan boom is underway. *New England Monthly,* two years old, is winning praise. Advertising sprouts like kudzu. We reach supersmart people, yet hope to be as fat as *Vogue*. Our conceit is that our readers' wallets follow their minds. In the eighties, some magazines are so plump and delectable that Tom Wolfe says they're probably edible. In addition to publishing fine writers like Joe Nocera, Renée Loth, Jon Harr, Annie Proulx, Tracy Kidder, Ben DeMott, Adrian Nicole LeBlanc, Ward Just, and Barry Werth, *NEM* offers readers BMWs, Johnnie Walker, designer clothes, jeweled watches, fine meals, and sumptuous resorts.

Jan Morris travels from her native Wales to our Down East coast to write for *NEM* about Bath Iron Works shipbuilders. Guy Martin covers a paper strike. Barbara Grizutti Harrison visits Vermont's Northeast Kingdom, where God-fearing parents beat their kids. Sarah Crichton shows us snotty "Beaches Where You're Not Wanted." Richard Todd goes sailing with the New York Yacht Club. Big, bearded, handsome Glen Waggoner is "The Man Who Ate New England," our best cover image (except for a glorious female lifeguard). Glen is bibbed, grinning, tucking into lobster, steamers, hamburger, pizza, clam chowdah, pie, and more pie—dishes perfected in New England.

Jon Harr discovers Jan Schlichtmann. Incongruously, the Porsche-driving lawyer represents bereaved parents of kids with leukemia who are suing chemical companies for despoiling the water supply of a working-class city north of Boston.

Jon leaves to write a book about the suit. We scratch our heads. Kids with cancer? Chemical companies? Huh? Woburn, Massachusetts, isn't New England's version of Santa Monica. It's more like Long Beach, with no ocean or good jobs. "Before you're done, you'll be scrounging for quarters in the car seat," Dan warns Jon.

Five years later, his advance long gone, his manuscript overdue, Jon ruefully calls Dan to admit that he's just rummaged through his Corolla for enough change to exit the Mass Pike. Never mind: *A Civil Action* is a tour de force. In the movie that ensues, John Travolta plays Jan, supported by actors named Shalhoub, Gandolfini, Macy, Lithgow, and so on.

In May 1986, *New England Monthly* is a finalist for the National Magazine Award for General Excellence. The awards gala is the magazine publishing industry's biggest funfest, our Oscars. The ceremony is in the Waldorf-Astoria Grand Ballroom, a brocaded, balconied wedding cake, a glamorous dowager soon to be overrun by schmoozing careerists and surly waiters. Across the long hall from the ballroom, a cocktail reception precedes the awards. Two bars quench a thousand parched throats. Later, magazine mavens will take the afternoon off. Lee Eisenberg, Dan, and I are about to broach the din. White wine fuels a gossipy tide that rolls our way. We pause under the entry. Lee, the editor of *Esquire,* stops, so we do too. He confesses: "I hate going in there. So many people in that room *hate* me."

"Me too," Dan agrees. "I hate *so many people* in there."

Later, we'll win, as will *Esquire,* despite all the free-floating animosity.

MAN ON THE ROOF

When I wasn't driving to Boston, New York, or Portland, or flying somewhere, I spent far too much time on the slate roof of our two-hundred-year-old home fighting winter, staving off invading slush. To motivate myself, I imagined the freezing runoff was akin to North Koreans trying to sneak through my private, tiny, frigid DMZ. A hundred and fifty inches of snow fell in our first winter on Norton Hill Road. Seven feet of falloff from the roofs blocked the view from our dining room.

We'd have been better off living in an igloo. Many New England homes are tripartite: a big house is attached to a small house connecting to the barn (so you could stay inside as you went about your chores). Up on the roof, it's you and your shovel, roof rake, and axe along with fate and the laws of inertia. Ice dams grew monstrously in January. A foot of snow on Monday, three inches on Wednesday, and two feet on Friday—trouble. After storms, melting commenced. Heat escaping from our centuries-old house thawed snow. Frigid residue dripped over old slates, dribbled underneath, refroze, and remelted. A gray-white Slurpee stretched over the aluminum that protected the eaves, then trickled inside the attic into the house. Every few days for twenty years, I clambered up on our porch roofs, shoveling lower roofs and knocking ice on the highest roofs. The ridge of our house was thirty-four feet high. Even on dry days, the roof was too steep to climb safely. I scraped with a twenty-foot aluminum rake and whacked rime with an axe. When it worked, the melt ran into gutters and onto the frozen ground instead of through ceilings. Sometimes, melt crept under the shingles and down the walls. Errant axe blows drove holes through thin slates, and icy water rushed in. You've got to hit a jam just so. When it's dark and freezing and your hands are raw from whaling away, your judgment suffers. As I've mentioned, judgment isn't my strong suit. Occasionally, a thousand pounds of sheet ice dislodged with an ominous crack. Surprise! I'd lunge under the eaves for cover. A solid sheet hurtled down, trying to decapitate me. In some wintry years, dislodged snow piled so deep that I could climb up on the lower roof without a ladder.

In rare wise moments, I called Willie Gray. A tip-top farmer, house painter, maple sugarer, and slate fixer, Willie was at ease on roofs (before and after his hip replacements). Driving his battered painting truck up our hill, Willie hauled out his ladders and scampered up to fix the problem. He's twenty years older than I am.

However, over the years, the elements beat me. In another part of town, on Bug Hill Road, Kit and I built a well-sealed metal roof, erected a home underneath to hold it up, and sold our dear, leaky home. Whatever becomes of me, our new roof will outlast my tired carcass by decades.

20.

Tough Yankees

Not long ago, a young local man dropped a chainsaw on his leg. The whirring chain ripped through his denims and slashed deep into his thigh. The young man removed his belt, tied it above the bloody gash, limped to his truck, drove to the emergency room, limped inside, got in line, and called no attention to himself. People already in the queue noticed a red pool widening around his boot. "Please," they said. "Go ahead."

"No," he said, "no, I'm good. I'm all set. You go on. You were here first."

LOCALS

Throughout the nineteenth century, more sheep than people roamed Ashfield, Massachusetts. A hundred years ago, dairy cows replaced critters that made wool, lambs, and mutton. Presto change-o, dairy farmers replaced shepherds. Overnight, more cattle than humans lived here. In the 1960s, our people census fell to 1,200 humans. Townspeople had departed for warmer weather, longer growing seasons, better jobs, and clearer TV reception.

Some 1,900 people live here today. The town is semifashionable, as it was in the late nineteenth century when the intelligentsia came for cool summers and the countrified pace. To the west, the Berkshires attracted Melville and Wharton. Our tiny town drew smarties from Harvard and New York. Every year, a gentrified family who lived on a luscious estate called Little Switzerland crossed the Atlantic by steamship, descending from Europe's actual Alps. Booker T. Washington spoke at an Ashfield Dinner in the late nineteenth century. He wasn't the first African American to come here: Peter Wells, former slave, born in Africa, tilled twelve hardscrabble Ashfield acres.

Transcendentalists taught the world Yankee self-reliance. They stuck to their knitting, too, unless they saw an opportunity to lift someone up. Their ideas sank into New England's soul. Today, even gruff guys who couldn't spell "pantheist" if you spotted them the vowels tacitly accept their theories. Early in the twentieth century, for some reason (jazz, cocktails, snazzy cars?), city people, our summer people, went to warmer places. They discovered highballs and the sea. *Sodas! Gin!* They summered on coasts and islands rather than our minimountains. A century of decline set in here. Winters were hard and summers passed without cash infusions save from the hardiest visitors. Today, longtime Ashfielders are swamp and hilltop Yankees, Canucks, Mick Americans, or Polack Americans. Tribes intermarry. Men don flannels and cotton in sleet, freezing rain, or snow. In summer, they shuck outer layers and don T-shirts fragrant from cedar chests. They don't retire short sleeves until the temperature steadily drops below freezing. Older townswomen retreat within their homes, leaving only for supplies, bowling, or movies.

WICKABLE PEOPLE

Times change. Once again, our pastoral charms lure people From Away seeking relief from urban life. Newcomers fix old homesteads or build new homes. In a slow deluge of ex-urbanites, our native garb is inundated by an incoming synthetic tide of breathable, moisture-wicking, bug-repelling fabrics. Our seasons still don't welcome easygoing folks. Discrete green and white stretches divide brown periods called "spring" and "fall" by people who don't understand how trying this microclimate can be. "Mud season" is no euphemism: sludge oozes for weeks, snarling axles, sucking tires, and gobbling small children. Roughly twelve miles of our roads become rutted morasses, or disappear altogether. You think I'm kidding? Visit in early April. I dare you.

In "spring," streams swell over Bug Hill's beaver ponds and erode our ever-treacherous road. Wickable neighbors gripe: Why doesn't the town fix the darned road? We pay taxes! Our town isn't as indigent as scruffier adjacent towns, but still, we can't pave everything. Not enough people From Away have moved in. Plus, eco-sensitive newcomers hate cutting the trees that line our country lanes, so cars are relegated to narrow horse paths. Wickables forget that two centuries ago, woodsmen felled old-growth money trees with rapacious abandon, and sheep defoliated what remained of our greenswards. Trees stood only in marshes or as roadside adornments. Now forests are again overtaking open land.*

* In the mid-nineteenth century, New England was open fields, pastures, and orchards. But western fields proved more fertile than our crabbed, rocky plots. Locomotives, trucks, and highways let westerners send their produce, milk, and meat round the world. Today, 70 percent of our region is wooded again. Stony soil, brief growing seasons, and bitter winters test our remaining farmers. They specialize, go organic, and use hothouses. Barbara Kingsolver cele-

In spring '07, I wheeled from town in my trusty old black truck. Steady rain had left gullies, peninsulas, and canyons where once were roads. Returning home, I forded a culvert above our beaver pond. A couple of inches of water streamed over the road. The pond, normally barely deep enough to paddle a kayak across, looked like a shallow river at flood tide, but I forged ahead. Halfway across, the Toyota began slipping. There was no road under the two left wheels. I was losing traction. How ironic would it be, I thought, to drown in our pond. I rammed into 4x4 and stomped on the accelerator, making grudging progress, exhilarated, scared. After lodging the truck in a neighbor's driveway, I trudged home through a cloud of adrenaline and chemotherapy: happy, very happy.

NATURALLY FIBERED FOLKS

My coffee-drinking friends at Neighbors and Elmer's Store wear leather, canvas, wool, or denim jackets. Some hew trees. Brian and Moose are twins: big, bearded, Harley riders. Brian's a metal salvager who doubles as Main Street's unofficial mayor. He knows everyone and dispatches pungent advice. When they were kids, they were hellions. Maturing, they became vigilantes, conducting dispute resolution without court supervision. They've cut back on their potables recently: doctors' orders. They're mellowing. Fritzie, Brian's recycling partner, is a Marine for whom "grizzled" fits like a leather jacket. Ray Sears doesn't sit. He's a tree surgeon like his son, Randy. Ray, pushing seventy, played vicious basketball until his rotators failed. Irregulars include Don, Doug, Dick, Bob, Bert, Brad, Steve, Norm, Stub, Jim, two Arts, and three Jeffs. Skip, a mail-

---

brated our town cheese maker, Ricki Carroll, and Sidehill Farm's Amy Klippenstein and Paul Lacinski in *Animal, Vegetable, Miracle.*

man, wears a faded Seabee cap. He's the guy to ask about VA benefits. Barry, Tim, Dan, and Jake are masons, their rough hands like clamshells.

STEVE LILLY: DAIRY FARMER EMERITUS

Steve has time to sip a second cup now on weekends. Until a few years ago, he had no time of his own. He was a lifelong dairyman until the family farm split up. After his aunt rejected his buyout bid, Steve became a trucker. He misses the routine, although dairy work is as risky as deep-sea fishing or mining. Tractors roll, barbed wire cuts, and cattle stomp your feet. Unlike sinking boats or collapsing coal mines, farm disasters seldom kill more than one man at once. Farmers go down singly in small, unnoticed tragedies.

It's hard work. Have you attached a milking machine to an unhappy milk cow's swollen, crusty udders when the temperature is below zero? I didn't think so. (Neither have I.) Knocking frozen manure off a hundred teats, attaching pumps to frigid Holsteins—Steve doesn't miss that, he admits. He doesn't miss getting up at 4:30 A.M. Yet in memory, nice days predominate. He misses freedom. Work goes faster when *you* decide what to do. He roamed six hundred verdant acres on his own schedule. He didn't mind helping a cow through a hard delivery. That was *his* cow. He doesn't miss bag-balming sore udders or mucking manure. He misses sweet new-mown rye, wading streams, mending fences, stringing wire, fixing tractors, hearing birdsongs, haying, and stacking fragrant bales. Farming is part routine and part surprise. He misses both. He misses being his own heavily mortgaged, overworked man. Independence is precious, Steve knows.

For thirty years, he worked seven days a week, twelve hours a day, taking a week off in some years. He worked with his cousin Alan and their dads. Once there were fourteen dairy farms in town, each with twenty to a hundred head. The Lil-Ho Dairy milked up to two hundred cattle. Now, three dairies, two Christmas tree farms, and two truck gardens remain in town. Two former dairies including Lil-Ho raise beefers—easier to manage than wallowing Holsteins. There's no money in milk here anymore. Gigantic factories in California and Wisconsin with herds in the thousands (even tens of thousands) profit by grand economies of scale.

Generations of farmers turned old-growth forest into beautiful pastures and orchards through painstaking labor. Fields bracketed by woods became more beguiling as time passed, providing scenes that attracted new people. Actual farming is odoriferous, however.

Some Wickable people bitch about the by-products, manure and methane: flatulence; pee-yew. A Wickable couple moved to an especially scenic part of town called Apple Valley. They got a rolling view of cascading glens and fruit orchards, but they missed their antiseptic semiurban former surroundings. Neighboring apple growers used pesticides! Who knew? Apple trees aren't native to America, Johnny Appleseed notwithstanding, so chemicals keep bugs away. Another Wickable couple urged an old-timer to train his rooster to crow at a more seemly hour: daybreak was *wrong*. Grazing cows broke through a fence and lumbered across the newcomers' lawn, big, dumb hooves digging into manicured sod. As the farmer retrieved his herd, the Wickable couple complained: "You were careless. This is private property. It's posted! No trespassing!"

"Well," the farmer replied, "the girls don't read too well."

21.

From Old to New Media

When I wasn't working at *New England Monthy*'s headquarters in western Massachusetts, I was driving to Boston, Manhattan, Vermont, or Maine, or flying somewhere. Busy, busy. Our little magazine soared for three years, losing less money each year—$3 million in 1984, $2 million in 1985, $1 million in 1986—and garnering awards, until the economy crashed. We were building market share even as the ad market disintegrated. Taking a bigger slice of a disappearing pie didn't work: we couldn't make the pie higher. Before our soufflé collapsed, in the autumn of 1986, Dan and I sold our magazine to Time, Inc. . . . almost. The deal came unglued.* We'd burned through

* Read about it in a Stanford Business School case study by Professor H. Irving Grousbeck and Kevin Taweel: "Abstract Text: Bob Nylen and Dan Okrent were publisher and editor, respectively, of *New England Monthly,* a regional magazine the pair founded in 1983. Although not a financial success thus far—the magazine continually operated in the red—it was an editorial hit that won the coveted National Magazine Award in 1986 and 1987. By April 1988 Dan and Bob were convinced that the best course of action was to sell to a large,

six million venture dollars and were starting to eat into a $2.3 million bank loan. (I'm sorry for my role in the savings and loan debacle.) The board wanted my square head. The creative enterprise was fine, they said, but the business side was tanking. I gutted it out. Dan called me "the Lieutenant," his code for mulish bastard, because I wouldn't let him help shoulder responsibility for our troubles. The only way I could demonstrate authority was to absorb pain, alone.

As we were running out of money, Telemedia, a Canadian company, bought the magazine for real. Kit and I took an apartment in Boston's Back Bay so I could spend more time in New England's marketing capital, as Telemedia urged. However, by the time their anxious CFO had finished his undue due diligence, months later, bankrupt, the magazine was out of cash and energy. Canadians, nice people, finally closed the deal.

After Dan left, and then me a year later, Telemedia lost another $4 million in less than a year, a record. Dan had plotted his escape for years. He had tried to flee in 1986. I made him stay. He preferred the giddy rush of invention to drudgery and routine. I'd moved from Texas for his cockamamie idea, and now he was going to stick me with a stinking sack o' New England!?!? No, no, a thousand times, no! Then I, too, was gone. I hate bosses, even pleasant Canadians.

AFTER *NEW ENGLAND MONTHLY:* WAITING FOR WALDMAN

In 1989, I became an itinerant, foraging from our Ashfield base camp for freelance wages, Don Quixote indeed. I'm not to be trusted with a chain saw, and our town lacks pretentious jobs,

---

strategic partner like Time, Inc. With the support of such a partner, they felt they could grow substantially. Surprisingly, the Board of Directors rejected Time's offer. Bob and Dan were left to figure out: what next?"

so I taught (adjunct professor, Smith College), edited, wrote, and with Kit, started newsletters about media law and golf. I was the "Scruples" columnist for *Selling* magazine (yes, we understood that the notion was oxymoronic) and an expert witness for a law firm with low standards for expertise. I wrote for newspapers and magazines from the *Times* to *Fortune*. Mainly, I consulted: thirty-five clients, serially. I had no boss. A delusion: actually, I'd traded one boss for many. Yet because I determined how I'd spend the next hour of my sixty-hour workweek, and the next, technically, I was "free." The catch-as-catch-can work life Kit and I shared came without benefits, pension, or health care. Yet I had what my neighbor Steve Lilly had, would lose one day, and covet forever: independence.

I was my own moron, ready to pick up my lance and charge at the nearest windmill. When a potential client called, however, I undertook a surreptitious examination. Could this be my next start-up? Steve Waldman called in 1998. We had friends in common. His idea—*Belief,* a magazine about spirituality and religion—was a good one. Steve had just left *U.S. News*. Working at *Newsweek,* and at *U.S. News,* Steve saw that religious and spiritual themes made surefire covers. Jesus drew more readers than anything but health, sex, or newly dead celebrities. The Bible was hot. Yoga was hot. Fundamentalists were feverish. Buddhism was so hot it was cool. No single medium addressed the whole topic. Niche publications focused on narrow denominations, practices, and ideologies. No one looked at the big picture—as we planned to do.

I said: I'll raise the money. We'll be partners, if you add morality to your mission. Neither spiritual nor religious, I'm sanctimonious. I wanted to vent. We drafted a prospectus, crafted numbers, and in the winter of '98–'99 briskly marched through magazine headquarters. CEOs patted our backs. A media banker said: "Best magazine plan I've ever read." However, nobody offered a penny. Publishers are loath to fund other people's projects.

Venture capitalist Matt Harris, the CEO of Village Ventures, seized on the modest online portion of our would-be enterprise. *That's* worth something, he said. Do *that:* a twenty-first-century dot-com company, not a twentieth-century magazine. So we did. Neither of us had worked for an online company, much less started one, but we emailed like kids. We could do this. Online media created by print retreads like Slate and Salon garnered growing audiences. Slate founder Michael Kinsley was an alumnus of Charlie Peters's journalistic boot camp* like Steve.

By 1999, Salon, four years old, had burned through half of the $86.6 million it would eventually lose. New print magazines sprang up to cover the new high-tech industry, like *The Industry Standard, Wired, Fast Company, Red Herring,* and *Business 2.0.* Each sold tons of high-tech ads. Consumers shared an insatiable mania for online information. The next year, *The Industry Standard* would sell twice as many ads as *The New Yorker.*

In 1999, I was having trouble heeding Matt Harris's mandate. Forecasting print ads and circulation had been easy for me, but calculating page views, unique visitors, and click-thrus was terra incognita. We got help from Dan Ambrose, who'd already switched from print to electronic media.

As we started pitching Beliefnet, to our wonder, venture capitalists (VCs) started pitching us. Salesmen are accustomed to being treated warily, so being wooed was weird. Yet a bel-

* *Washington Monthly*'s gruff founder was an idealistic West Virginian who tortured talented journalists. Peters taught tough-minded "neo-liberalism" to future stars like Nick Lemann, Joe Nocera, Taylor Branch, Walter Shapiro, Gregg Easterbrook, Jim Fallows, Tim Noah, Jonathan Alter, Katherine Boo, Mickey Kaus, John Rothchild, Jon Meacham . . . and Waldman. Peters's tough love included a daily, fiery rain dance, a diatribe in which he told his terrorized young editor he was stupid and worthless. Though infuriating, Charlie did far more good than harm.

lows of venture-fund money was blowing cash windstorms into not-yet-hyperfunded online media. We became decision makers, not supplicants, an unsettling role reversal. "We're smart money," they all said, earnestly. "Do you want *anybody's* money, or our smart money?" VCs believe themselves to be adventuresome, bright, hip people. Compared to CPAs, they are, too, but with rare exceptions, their alpha dog is received business wisdom, barked loudly amid the business pack. Lone VC wolves howl in the mountains unheard. Most VCs lope in stride with one another, reluctant to get in front or lag behind. They answer questions about pay, staffing, hardware, and software with dogmatic certitude: "X—X—that's market. So plug in X." In other words, do it like everyone in our portfolio does it. Don't rock the boat. To create a new business, emulate existing companies. Originality is risky. All right! I could copycat!

That winter, after we landed six million bucks in upfront funding, Steve and I went to a party in a chic Manhattan restaurant with entrepreneurs, industry gurus, and Hollywood stars. As the party dwindled to a woozy, boozy end, our host VC's most senior partner told me that Beliefnet would be their biggest investment ever: a billion-dollar IPO was possible. The auguries were good.* They'd get better . . . before darkening.

Fast Company* sparked an online parody. "Fucked Company"—"Fked Company" to get around prissy search protocols—recorded the insanity of the high-tech tulip madness with scandalous, scathing posts from anonymous insiders. News of firings, downsizings, space shrinkages predicted the imminent demise of hundreds of tottering dot-coms. Fucked Company posting on April 12, 2002, after Beliefnet filed for bankruptcy: "Jesus Christ on a crutch . . . Mon Apr 15 . . . who the fuck gave these idiots $25 million in venture capital? [*sic:* actually, it was $26 million] Sure, they claim to have received millions of hits (mostly from the sort of redneck trash that think that Bob Tilton and Jerry Falwell actually talk to God on a first-name basis), but you have to consider that religious fanatics are so cheap that they use both sides of the toilet paper. This is just a cheaper version of Fandom.com, only where the patrons wear polyester suits instead of Star Trek uniforms. I hope that someone is planning to do some smiting for this mess."

SIMULATING A DOT-COM GUY

Clomping around Manhattan, I cut an absurd figure. Despite sporting Nixonian jowls, dewlaps, and liver spots that my dermatologist couldn't eradicate, I wore the duds affected by the high-tech kids in the tribe to which I so tenuously belonged. Seeing my period-appropriate shoes in the closet, I zoom back to 2000: I plodded through Silicon Alley in those wide-beamed, jumbo-sized clown shoes whose broad, flat, elevated heels and rubbery soles protruded like flotation devices on a tugboat's gunwale. There were limits to my nerditude. At an expensive hair salon a few blocks from the office, I didn't succumb to the blandishments of a Korean hairdresser who offered to make my hair "shiny." Shiny? Why shiny hair? Was she proposing to mousse my once-blond locks in the wet style of the day? No, she said haltingly, but language failed her.

The salon's English colorist translated. "Shiny," he said, meant removing gray. She wanted my hair to be more suitably youthful. She'd picked up on the incongruity between my costume—blue shirt, black pants, Bozo shoes—and aged coiffure. But trimming sidelocks down to the skin wouldn't erase the gap between my dot-com guy mode and my age. Worse, it revealed more liver spots. No thanks.

Moreover, I never considered adopting the rip-stop nylon trousers our technology chief, Ole Peterson, wore. He had a Ph.D. in computer science from Sweden. I let Ole hire twenty Jamaicans, Russians, Chinese, Trinidadians, Croatians, Serbs, and Canadians. Ole hated Americans and Swedes equally.

BEST DOT-COM MEETING EVER

In 2000, a megacelebrity asked his counselor—our contributor Rabbi Shmuley Boteach—for introductions to acquaintances in finance and new media. So Steve Waldman, Tony Uphoff,

Highland Capital VC Jo Tango, forty strangers, and I met in the Four Seasons hotel suite of the most recognizable human on the planet. We munched finger foods and evaded jumpy PR ladies and the Good Rebbe in the star's spacious living room.

More or less on time, the King of Pop strode from an anteroom: Michael Jackson went straight to work. A young man assisted, holding two dozen illustrated storyboards. Jackson wished to build a Peter Pan theme park. A misapplied Band-Aid held his nose to his face as he spoke diffidently, then with mounting confidence as his voice dropped from alto to tenor. It wasn't a bad idea, aside from the unbelievably creepy factor. Theme park? Peter Pan? From a guy living a pedophilic life that J. M. Barrie only simulated? Hmm.

Mr. Jackson took financial questions for fifteen minutes. His concentration began slipping. He lobbed grapes at his colleague, who reciprocated. Rebbe Shmuley asked us to pose, one by one, for photos with M.J., and oh, by the way, how about donating to a new charity to benefit kids? Each of us in turn grasped the naked right hand of the famous germaphobe, flesh-to-flesh, and chatted with him, too.

Subsequently, I coughed up a hundred dollars for the charity, but no photo. I don't know what Shmuley sought in the way of cash donations, but quid pro quo for a photo keepsake was obviously more than a hundred bucks. As I recall, the charity was called "Save These Children."

22.

Why Kit Manages Our Finances

Once I handled family finances in a manly fashion, taking risks and going for big wins, like buying American Motors in 1975 on the launch of the Pacer—in retrospect, America's worst car. What can I say? I liked the idea of driving a six thousand-pound sunroom, a car that got fifteen miles to the gallon. But starting Beliefnet.com required long workdays and commuting from Brooklyn to Massachusetts every other weekend. Kit had already taken over the checkbook and taxes. Now she also handled what we called our "investment portfolio." I ceded control reluctantly. Men should hold the purse strings, right?

Frankly, Kit was motivated to act by an unfortunate investment we'd made in 1981 that haunted us for nearly a decade. Okay, *I'd* made the investment . . . in a fraudulent company, as it happened . . . but I'd thought I was doing well by doing good. To foster energy independence, President Jimmy Carter encouraged putting money in companies that reduced energy consumption. That year, a financial adviser urged *Texas Monthly*'s senior managers to buy shares of Organized

Energy Services, which made complex thermostats. For every dollar we put in, we'd get $2.50 in tax credits. At the time, the highest tax rate exceeded 50 percent, so we'd get bigger tax breaks than we paid! I claimed nearly $150,000 in tax losses in 1981, '80, and '79, using our accountant's conservative formula. Plus, we owned a bit of a socially responsible business! Too good to be true?

Not only did Kit and I lose our original $62,000 investment: the IRS back-billed us for catch-up interest for each of the five years that had elapsed since the initial filing year. At the time, Kit and I had $400,000 in savings and a million dollars in *NEM* stock (on paper). We owned a house, four TV sets, a VCR, two lawn mowers, and two Nordic cars. We thought we were rich. Okay: I thought we were rich. In 1986, bills arrived for $446,000 from each of two IRS offices, nearly a million bucks all told.

Kit thought that a more prudent investor (say, her) might not have made the OES blunder. A funny thing: we've fared better under her dominion than under my M.B.A.-driven financial rule. Her B.S. in education has produced gains, especially from real estate. Recently, I noticed that our joint holdings are all in Kit's name. She tells me that my risk-taking ways mean I'm more likely to get sued than she is, and thus our assets are safer in her name. Does that make sense? She assures me she's being reasonable. Hey, okay. I'm man enough to leave bread on my family's table if my raggedy ass goes to the Big House. Kit's tough.

Were you to compare us to celebrity couples, we'd like you to think that we're Spencer Tracy and Katharine Hepburn in *Desk Set*, cooing and squabbling, but we're probably closer to Courtney Love and Kurt Cobain, except that Kit would never have anything to do with Hole or wear that much lipstick or mascara.

• • •

In 1999, Beliefnet opened shop in temporary offices in 26 Broadway, five blocks south of the World Trade Center. We moved north before the buildings were vaporized. When the big, ugly slabs collapsed, suddenly the city missed them like unappreciated, boring, but reliable relatives. At the time, we were on vacation, and therefore neither in Ashfield nor in the Brooklyn Heights apartment where I'd been spending most of my time since 1999 as Beliefnet started. Returning for a few months to Brooklyn before selling the apartment (and recommitting ourselves full-time to Ashfield), in that brilliant, strange fall of 2001, I ran or rode my bike over the Bridge dozens of times, coughing through the ever-present smoke, to peer through slits in the plastic-draped wire barricades keeping idlers from gaping at the crime scene.

On 9/11, the borough's first fire responders had torn across the Brooklyn Bridge and raced up doomed stairwells in the World Trade Center, leaving quiet firehouses near our part-time apartment. Twenty Heights firemen had died. Black bunting draped the brick buildings. Before 9/11, Heights residents strolled past firemen who were standing in truck bays without seeing them. Previously invisible, firemen earned the respect they'd always deserved. For weeks after that terrible day, watching trucks roll off afterward to smoldering Liberty Street, Brooklynites wept, blasé no more. When cops blazed by, we waved. On the Esplanade overlooking the East River, ten thousand votive candles flickered in the crater's wind. Photocopied posters of the "missing" were everywhere.

At loose ends, I had no job. I'd left Beliefnet's day-to-day operations: I was in Tony Uphoff's way. Tony was the big CEO I'd hired to run the business. How big? His Italian diving wristwatch looked like an alarm clock. I tried to resign twice, but

Tony fired me instead—for the board, he explained. Apparently smart money isn't always graceful money. I was superfluous. Tony didn't like sharing authority.

That autumn, as a new war began in Afghanistan and preparations started for the invasion of Iraq, my doddering peers and I fretted in our living rooms, looking at volunteers do war's dirty work. Old GI warhorses don't die. Grazing in green pastures restoreth our souls. We no longer gallop to the fray. We watch TV. Meanwhile, no one in the executive branch of government called for sacrifice. No draft, no new taxes: no problem. The president beseeched us to shop. Rich people got richer, bought bigger yachts, and sheltered more income as Walter Edward Martin, a teenaged Ashfield Marine, slogged through 120-degree heat in Fallujah. Ashfield's Scott Pichette, thirty-four, flew helicopters for the Navy, earning a third of the pay he'd have made by joining Blackwater, the private security service. Warren Gray (Willie's son) and Paul Monahan served; Paul went to Afghanistan. I lived the new war vicariously, watching, reading, and working as a consultant to a group of historical magazines.

23.

The Beginning of What Proves Not to Be the End

On April 6, 2004, I played noontime basketball at the Northampton YMCA. Over the years, most of my athletic peers had quit—hurt, distracted, or just wised up—but I persevered. "You inspire me," younger men said. They meant: "Still here, you old coot?" I ignored evidence that my time was up. My knees were sore and my back ached. I couldn't defend or rebound. Still, many people my age, a week shy of sixty, are sedentary—or dead. What kept me going? A paucity of shame. My only move was a dilapidated jump shot. My accuracy had waned. My favorite nickname, "Automatic Bob," had eroded to "Semi-Automatic Bob," "Semi," "Bob," and finally, "Old Bob."

My disintegrating body stumbled down a worn path. As John Kenneth Galbraith was nearing ninety, the ex-ambassador and Kennedy confidant wrote that he'd involuntarily entered the "still" phase of life. Friends who bumped into him on Cambridge sidewalks asked: "Still walking, John? Swimming? Writing?" Annoyed by inane queries, Galbraith still knew that this sort of stillness—quiet endurance—beats the moribund alternative. He died in 2006, still sentient.

If you aren't a fake old jock like me, you may not know that a shot that swishes through the net can make an ordinary guy feel like Reggie Miller. My late friend John Jerome described the nanoseconds that unify and transcend sport as "sweet spots in time." You enjoy a kinesthetic thrill as your racket strikes: *pow*! When the fat part of your bat rockets a ball to the stands. Or you cast a lure to the precise pool of water beneath which a trout lolls. Say you're facing a dogleg left. You drive your Titleist 263.5 yards, gently hooking, plunking in the fairway. Sweet indeed. The glory of play is that even rickety codgers enjoy giddy moments. Sure, they scamper away as fast as they come. Our faces turn gray-red, we gasp . . . *O tempora! O mores!* Sweet spots in time are fleeting pleasures. Isn't all joy always over too fast?

Sweat is good. Pushing sixty, I was a player. Fifteen years had elapsed since a big goon on an opposing basketball team had shattered my arm over his shoulder, transforming my left elbow into a sack of jacks. A five-hour surgery gathered shards and held them together with a bolt, pin, and sheath. On my cast, my friend Dick Todd (whom I later induced to become editor in chief when Dan finally left *NEM*) intermingled Percy Bysshe Shelley with the legendary Boston Celtic: "Hail to thee, blithe spirit! Bird thou never wert." Despite my damaged alloy arm, I huffed up and down the court again, happy to struggle toward the same pointless team goal. My hand, shot; nerves, disconnected: no matter. I'm right-handed. Two or three days a week, winning one for the Skins (or the Shirts) was more important than anything. Endorphins are their own reward. Shuffling over the YMCA hardwood, as my man whisked by I grabbed his trunks. My profanity provoked the staff to tape this sign to the cinder-block wall: "Please Don't Swear!" (It could have read: "Cool it, Old Bob," but rudeness is un-YMCA.) I ran, too; walked, biked, golfed, and snowshoed.

Although she doesn't play hoops, Kit Hopkins Nylen and I have been best friends for forty-five years. (She says forty-four; I say forty-six; we compromise.) We aren't cooing, uxorious lovebirds. We bicker and jab like judo partners. Luckily, our cauliflowered ears no longer transmit each painful blow. We enlist weary friends and our put-upon daughter to referee our spats. Some mornings, Kit tells me to shut my flapping lips. Kit and Cassie call me "Old Bastard." Don't stand between us when hot words or warm spittle is flying.

Where was I? Life that April wasn't perfect. My career was fading. My ambition, once a fiery oven, had cooled. My work had tailed off to consulting for some dinky companies. Challenges kept me alert but didn't tax me. That was okay: we'd set aside funds for slushy days. My business life receded like light dimming on a summer evening, slowly, inevitably. I wasn't desperate to hang on. Soft, soft, sweet candle. On the whole, my life was—no, is—fine. Better than fine.

TROUBLE IN PARADISE

One tumultuous week after what proved to be my final lackluster b-ball game, I celebrated my sixtieth birthday and got the formal results from my first colonoscopy: ass cancer. "Colorectal cancer, stage III (b)" was too respectful a term for the sordid truth. Days later, Christopher Moltisanti, Tony Soprano's psycho cousin, ominously told his *paisanos* that getting whacked wouldn't be so bad. A violent death, he said, would be better than going out as his aunt had gone: "Her ass got eaten out by cancer," he said, shaking his head, disgusted.

Treatment began immediately: three months of chemotherapy and radiation, then a five-hour surgery on July 31. Before operating, my highly regarded sphincter-savior confidently told me: "We'll save your bottom." (His Web page says saving sphincters is his specialty.) Ordinarily, I call a spade a shovel, but if you call my tailpipe my "bottom," not my cloaca, be my guest, thanks. Subsequently, I found that a somewhat saved, semi-functioning bottom is not what it's cracked up to be. However, I appreciated Dr. B.'s euphemism for my least attractive parts—even his medical "we." Despite their infantilizing effects, substitutes wear better than clinical Latin.

I awakened with an L-shaped scar from my belly button to my pubis. A pink chunk of large intestine protruded through a hole in my tummy. Surprise! I thought Dr. B. would go in through the direct access route. Instead, Dr. B. drilled through the top. Better light?

Such as it was, this was my first vacation in years. We took luxurious hospital accommodations with flat-screen TVs, a view, and a separate bedroom where Kit and Cassie could sleep, as well as an enticing menu (from which I couldn't make a selection: I was "nil by mouth"). In our lush pavilion suite, I awoke with a fever, a colossal headache, and waking nightmares. In our spacious private bathroom, NVA, Viet Cong, former investors, and bad guys attacked me.

RIDING BACKWARDS

Back at home: adjuvant chemo. In a single week, my chemo bill was $11,089. That wasn't unusual. Kit's health insurance is a godsend. Then infections caused my diabetes to go nuts. In fall 2004, I made five trips to the emergency room. Mysterious new ailments devolved into infections. A comical teeny rupture inside my belly button, and a life-threatening deep visceral one: together, they made me dull, fevered, and pain-besotted. Infection, cancer, and diabetes conspired. My frayed, tender posterior left me reliant on opiates. In REM moments, combat flashbacks mingled psychedelically with business catastrophes. One minute I staved off sappers; the next, I was making a pitch, nude. Dreams ended with me spelunking naked into urban tunnels, escaping aliens. These dreams melded into one. Frantically escaping, I dropped bare-assed into a cul-de-sac, got trapped, and exploded. In recent dreams, I scour, bleach, rinse, and vacuum, as I do when awake, trying to expunge the ever-present crud of life with a stoma.

That fall, my new predicament confused medical America. Big-city doctors exercised dibs over my aching body, insisting that I come to Boston for a look-see. Two pleasant EMTs drove me to the epicenter of all medical knowledge, the Harvard Medical School's complex in Boston. The team was willing, they had a map, but between them they'd driven to Boston maybe four times in their young lives, and neither had driven this aged warhorse more than two hundred miles. The odometer said 245,000 miles. Sprung springs said more. They strapped me to a gurney and pushed me aboard, my big feet flapping over the end. Off we went.

By default, I was the navigator, and frankly, my directions weren't great. My concentration was poor. Our 120-mile journey took three agonizing hours. The ambulance's suspension was shot, and potholes drilled my organs like jackhammers. Clamped and buckled, I couldn't budge, just shift my gaze from the rear window to a side porthole and back again. I was looking at receding signs advising drivers who were headed west about their upcoming exits. Our east-aiming vehicle had already passed these exits. On our side of the highway, I saw the backsides of blank signs.

Yet I'd made this trek a bazillion times, driving parallel to drivers reading newspapers, writing memos, brushing their hair, plucking eyebrows, or arguing at 80 mph. Starting at Worcester, which Bostonians think delineates their Hub of the Galaxy from the vasty ends of the universe, I perked up, alerting the EMTs what to expect. Ah, yes, we're coming to I-495. Route 128 is about twenty miles ahead. We're getting close. Get in the right lane. Take this ramp. Look for Route 9 east. Exit right. Go left to Brookline. After the second Dunkin' Donuts go left. Oops! Too early! This is an alley. (There are an infinite number of identical Dunkin' Donuts on Route 9.) Try again.

After checking in to the ER, I spent a restive night. My closest neighbor watched TV until sunrise with the volume turned to "Deaf People in Charlestown Can Hear This." The next morning: interventional radiology. Real-time X-rays guided a team of radiological surgeons as they inserted a catheter through my right buttock, snaking it into my abdomen. The business end of the device reached the abscess that was the cause of my misery. Eureka! The catheter jutted out from my butt for six weeks, draining into a plastic pouch I carried in my left trouser pocket. I was packing a stoma appliance and a drain bag: Two-Pistol-Pouch Pete. Sitting for a few excruciating minutes at a time, I delicately pivoted between a sore anus and a plastic butt rivet. Driving was parlous. Working and thinking were all but impossible. *But I'm alive!* I reminded myself. No income, but who cares?

DOWN IN THE BASEMENT

Recovering, relapsing, feeling useless, I did what Granddad and Dad designed me to do: hard work. It's therapeutic. I descended into the unfinished basement a step at a time to smooth the walls and ceiling. Brother John came to visit: hee hee hee! Here's your roller, Johnny! We co-labored: taped, spackled, painted, and inhaled a ton of wallboard dust. Our work withstood cursory inspection with low lights.

After John went back to Delaware, emboldened, I bought a truckload of easy-application tongue-and-groove floorboards.

Laying down the first four rows proved devilishly hard, however. Instead of popping a new board on, each strike of my carnival whack-a-board game loosened a previously nested pair: the board on the far end popped off. I needed a third hand to keep the jerry-rigged mishmash from disintegrating with each blow. While I was juggling a rubber mallet, keeping drainage and ostomy pouches dry—try it some day—an eighty-pound pallet fell on my right foot, re-breaking two bones that I'd broken playing geriatric basketball the previous year. Fine: I couldn't sit, think, hammer, or walk. I hired a flooring expert and retreated to the bedroom. The floor looks nice. You tell Bert and Nels: I can't.

CURED

Little by little, I got better. The first ostomy was reversed. Pooping again wasn't quite the joyous activity I had grown to imagine it during the previous seven months, but it was a step toward normality. In May 2005, Ron Miller removed the chest port he'd surgically implanted a year earlier. OxyContin and fentanyl patches made lingering pain tolerable. Cured.

As remissions go, however, this was short-lived. In August 2005, oncologist Deborah Smith sighed, "This is the worst part of my job." Blood tests and a CT scan showed four liver lesions: full-blown metastasis. I sought an oracular insight. Reluctantly, Dr. Smith said that on average, a patient in my particular circumstances might live a year or so. Mercifully, she added, "Some people in your situation survive many years . . . and live well." After a similar diagnosis, one putatively doomed patient, an engineer, had told Dr. Smith that he planned to read fifty books in the next six months to die well read. A half year later, undead, he went on reading: two hundred, then three hundred books before he quit, weighed down by the knowledge he'd gained.

"Don't worry," Dr. Smith told him. "It's not the books."

She assured me: "You don't have liver cancer. It's metastatic colorectal cancer." The distinction was lost on me until Google revealed that mine is the version you want. When cancer starts in the colon it goes (if not to the liver) to the lungs or brain. Lungs and brain don't regenerate. Only our skin and livers are able to regrow, so I was better off than I might have been. A few months later, an agitated man of my years butted ahead of me in the MRI line at Yale. "My case is urgent," he said, loudly. Sitting down, he explained why he was in a hurry: "I have liver cancer. You know what that means?"

Soon, another problem—my worst ever—a bladder fistula. A local urologist declined to examine my nightmarish symptoms. At one point—forgive me—I flatulated and pooped from an orifice not designed for these duties. (Mega-sorry.) Shenanigans that would fascinate twelve-year-old boys didn't interest him. Since pelvic radiation had caused my plumbing to collapse, urinary surgery wasn't viable. Why bother? he told Dr. Miller. Antibiotics could help. I was taking antibiotics. Dr. Miller considered alternatives. One was to divert my "fecal stream," as he considerately called my sewage system. This unusual bypass, seldom discussed when dinner-party chat turns to medicine, rerouted my plumbing in January '06. (At dinner tables, chest cracking, botoxification, seed implants, gall bladder excisions, and electroshock therapy are less taboo.) Bypassed, the fistula became quiescent. Moot. It's still there, ready for mischief, but in solitary confinement.

Recovering, I shared a hospital room with a Cambodian man whose Laotian wife never left his side. Both of the twenty-five-year-old breadwinner's lungs had collapsed over the course of six months. Their friends, night-shift workers, gathered in our room at 11:00 P.M. and chatted quietly in English, their shared language, until dawn. On other hospital stays, I shared rooms with an eighteen-year-old appendicitic, old dudes with bad kidneys, knees, and stomachs, and a twenty-year-old Boston College student who'd hurtled involuntarily through a barroom window. I don't like sharing quarters, but when you're sick, living with someone who is equally miserable helps both roomies buck up. You each pretend bravery.

A bonus: after the new ostomy, my pain receded, then disappeared for the first time in eighteen months. After a few sleepless days and nights, writhing with a serious jones, I kicked fentanyl and OxyContin. Perhaps I'm stronger than Rush Limbaugh. Woody Allen's line dances in my head: "It's not that I'm afraid of dying—I just don't want to be there when it happens." Twinges, bleeding, and aches remind us that we're alive.

24.

The Spurious Cancer-as-War Metaphor; Some Un-Ironic Heroes

Susan Sontag objected to cancer's ubiquity as metaphor for every bad thing that rides down the pike or slides down alimentary canals. After her tumors were found, Sontag heard afresh how callously cancer was discussed. Her disease was pernicious shorthand for "doom." Once, tuberculosis was a watchword for bodily disintegration: "consumption" meant slow death. Cancer had supplanted TB as an acute illness reified into extra potency, its victims stigmatized.

Even now, some dope kvetches every day about a tumor growing on some institution. Sloppy journalists use physical maladies to symbolize already noxious phenomena. Undesirable and fearsome by definition, diseases stand for moral decline and societal corruption. People afflicted with cancer were until recently regarded as pariahs. Cancer's healers made the disease worse by lying to their charges, treating them like children too weak to learn their true prognoses. In *Illness as Metaphor,* Sontag decried the clumsy way so-called experts induced guilt in sick people. Phrases like "cancer personality," "the cancer growing on the White House," "cancers in popular culture," and "cancer on our health care system," to name a few, created a myth that cancer was the worst curse to befall humanity, ever. Reporters and self-help authors relied on cancer as a stand-in for punishments, hexes, and miscellaneous bad luck. Cancer became ubiquitous. To be sure, cancer is wretched. Saying that X was "like a cancer," however, became a mindless way to suggest the unspeakable.

The cliché offended Sontag. Tumors, tumors everywhere, but none to make us think. She was right to complain, but she ignored one oddly flattering new cancer metaphor: suddenly, sufferers were brave combatants, warriors who resisted disease as Marines resist enemy attack. In short, within a generation, sufferers had metamorphosed from pariahs to heroes. Yet no matter how tough we are—Ms. Sontag was as valiant as we come—the metaphor is flat wrong. We aren't the combatants in this kerfuffle any more than the green fields of south central Pennsylvania fought the Battle for Gettysburg, or the muddy, rat-infested trenches in the Marne Valley clashed in World War I. The ruined buildings of Stalingrad didn't beat the Germans in World War II. The reeds and estuaries of the Mekong River Delta didn't defeat Americans.

To be sure, pundits posit that good antibodies and bad cancer cells fight one another, combat of a kind. An unseen enemy contests our lungs, kidneys, and brains. However, we, the becancered, are combat journalists in folding camp chairs, watching. Cancer attacks. Our cells and antibodies respond to the siege. Our wills resist, but in interior skirmishes, our immune systems fight. Or not. Our bodies and minds wage this battle only in a cosmic sense. Our bodies are the battlefields, not actors moving on them. Our defenders are our oncologists, radiologists, and surgeons. We don't do much beyond nodding yes or no to the next course of treatment. As fighting takes place in our tender, flagging bodies, we pour boiling oil over battlements atop our foes, scalding ourselves, too. Heroically!

WHAT'S WORSE?

When I was a kid, my friends and I played an idle game. In combat, what body part did we want hit? Military service seemed inevitable, as we grew up amid impending nuclear annihilation, walking hallways lined by Civil Defense warnings. Ergo, wounds would happen. Not death: maybe him or her—not me. Losing an eye? Okay. You'd have another eye and a swell black patch for the hole, like a pirate.

No? Well, an ear? Lip? Nostril? Arm? Leg? Flesh wounds were okay. "Flesh wounds" were of little consequence to our movie heroes, unlike, say, being gut- or head-shot. "Flesh"—some unknown flabby part, no bones, veins, arteries, or sensory apparatuses. Maybe our heinies, which we believed were nerveless. (However, I can testify that there are neurons in our keisters.)

Now I play "What's worse?" Though unpleasant, cancer is far from the awfulest disease to afflict us. For example, neurological disorders are worse, like multiple sclerosis, muscular dystrophy, Alzheimer's, and ALS. (Rank that quartet alone: I dare you.) Paraplegia is worse. Quadriplegia is unimaginable. Bad respiratory problems? Much worse. Iron lungs! Emphysema is horrible. You drown, slowly. Cystic fibrosis? Worse than emphysema. All breathing maladies, even the so-called Old Man's Friend, pneumonia, are death by suffocation, but cystic fibrosis makes kids gasp for every breath starting when they're tragically young.

Blindness is awful. Third-degree burn victims' pain is unendurable. Surviving, even tenuously, depends upon having one's flesh debrided in ghastly flensings. Scars tighten, encasing bodies in prisons of integument. Victims of advanced psoriasis suffer similar fates. Scarred skin tautens and cripples, toes and fingers webbing together. Rheumatoid arthritis cripples, too.

We haven't gotten to tropical diseases like malaria, river blindness, or elephantiasis, and we won't. Cancer isn't so bad in the context of flesh-eating bacteria and HIV-AIDS. Yet for a while, I confess, I thought that rectal cancer was the worst disease that one could get. It's even hard to explain where the damned thing is. "Colorectal" is a palatable version of "rectal cancer," but anal cancer, sphincter cancer, cloacal cancer, or poop-shoot cancer is all bad. Mostly, it was the worst disease because I had it: solipsism rules. So I began asking: Okay, Mr. Pitiful Smarty-Pants: Where would you prefer the problem be sited, were it your choice? Left testicle? Right leg? Amygdala? Frontal lobe? Nipple? Prostate? Cheek? Tongue? Ear? The answer, of course, is nowhere, but there are especially bad places, and they aren't on (or in) your bum, not even mine.

I asked Dr. Smith what cancers she found most difficult to treat. She said: "Aesthetically? Well, head cancers, particularly ear, nose, or throat cancers. Tongue cancers. Sinus cancers. Anywhere around the mouth: they're the worst. No doubt."

Personally, though, I almost get why some people say they're grateful for their diseases. Paraphrasing Churchill and Teddy Roosevelt, who were speaking of being shot at to no effect, nothing concentrates the mind like an imminent death warning. Years later, if you're still here, you realize that you've seen, heard, smelled, and tasted—better. Small pleasures give you more joy. Annoyances bother less. You love your family more than possible. Everyone is happy, except perhaps kindly friends who showered you with affection after hearing your diagnosis, thinking what the heck, he was an irritating bastard but now he's checking out. Expecting you to leave by overnight bus, belatedly they discover that you're a walking, talking anticlimax. (Still.) It's hard for them to say hello when they've already said goodbye, but you can deal with disappointments like these.

The perfect death is supposed to be one in which you quietly slip away in mid-dream. However, if your loved one died that way, you know how the bereaved greet death that comes without warning. Spouses, kinfolk, and friends don't have a chance to say farewell. So let's be frank. All disease, every death whether it be fast or slow, stinks. Which way is worst? It's a flat-footed ten-billion-way tie.

WHAT I KNOW ABOUT INFUSIONEES

We share treatments in rooms no bigger than a confessional or jail cell. That intimate space, our shared lethargy, and the reassuring nursely bustle make shy people talk and make telling secrets okay. Unlike the medical staff, patients aren't bound by confidentiality pledges. In those rooms, malignant melanomas, Hodgkin's disease, and cancers of the lung, skin, brain, and pancreas are common. Curiously, the only rectally cancered people with whom I've shared space in the Barcalounger room have been women thirty years younger than me, mothers who scarcely fit the disease's archetype: sedentary behavior, fatty meat, smoking, drinking heavily, and getting too old. Exchanging intimacies, you make friends in a hurry. Then you're gone, weaving your separate ways to the parking lot. No phone number exchanges. You meet again by chance, months later, discover new shared indignities, reveal fresh complaints, then part company again. You don't see Monty or Susan for a while. You ask. A staffer sighs, reminding you that privacy rules prevent them from discussing patients.

An irony: you know more about Joe and Gertrude than they do, but they can't say diddly-squat. Is she . . . alive? Yes: they'll say that much. Should have asked her for that number, even though discussing illnesses—all you have in common, really—over the phone will shorten your lives in proportion to the time you spend reminding one another that you're terminally ill.

MARJORIE WILLIAMS: STRUCK BY LIGHTNING

Williams was forty-three, fit, busy, a mother of two with a great career, happy, when a check-up in 2001 revealed a terrible surprise: advanced liver cancer. Cancer dispatches few organs as fast as it does the almighty liver. Her prognosis was as bad as it comes: stage IV (b). "There is no V, and there is no (c)," Williams wrote in *The Woman at the Washington Zoo*. When I read her book in 2005, my liver cancer was freshly diagnosed: her stark summary struck me with a force that I didn't feel when I read the Merck Manual or *How We Die*, in which Dr. Sherwin Nuland described his brother's gruesome death from colon cancer.

Williams and her husband, Timothy Noah, had shared an engaging 1998–99 "Breakfast Table" column in Slate. Sitting together, typing, feeding their kids, they exchanged digital messages over cereal and muffins. In the net's salad days, their ripostes were reasons to go online. They were an elegant, dry pair, Hammett and Hellman transmogrified by the New Medium. Williams was a reporter and columnist whose day job for *Vanity Fair* entailed profiling important people in our most self-important city. Later she wrote a tart weekly column in *The Washington Post*. Before her terrifying diagnosis, Williams had no warning of a physical problem except for a slow and not unwelcome weight loss.

Though no kid (her son was eight, her daughter five), Williams attributed her slimming figure to a new jogging regime. After her daily trot through Rock Creek, she took womanly pleasure in admiring her new svelte form in the mirror. Then, shock. "Why me?" she asked, as most of us will ask one day.

(Or already have.) The news that we're mortal, now, not twenty years from now, stuns us no matter what our ages are. Why this? She'd had no liver disease, cirrhosis, or hepatitis A, B, or C. She'd quit smoking, though she'd started briefly again then stopped not long before the awful news. Why this? A wise healer said: "Lady, you got hit by lightning." Her condition wasn't operable. Stage IV liver cancer doesn't respond to surgery, radiation, or, frankly, anything. Still, Williams got chemotherapy for three years. Poisons kill more bad than good cells, one hopes, temporarily stifling or at least palliating the disease. The recipient of all these exotic, toxic fluids may enjoy an active life, and even if not recovering, die more slowly (and less painfully) than by forgoing treatments.

"Liver cancer is so untreatable because chemotherapy has little effect," Williams wrote. "Localized treatments can slow the growth of the tumor, or tumors, in the liver. (Chemo may be pumped through an artery directly into the tumors; the tumor may be ablated with radio-frequency waves; or frozen; or localized chemo pumps are installed to blast them directly.) But if the cancer has spread, medical textbooks say no therapy can stop it or even slow it down much. Chemo has about a 25 to 30 percent chance of having any impact."

Yet Williams mounted what she allowed herself to call a "miraculous" resistance. As her family and friends cheered her on, she undertook a cancer patient's homebound, motionless equivalent of Lance Armstrong's post-op runs over Europe's mountains in the Tour de France. Given the cruelty of her ailment, defying death for thirty-six months was a grand feat. "Whatever happens to me now," Williams wrote, "I've earned the knowledge some people never gain, that my span is finite and I still have the chance to rise and rise to life's generosity." She died in 2005, living, raising kids, writing, loving, until the end. Life goes on until one day: it stops. Or you stop it, as some people do.

HUNTER THOMPSON

Before he was fired at *Time* magazine for sassing his bosses, Hunter S. Thompson was a copyboy. He spent idle hours retyping Fitzgerald's *The Great Gatsby* and Hemingway's *A Farewell to Arms* to decipher how the masters strung words together. Soon, Thompson invented his own strange, original style, smooshing fact and fiction.

By 2005, his beach-bum good looks were kaput. The guy who'd ridden with the Hell's Angels (before they kicked the crap out of him) was done. The postmodern bizarro New Journalist, the protagonist in his own news reports, the man who invented gonzo journalism, the guy who called his best work "irresponsible gibberish," a clown-beast who feared and loathed his way across America, once spraying diners in a crowded restaurant with Mace for the hell of it . . . that guy was spent. Finito. Drugs and booze got him. At sixty-seven, Thompson was painfully aware of the toll his reckless life had exacted. While talking on the phone to his wife, Anita, Thompson blew his brains out. At the time, he was in the back bedroom of his Woody Creek cabin. Mrs. Thompson was at the gym. His son, daughter-in-law, and grandson were in the adjoining room. His suicide note said:

> No More Games. No More Bombs. No More Walking. No More Fun. No More Swimming. 67. That is 17 years past 50. 17 more than I needed or wanted. Boring. I am always bitchy. No Fun—for anybody. 67. You are getting Greedy. Act your old age. Relax—This won't hurt

After Gonzo died, Johnny Depp paid for the funeral. George McGovern, John Kerry, Ed Bradley, Bill Murray, Sean Penn, Josh Hartnett, Lyle Lovett, and John Oates partied heartily, as he'd hoped. His ashes were shot from a cannon atop a 150-foot tower that he'd designed himself.

PAPA

Ernest Hemingway and William Faulkner dominated U.S. letters. Papa Hemingway's terse prose and craggy face symbolized American masculinity. Unlike Faulkner's prose—discursive, dreamy, recondite—Papa's was easily parodied but seldom matched: a generation tried and failed. His stoic protagonists struggled to achieve grace under pressure. Papa didn't just describe a he-man's life. He lived it. As an Italian army ambulance driver in World War I, he was wounded badly by shrapnel and a bullet. He recuperated on Lake Como like his character Lt. Frederick Henry. Papa could be an unpleasant bully who argued with fellow drunken Parisian geniuses; he cheered bullfights and covered Spain's civil war. In Africa, he shot big game and climbed Kilimanjaro. He boxed, knuckles bare. During World War II, he converted *Pilar,* his fishing boat, into a Q-boat, a miniature sub chaser. As a war correspondent, he watched the Normandy invasion. When the Germans fled Paris, he was there, leading a partisan group that chased Nazis from the street. (Historians sniff that Papa merely liberated the Ritz Bar.) His drinking was prodigious, legendary, and destructive, but he earned the U.S. Bronze Star for his correspondence. He already had Italy's Silver Medal. In his fifties, he grappled with marlins in warm water between Cuba and Key West like Santiago, the hero of *The Old Man and the Sea*. A world-class raconteur and small-bore confabulator, he was unfaithful to four wives.

To succeed, one must endure, he said: "*Il faut durer.*" Yet his Herculean drinking and shock treatments for chronic depression precipitated declining health. Gifts fading, Papa ended his life grotesquely. Resting his chin over a prized double-barreled shotgun, squeezing both triggers, he blew his deteriorating brains onto the ceiling of his fishing cabin in Ketchum, Idaho.

WOOLF: "ON BEING ILL"

In 1918 and 1919, influenza, the worst disease since the Black Death, killed forty million people. No respecter of artistic talent, the flu hit Bloomsbury and East End slums alike. Virginia Woolf was one of countless Londoners stricken by the pandemic. Though sick and bedridden, ever the reader, Woolf turned to books for solace. Her search was fruitless. Great writers had given sickness little heed through the ages, she discovered. Love and war had received epic attention; romance and courage were constant subjects through the millennia; but Woolf searched Homer, Shakespeare, Milton, Pope, Keats, and Wordsworth in vain for insights into so much as coping with a simple headache. Illness is commonplace. Oddly, as it reduces one to somnolence, illness enhances perceptions. Yet illness was taboo—a subject feared but not discussed, neither by literary masters nor Woolf's contemporaries.

When one is sick, Woolf wrote, healthy people walk by unaware in the hearty "army of the upright," marching to some metaphorical battle somewhere else. The sick march nowhere. After a while, Woolf stopped resisting. She went AWOL.

> Directly the bed is called for, or, sunk among the pillows, as we raise our feet even an inch above the ground on one another, we cease to be soldiers in the army of the upright; we become deserters. They march to battle. We float with the sticks on the stream.
>
> It is only the recumbent who know what, after all, nature is at no pains to conceal—that she in the end will conquer; heat will leave the world; stiff with frost

we shall cease to drag ourselves about the fields; ice will lie thick upon factory and engine; the sun will go out.

NOT BEING U. S. GRANT

On Memorial Day, Ashfield pays homage to the statue of a granite Union soldier: four feet tall, he stands on a pedestal wearing a campaign cap, holding a stone musket. His face and mustache have been smoothed by acid rain, his features are blurred into realistic immaturity. In the cemetery behind our little Everyman, schoolchildren place crisp little flags, marking graves of Ashfielders who died in "the War of Nationality." In all our wars, men with names like Lilly, Williams, Gray, Graves, and Howes reappear. Considering them, I remember the unlikely Ohioan who led them.

General Ulysses S. Grant's feet were surprisingly dainty for a man who left such a huge legacy. I admire Grant, but I'm happy to know that I'd have towered over him had we been contemporaries. Robert E. Lee also loomed over his short, slouching rival at West Point. In the Mexican War, Lee was Grant's superior. Grant shunned grand uniforms like the one Lee wore to Appomattox Court House. Grant accepted the surrender of the Army of Northern Virginia wearing a soiled private's blouse to which he'd hastily strapped general's stars. Biographer Josiah Bunting reports: "One of Grant's own staff officers . . . said that Grant was 'covered with mud, in an old faded uniform, looking like a fly on the shoulder of beef.' "

History buffs prefer gallant Lee to taciturn Grant, perhaps because of the romance of the lost cause, as well as Lee's silvery mane, blue eyes, and neat beard. He looked like a benevolent biblical prophet. Men revered him. Intrepid, he loved attacking. Yet although he started the war with fewer than half of Grant's forces, Lee lost more men. Recklessly offensive, he doomed his army. Somehow even Northerners believed he was compassionate; Grant was denigrated as a butcher.

"U. S. Grant" was an accidental name bestowed on Hiram Ulysses Grant at West Point. A clerk substituted an *S* for the *H* that his parents had given him, and transposed the old *U* and the new *S*. A felicitous clerical bungle created a wondrous brand for the man who would embody the Grand Army of the Potomac. HUG might have had trouble beating Lee's renegades: U.S. prevailed. In sepia portraits, Grant looks big, but he had presence, not bulk. He entered the Point as a skinny seventeen-year-old, five feet one, weighing under 120 pounds. Although he grew seven inches at the military academy, he remained slim. Unlike his gaunt but well-kempt friend William Tecumseh Sherman, Grant was disheveled. Nonetheless, Hiram Ulysses Grant was the Point's best horseman—riding was the only college activity at which he excelled.

When he was fatally ill, Grant wrestled again with war's dogs. He remembered every melee with clarity, but the war's blood cost prevented him from savoring his triumph. The staggering number of Union and Confederate losses would overshadow the casualties America would suffer in future conflicts, save World War II. Compared to overall population, the Civil War's death rate was six times what it would be in World War II. Grant's memoir closes by hoping for no more wars: a perpetually vain wish he shared with most other blood-soaked generals and admirals. After Lincoln's assassination, the nation worshipped Grant and "Cump" Sherman as its military saviors. Adulation propelled Grant into the White House. (Sherman famously refused the honor.) Both old friends dreaded public speaking. A decent manager, Grant was a lackadaisical political boss. In the White House, he missed the intense physical challenge with which his brilliant nemesis, Lee, had presented him. Grant preferred crisp confrontation to inchoate politics.

He was no stranger to trouble. After his heroics in the Mexican-American War, his farm failed. He was reduced to hawking firewood. His business sense was flawed: not his integrity, though as president, he let scalawags flatter him. Venal men sullied his good name. When he strolled from the White House to the lobby of the Willard Hotel seeking refuge from routine, favor seekers surrounded him. Watching their shenanigans, reporters called his supplicants "lobbyists." An unfortunate new pseudo-profession was born on his watch. After the presidency, he lent his name to a Wall Street financial enterprise. Young Master Ward, a friend of Grant's son Buck, swindled the Grants and their investors. Grant & Ward went bankrupt. Investments in other failing companies impoverished him.

Yet in every crisis, personal and professional, Grant was unruffled, scrupulous. During a rift over the presidential election in which his successor, Rutherford Hayes, and his opponent, Samuel Tilden, appeared to be tied, their supporters threatened to fight one another with fists and guns for the spoils that accompanied the nation's top job. Serenely, Grant defused another potential civil war.

After his presidency ended, Sam (as his friends called him) and Julia Grant traveled. Kings and emperors feted them, bands played, throngs cheered. Returning home, facing financial crisis, reluctantly, he recollected the Battle of Shiloh for *The Century Magazine*. The first draft was tortuous, stiff prose, until he stopped writing as he thought he should and addressed readers as directly as he'd written his military orders. The ensuing issue sold out. *The Century* asked Grant to write a book. He agreed. Happily, his friend Samuel Clemens, whose alter ego, Mark Twain, knew that publishers were untrustworthy, offered to publish the book instead for higher royalties and a big advance.

One minute, Grant was a healthy man who would write his way out of hock; the next, as he bit into a peach, pain seared his throat. Disrespected by moralists, indebted, Grant was dying of advanced cancer. He lost weight. His face was emaciated. Yet blessed by Clemens, Grant's book could end his family's financial woes. Speed was essential. Talking was hard, but Grant dictated to gain time. Eventually even whispering was too much: eating, impossible. Sipping liquids, he scribbled with whittled pencils. When visitors paid respects, he answered spoken questions with good-humored longhand notes. Cocaine helped.

In 1884, as he was recording 1862's dire events, a hemorrhage nearly killed him, but he rallied. His narrative tightened. There was never much meat on him except the sinews that made him a gifted rider. Nonetheless, he worked four hours every day, his memories crackling like muskets. His precise communiqués had been keys to his success; his best orders, laconic soldierly haiku. Reporters had sneered that he was an insensitive brute. They were wrong. Humble, generous, Grant was no butcher. True, he could lead in adversity. Now the drug that eased his pain freed him to probe his heart. He wasn't sentimental, but he wrote with moral force.

Instead of engineering texts, he'd read novels at the Point. He put his literary knowledge to use as he wrote. Moreover, he recalled every battlefield declivity and ridge. Although he'd seemed coldly unaware when his men had fallen around him, he evoked his men's sacrifices, rechecked facts, agonized over each name, and credited all his enemies except Bobby Lee. He thought his rival more daring than wise. Despite his resentment over accolades the press had bestowed on the rebels, even his old foes visited during his last days. His posthumous book, America's best war history, led to national reconciliation. On July 23, 1885, four days after correcting his galleys, Grant died.

His men thought his body had been amalgamated from iron, hardtack, and gunpowder, but it failed. His illness took two fleeting sentences in his book. Disease wasn't discussed in his harrowing era. Grant accepted his fate. Confederate and Union generals escorted his casket before a million mourners. Royalties to his family reached five hundred thousand dollars: $10 million today.

G. WASHINGTON: STOIC

Rather than run for a third presidential term, George Washington retired to bountiful Mount Vernon. Like the Roman general Cincinnatus, Washington was a rare man who gave up power voluntarily rather than have it wrested away. His life was good. "Throughout his final retirement Washington experienced no debilitating injury or discernible deterioration of physical or mental powers," his biographer Joseph Ellis writes. "His long midday rides provided him with more exercise than he could manage during the presidency; making him more trim and fit than he had been in eight years. . . . Aging gracefully, [he was] putting the lie to all those Jeffersonian rumors of his imminent descent into senility. Friends who recommended special diets or health potions received polite rebuttals that suggested a man at peace with his mortality." In his remarkable will, Washington wrote: "Against the effect of time and age, no remedy has yet been discovered; and like the rest of my fellow mortals, I must (if life is prolonged) submit."

"His stoicism on this score was real, not a brave pose," Ellis says.

> When the grim reaper came, he was vulnerable only because he insisted on making his daily rounds with disdain for a sleet storm that drove everyone else to cover. . . .
>
> Washington had ridden in a storm for five hours, but in order to promptly entertain dinner guests, he de-

clined to change from wet clothes. The next day, though hoarse and uncomfortable, he marked trees for cutting. He presumed that he'd caught a cold, and sought no special care. "Let it leave as it came," he said.

That night his breathing worsened. Washington got the best medical care available at the time: Four bleedings extracted more than five pints of blood. Blistering agents were applied to his neck. Laxatives purged him. He probably suffered a virus infection of the epiglottis.*

He died as a Roman stoic, not as a Christian saint, Ellis says. History doesn't suggest that he saw angels in his last hours. The only place he knew his body was going was underground. No ministers were present at the deathbed: no prayers were offered. His wife, Martha, three female slaves, and a manservant were on hand. "Eventually Washington ordered his doctors to cease their barbarisms and let him go in peace," Ellis writes. " 'Doctor, I die hard,' he muttered, 'but I am not afraid to go.' " The manservant had been standing for hours when Washington asked him to sit. Controlling this last small decision, after the man was seated, he said, " 'Tis well."

* Ellis writes, "Epiglottitis is an extremely painful and horrific way to die, especially for a man as compulsively committed to self-control as Washington. As it swells, the epiglottis closes off the windpipe, making breathing and swallowing difficult, eventually impossible. The fully conscious patient has the sensation of being slowly strangled to death by involuntary muscles inside his own body. The last hours must have been excruciating, since he was essentially being tortured to death by his doctors at the same time."

25.

Foolishness Continues; Backwards, to Infirmity

In a light snowstorm six months after my 2006 Bug Hill Ice Capades, I helped Mary Schjeldahl move. She'd taught me yoga: I owed her. *Boing!* A mound of inguinal muscles, a goose egg, sprang on my groin, growing as I lugged fifty boxes to the second floor. Ouch. In 2004, I could do 150 sit-ups. Stomafied, herniated, a half-sit-up was beyond me.

A few weeks later, I was backing my new 4x4 ATV from the truck. Cassie guided me. The right ramp kicked from an unsteady base. My silly old carcass went reeling. Four hundred pounds of shiny red Honda Rancher fell on me. The handlebar missed my stoma by three inches, breaking two ribs.

Summer arrived. Free of chemicals, feeling strong, I hopped on my mountain bike, my first ride in years, pedaling slowly at silent-movie speed, as if riding a Victorian relic with a big front wheel. On my fifth ride, I lost my balance. My new truss hitched up my manliness. When I came down: yeow. Epididymitis ensued—a squashed testicle, or seminal vesicle, or both. More antibiotics. By midsummer, a girdle of trouble ached below my mangled belly button: hernia, stoma, broken ribs, and mashed testis—suitable for display in Philadelphia's Mutter Museum, home of the World's Biggest Colon. My torso was a blueprint for failed trolley lines. Scar tracks ran every which way. No more Speedos for Old Bob.

As time passed, chemo continued: one session during three of every four weeks. Each dose infused by Dr. Smith's staff, Pat, Kelly, Nancy, Karen, and Diane, flattened me. Diabetes joined in cahoots. My bewildered immune system went stuporous. Then a week later, gaining pep, I'd go back into the woods with Kit, Cassie, and the dogs. We hiked, chopped, whacked, and made new trails. Friends brought meals and buoyed my spirits. Then more healing poisons, downtime, recovery, repeat. Jackie, the receptionist, did me a world of good by calling me "a hip, hot, happening dude." (Give that woman a raise!) Meanwhile, my new stoma prolapsed glacially, a few slimy micrometers at a time, into a fleshy stalactite. By the fall, my colonubbin, newborn and cute in January, a winking pink coquette, had grown apace. The distended sight might have caused Florence Nightingale to abandon nursing, but physical oddments depicted in *Ripley's Believe It or Not!* have fascinated me since I was twelve. Holes drilled in skulls, arrows through faces, windows on stomach digestion, are better than TV.* I bore up. The bemused observer inside me watched detached as the rosy button protruded like Babar the Baby Elephant's trunk. By late summer, three pounds of inside-out large colon, pink, glisten-

* From Nicolson Baker, *A Box of Matches:* "I recall a cowboy movie in which a man was shot near the heart with an arrow that had a detachable head. If he pulled the arrow out, the head would stay in there and he would surely die. So he had to push the arrow all the way through his chest and out his back, remove the arrowhead, and then draw the unarmed shank back out from the front. He grimaced and trembled, but he lived.

"Nothing like that has happened to me. I've just ridden my tricycle, gone to school, greased my bicycle bearings, gotten a job, gotten married, had children, and here I am."

ing, dangling pendulously, ruined my self-esteem. My golf game degenerated. Too much flesh was swinging without whacking the ball. The Venetian merchant's metaphorical pound of flesh took form as an ugly remora. Disguises, Hawaiian prints and flowing Guayabera shirts, didn't work. Biking shorts joined Speedos in the Goodwill bag.

In September '06, feeling strong, I met three aged fraternity brothers, Casserole, Hose-Nose, and Pudgy Bear, for an unofficial golfing reunion in northern Idaho. On our second day, my stoma appliance, an unwieldy two-part affair, a Rube Goldberg contraption attached by expensive stickum to my midriff, separated during an awkward backswing. As I hooked my drive, effluvium cascaded over my two-toned golf shoes. Drizzle transformed me into a cow patty in a $5,000 golf cart. Mortified, was I. That night, we watched a nostalgic college DVD prepared by Casserole, our host. He presides over a big bank in Seattle—which you'd doubt when he guffaws. To hide my shame, I told old stories and drank slushy vodka from a semi-frozen bottle, "like a pirate," Casserole said the next morning. Bemused, my brothers stuck to wine. Ah, me. Self-medication compounded my shame. Brothers forgave me. They'd seen worse: they'd done worse. They understood childish misbehavior. Bouts of adolescent insanity inflamed by beer, Stumplifters, and Purple Jesuses had united us in the first place.

The Brothers knew I'd been busy during the summer. Before our outing, I'd gotten two PT scans, a CT scan, an MRI, three X-rays, two sonograms, a second colonoscopy, and a biopsy. Eleven doctors had treated me for four problems. My right eye was lasered for retinopathy. A new EKG revealed an elevated R factor. They surmised I'd had a silent heart attack. (Wrong: hypertension had twisted an otherwise strong heart muscle.) Yale surgeons had decided I was a candidate for a new, aggressive resection, curative, not palliative. After my return, more tests: surgeons reconsidered. Tumors were growing too fast for surgery. Was that ill-advised Idaho vodka slushy to blame? In November, with nothing else going on, I fixed my painful non-life-threatening hernia and ostomy. Bye-bye, Babar.

In a month, I was better. Occasional intestinal blocks required dashes to the emergency room, but life was good. Not much pain. For a nearly dead man, I was in excellent shape. Sometimes, as I walked through the woods with our goofy dogs, sweating, whacking tree limbs, dappled by sunshine, euphoria swept over me. Sometimes, being unable to think ahead is a blessing.

TOUGH POLS, TOUGH JOCKS, AND MORE: THE VOTING RECORD

Americans usually vote for tough candidates. For years, U.S. politics boiled down to one rule: tough guys beat wimps. Daddies creamed mommies, until Nancy Pelosi became Speaker and Hillary Clinton was reborn with totemic testicles. Impugned as "soft," telegenic candidates demonstrated moxie or got buried in electoral mud. Smash-mouth, trash-talking guys won. Wussies lost. Whatever their defects, virile guys like JFK, LBJ, Dick Nixon,* Ron Reagan, Bush the Younger, Mayor

* "Virile" might not be the best adjective for R. Milhous Nixon, but he pursued manliness starting as an undersized Whittier College lineman. Marilyn Young transcribed a conversation between Nelson Rockefeller and Nixon (speaking in the presidential third person): "Some senators think they can push Nixon around. Well, I'll show them who's tough." Stanley Karnow quotes Nixon admonishing Henry Kissinger and Alexander Haig to "hang tough" while negotiating with Premier Brezhnev. David Halberstam refers fifty-one times in *The Best and the Brightest* to American leaders' aspiration to be seen as tough. "Kennedy was tough," Nixon said, grudgingly. Johnson saw himself as "a tall tough Texan." George Ball might have been a dove, but "there was nothing soft about him: his approach was tough and skeptical." Robert McNamara was "forceful and tough; the advocate of escalation." Johnson worried: "Was Hubert Humphrey tough enough?"

Rudy, the Governator, Shoot-'Em-Up Dick Cheney, Rummy, Tom the Termite Hammerer, and POW John McCain got big jobs. Howard Dean had a mean streak. Reagan and FDR embodied the American political paradigm: popular, friendly, and handsome, but tough as ground glass.

THE MILITARY

Craggy, aggressive soldiers—Tommy Franks, Colin Powell, David Hackworth, and Norman Schwarzkopf—evoked iron-butted American warriors like Puller, Patton, Halsey, Black Jack Pershing, Grant, and Lee. In their days of gore, Alexander, Caesar, Khan, Attila, Bonaparte, and Lord Nelson didn't give gold stars or back rubs. Until the mid-nineteenth century, British officers flogged their men. Churchill putatively said, "Don't tell me about the gallant history of the British Navy. It's all rum, buggery, and the lash."

U.S. Marines embody America's martial resolve. Neatly tonsured men and women refute the spurious argument that ours is a nation of weenies. You want tough? Here's a squad of jarheads, ma'am: semper freaking fi, as rough-and-tumble kids as we've got, except RECONDO, SEALS, Rangers, Special Forces, Hell's Angels, Banditos, or Warlocks.

Americans love rugged actors who play take-no-prisoner soldiers, like Stallone, Willis, and Norris. John Wayne was the prototypical U.S. cinematic warrior, but Wayne's star dimmed partly because he remained a sound-stage hero as contemporaries like James Stewart and Clark Gable served in the fighting war. In my time, Army instructors warned us, "Don't pull a John Wayne" (i.e., hotdog or grandstand). In recent war movies, however, tough combatants (Fred Thompson's roles notwithstanding) are often ambiguous moral figures. "I'm relieving you of command, Staros," Colonel Tall says to a popular company commander in *The Thin Red Line,* based on James

Jones's Guadalcanal novel. Nick Nolte plays Colonel Tall as an old-style military fanatic willing to sacrifice men for ambition. Nolte caricatures Wayne's granite demeanor. Tall tells Staros: "I don't think you're tough enough. I think you're too soft. Too softhearted. Not tough-fibered enough. I think you let your emotions govern you."

WAR MOVIES

Friends sometimes ask me for cinematic reality checks. They wish to know if a film—say, *Platoon, Flags of Our Fathers, Letters from Iwo Jima,* or *Saving Private Ryan*—captures authentic raw combat. Tracking Tom Hanks's uncertain, terrifying progress across a hellish Omaha Beach scene raked with flying metal strikes moviegoers as particularly true: gore, clamor, fear, it's all there in apparent verisimilitude.

Well, sure: it's the same. Good war movies are indeed war zones, with some caveats. For one thing, your movie theater should vibrate with the force of an earthquake to set the mood: not just any old earthquake, either, but one that falls between eight and eleven on the Richter scale. The noise should be powerful enough to blow out eardrums and rattle the teeth of everyone in the first seven rows. Ideally, a tsunami of dirt, flesh, and metal should follow the sonic assault. Moviegoers should be encouraged to writhe on sticky popcorn, Jujubes, Hershey bars, and dried Coke encrusted on the concrete floor, simulating gore. Yeah, sure. That's it. If the cineplex management shoots metal shards through the air; if people around you scream in panic, pain, and delirium (preferably all three) crying for Mommy, a medic, or euthanasia; if you, yourself, are on fire, wriggling; and for the sake of argument, you're bleeding, vomiting, and losing control of your bodily functions . . . well, sure. That's real: as real as it gets.

Years after our war ended, Bill Broyles and I watched *The*

Deer Hunter and *Apocalypse Now* in Austin theaters. Neither captured our war, not even surrealistically, we concurred. After the Vietnam Memorial went up (rather, down, ignominiously yet movingly), Bill went to Washington to read names on the polished granite for himself. The memorial's message was: dig deeper, GI. Bill went back to Vietnam in the eighties. *Brothers in Arms,* Broyles's autobiography, describes revisiting the tropical nation whose fierce people had tested him as a Marine platoon leader. Bill sought former enemies, hoping to see the war through their eyes. Later, he created *China Beach,* a TV drama set by the Navy hospital* outside Da Nang. Bill's a mountain-bike-riding, bone-breaking, jeep-flipping, multiply-married, oft-moving guy. After he wrote *Apollo 13* and *Castaway,* his *Jarhead* screenplay turned Anthony Swofford's first-person account of a Marine sniper in the First Gulf War into a wrenching movie, with no combat.

In *Jarhead,* before heading to fight in Kuwait enchanted Marines watch *Apocalypse Now.* Col. Robert Duvall's helicopters ravish a defenseless village. Women and children are strafed. Swofford's mates whoop and holler: "Get some!" Helicopters swoop, speakers blasting "The Ride of the Valkyries." Swofford realized that even antiwar films are warnography. Orgies of violence, they celebrate what they purport to mock. Bill Broyles knows soldiers love cinematic adrenaline rushes, as did Kubrick, Ford, and Huston. There it is. Middle-aged men plan wars, both real and cinematic. Young men get off on both kinds.

TOUGH BUSINESS

Computers, luggage companies, poultry breeders, Dodge Rams, Ford trucks, and Master Locks boast of sturdiness. "Tough" is

* A Navy doctor patched my ear together at China Beach, but I didn't swim. Sentry boxes and concertina wire meant "Surf's down, dude."

superlative adspeak, like "new" and "free." Emery boards, credit cards, and Apple iPods are all tough stuff. After Carly Fiorina ran Hewlett-Packard, she wrote *Tough Choices*. GM's Rick Wagoner fired thousands of workers. Critics attacked him for poor performance but he declined to step down. "I wasn't raised to cut and run when times get tough," he said. I'm looking at a magazine ad. A bruised six-year-old boy stares at me through blue reflecting glasses, ginger hair sticking up in tufts, arms folded across his T-shirted chest, a crusty scab on his pug nose. He poses like a miniature wrestler. The headline:

> Even tough guys have a sensitive side.
> Introducing Wet Ones® Sensitive Skin . . .
> He may look macho but he's still your baby.

Reporters hounded President Bush to tell them: What were your mistakes? Furrowing, squinting, the president admitted, perhaps, maybe, okay, that he'd talked too tough, as in: "Bring it on!" and "Wanted, dead or alive." Otherwise: no problem. Losing two wars, popularity sagging, Bush hung tough.

THE PLAYING FIELD

You want tough? Watch meat-grinding football, any game, high school or pro. Three or four players will be hurt: one, seriously. Heads will concuss. Blood trickle. Bones sprain or break. Retired NFL pros have knees, shoulders, and skulls that look like epidermal railroad yards of scar tissue. A photo essay in *Play* magazine depicted injuries five pros sustained. Junior Seau's injuries included a torn shoulder, a fractured vertebra, bone spurs, and a broken toe. Running back Fred Taylor suffered eleven serious injuries; linebacker Reggie Williams, fifteen, including knee replacements; quarterback Steve McNair, twenty-one; and lineman Mark Schlereth, twenty-nine. Looking at his disfigured hands, Schlereth said, "Everyone chips bones and breaks fingers in their hands. You don't even think about it."

Few soccer players bleed in international games, but players flop in mock agony. A teensy head butt got Zinedine Zidane tossed from the France-Italy World Cup final. Who hemorrhages in cricket? Baseball? Groins are pulled, arms strained, and pitches bruise. Big deal. Maiming happens in America's Game.

Lounging on comfy couches, we watch *Gladiator,** the Super Bowl, *Survivor,* NASCAR, *Lost,* and *Ultimate Fighters.* Voyeurs, we crave vicarious fortitude. When the going gets tough, sedentary tough guys watch.

What kind of love do we like? Tough love. Don't like it? Tough, buddy. Green Bay fans and business magazines adored Jack Welch and Vince Lombardi, mean bastards. *Fortune* serially named Neutron Jack "America's Toughest Boss," a superlative that decorated so many covers in the eighties and nineties that I stopped counting at twenty.

One Super Sunday, *New York Times* columnist David Brooks wrote: "On this holiest day of the year, when Americans gather, overeat, and enjoy the outpourings of our great ad agencies, we reflect on the core myth that animates our nation. No, I don't mean the Western—so 19th century. I mean sports movies, epics that define contemporary America."

Coaches evoke "flinty, uncommunicative" men's men who ruled until America became feminized in the sixties, organization men were scorned, and ambition itself was attacked. Today, men demanding order are the rage again. "Tough coaches may be scarred inside, but they project confidence and calm," Brooks wrote. "The 1960s happened. Vince Lombardi won."

* "In Rome, private companies sprang up to provide for the torture and crucifixion of troublesome slaves, relieving estate owners of the need to deal with them. Crucifixion is one penal market niche that American companies have not sought to exploit."—Cullen Murphy, *Are We Rome?*

IT'S NOT JUST FOOTBALL, BUDDY WRANGLER

Consider the skinny Texan who conquered the Alps more impressively than Hannibal's elephants. Everyone admires cancer-beater Lance Armstrong (except French sticklers for body purity). Metastasized testicular cancer to the brain and lungs, stage IV, kills most mortals. Not even superhumans whose physicality rivals Armstrong's are exempt from the terrible odds that confronted him. His doctor thought he had a 2 percent chance of surviving, data so dire he didn't share them with his patient. After surgeries on his genitalia, brain, and lungs and debilitating chemical treatments, merely recovering and getting back on a bike make him a hero—forget racing. Winning the Tour de France seven times? An astonishment. Steroids, doped blood, kryptonite injections, jet fuel, food additives, methamphetamines, Bazooka chewing gum: Who cares? Whatever he did or didn't take, he amazes.

Although testosterone and aggression are linked, one needn't be male to be a tough cookie. Women have excelled in our toughest contact sport, starting with the Amazons. Jeanne d'Arc's charisma beat the English. Elizabeth I defeated the Spanish Armada. Golda Meir beat the Arabs. Maggie Thatcher whipped the Argentineans. "Don't go all wobbly on us, George," she admonished Bush One before the Gulf War. In Iraq, pilot Tammy Duckworth lost her legs, then ran (or crutched) for Congress. Pan-broiled perfectionism, thy brand is Martha Stewart. Oprah Winfrey didn't climb TV's slippery pinnacle by simpering. Speaking at her alma mater, Edinboro University, Sharon Stone said: "It's very hard to be from here. Pennsylvania's a tough place with tough people. The weather's tough, it's tough to get work, it's tough politically. But it has served me well and I am so proud to be from here."

Toughness isn't a synonym for manliness. In *Manliness,* Professor Harvey Mansfield pines for the days when men were men and women cooked, but he undercuts his arguments, admitting he vacuums and washes dishes. Oxymoronically, Dr. Mansfield grants that Golda Meir and Margaret Thatcher were manly women. His claim to fame? A harsh grader, he gives Cs, the Ivy League professor's version of smack-down street fighter. Mother Teresa defined compassion yet was hard as a yogi's nails, solacing dying Indians with Christ's penitential lessons and rudimentary medical service. Toughness absorbs nobler traits—courage, valor, resolve—as well as a less admirable quality, hardheadedness.

Populist Barbara Ehrenreich, author of *Nickel and Dimed,* is an unlikely student of war, being a lefty as well as a 100 percent girlie-girl. Nonetheless, she wrote *Blood Rites: Origins and History of the Passions of War.* Why are we so warlike? she asked. Are humans, especially men, just naturally cruel beasts? Studying anthropology, history, and psychology, she answered no, years before Harvey Mansfield created his paean to pugnacity. Men aren't instinctive killers, she said. Rather, our ancestors were hunted. For eons before they became predators, humans were prey. Cro-Magnons were better runners than fighters. Stronger, more terrible creatures ate our ancestors for millennia before they wised up and banded together. Working cooperatively reversed the deadly game. Humankind became resilient under duress.

WHAT'S WRONG?

Yet we have a problem, friends, don't we? Toughness is impure. Vulgar. Rude. Mother Teresa, Sharon Stone, and Jeanne d'Arc aside, "toughness" is cruelty. Gruff stamina, resilience, and endurance are good traits, yet toughness is vindictive, too. Aggression is respected in sports, combat, and business, but let's be frank: tough *hurts*. In *US Guys,* Charlie LeDuff shows how painful our quest for toughness can be. A hard-drinking, two-fisted guy who wrote *The New York Times*'s drinking column, "Bending Elbows," putting his liver on the line, LeDuff describes Oakland bikers, Civil War reenactors, gay cowboys, semipro football players, and a couple of Detroit murder detectives. LeDuff love-hates "angry, forgotten middling Americans." It's hard to warm to them, but then again, they don't want your warmth.

In our little hill town, the dark side of our laconic manhood and stern womanliness is spousal abuse, closeted addiction, and DUIs. Years ago, a local man killed a sibling. When he got out of prison, his parents welcomed their prodigal Cain home; he bilked his parents in a check-kiting scheme.

Marriage, lovemaking, child rearing—the humdrum stuff of daily lives—should be shorn of aggression, should they not? After all, who wants a tough spouse? Who needs a tough teacher? (Okay—a prospective delinquent.) Who wants to be on the receiving end of a hypodermic wielded by Nurse Ratched?

26.

Becoming a Little Bit Stoic

As I was failing in 2004, trying to be tough enough, rallying, then drooping in 2005, rallying again, sagging again, Dr. Miller lifted my spirits during his second through fourth operations by telling me that I was a glass-half-full kinda guy. Meanwhile, Dr. Smith suggested that my strange, upbeat attitude might have helped me escape the fate that her composite metastatic data had predicted in 2005. Maybe doctors thought well of me because I didn't blubber much. Their view of my comportment, though wrong, was useful. If I could fool caregivers into thinking that my jaunty acting was real, maybe by adding a pinch of self-discipline I could shrivel my pain. Opiates (Dilaudid, OxyContin, morphine, fentanyl patches) helped with the worst stuff. Yoga, acupuncture, stretching, and getting pricked beneficially also helped.

Why not close the East-West circle? Go Grecian? Subduing trouble, I decided to become a stoic, a thinking man's tough guy. In crisis, we look inward. Famously, milliseconds before a car crash, axe blow, or pistol shot, time slows. Our lives flash in slo-mo. Tunneling into memory is a standard route from here to the hereafter. We talk with God, Jesus, Allah, Rama, the Virgin Mary, Buddha, Dionysus, or Pan. Personally, I ruled out no god, certainly not the One, but I also sought Zeno of Citium.

Ancient, Greek, and tough, Stoicism's details and practices were mysteries to me. Mind over matter? In my imperfect understanding, Stoicism would affirm my sense that people of action prevail, or at least that men endure even though, or because, they lack complicated thoughts. Unless you've read the Greeks, you probably learned about stoics in stories about people grappling with difficulty. Their houses burned. They lost limbs. More often, they sprained joints, mud-wrestling or ping-ponging, yet played on, persevering. "Stoic" is usually a lofty synonym for "tough" that invests periodical prose with a thoughtful if imprecise glow. The usage isn't wrong, just simplistic. Most often, we see stoics as jocks or poor stricken sods. After earthquakes demolish their homes, people standing blankly in the rubble are stoics. If you're Australian, English, or Irish, stoics are hardheaded rugby players who get back into the scrum despite knotted ears and broken teeth. Although the original Stoics were an austere lot with rich inner lives, in modern usage, a stoic is groggy, barely breathing, and oblivious.

Penguin's handsome little *Marcus Aurelius' Meditations* paperback caught my eye. The philosopher-emperor made sense. I bought *Seneca, Plato,* and *Socrates,* too. What I thought I knew was wrong. Stoicism isn't a prescription for old age, for example. Aurelius said: Anticipate death *now,* whether your health is perfect or perfectly terrible. Quit listening to other people. Satisfy yourself. Before Christ showed us how to endure suffering, Zeno encouraged Athenians to control themselves. Keep cool! Emotion distracts. Be levelheaded, seek wisdom. Help the needy, ignore the chattering yammering crowd.

Zeno delivered his pungent messages while standing on a porch. (*Stoa poikilē* means "painted portico.") Verandas don't evoke profound ideas, but the breezeway opened Greek minds. The fresh air of new ideas cooled their heated brains.

"Stoic" came to mean unemotional, indifferent. Today, we see such people as wooden robots. Eradicating "passion" conjures burning stacks of bodice-ripping novels. Perish the thought! Etymology confuses us. Passion now means salaciousness: resisting it signifies de-sexing ourselves. Misery! Yet Stoics didn't want to kill melodrama—or sex. They weren't anti-feeling. They didn't want to *extinguish* emotion. They avoided emotional *trouble*: To the Hellenes, "passion" was "suffering." Apatheia limited suffering, but didn't mean refusing to cheer. Apathy wasn't indifference. Apathy, clear judgment, mirrored Buddha's truths: all life is suffering (*dukkha*), suffering is rooted in desire (*samudaya*), and meditating frees us from suffering. The Gospel of James teaches the same practice: become indifferent to worldly claims. Think long term, Christians! Religion aims at forever.

By mastering emotions, Stoics believed they could find peace. This tantalizing message is hard to grasp. Romans like Seneca, Marcus Aurelius, and the Catos were Stoic. Cicero followed Stoic moral tenets, too, but he was an Eclectic. (You thought "eclectic" meant collecting funky art.) Zeno taught that moral law was roughly the same as natural law. Behave the way you should. He engineered the first back-to-nature movement, anticipating the Golden Rule as well as "ashes to ashes, dust to dust." The unified Stoic view of the world placed ethical behavior at its center, borrowing the Cynics' idea that goodness is in the soul and in self-control. "Follow where reason leads." Logos, universal reason, is in all things. "I think, therefore, I am," Descartes would say: Stoicism in a French chestnut.

Stoics didn't seek pain. They weren't masochists. They thought: if destiny chooses you to suffer, suffer well. If fate makes you a gardener, be a good one: don't fret because you aren't a priest or a poet. Envy wastes energy. Sturdy Cicero and Cato made fine public servants.* Like Socrates, Stoics held that unhappiness results from ignorance. Stoicism is a way of life. Here's the hard part: practicing.

I'M *NOT* ZENO AFTER ALL

In *Meditations,* Marcus Aurelius offers thoughtful routines. For example: "Say to yourself in the early morning: I shall meet today ungrateful, violent, treacherous, envious, uncharitable men . . . I cannot be harmed by them, no man will involve me in wrong, nor can I be angry with my kinsman or hate him; for we have come into the world to work together." Be alert, think about problems, and solve them before they paralyze. Philosophy is active: let's help one another. Rank and wealth shouldn't matter.

On reflection, much of Stoicism is alien to me, especially reflection. I can't say that I *practiced* Stoicism. I studied it, after a fashion; decided I got it, more or less, and went about my life, considering its lessons every now and then. To my dismay, pretending to be Stoic got harder when I read *Ideas: A History of Thought and Invention, from Fire to Freud.* Peter Watson explains Nazis, Druids, economists, Pagans, Babylonians, Jews, Christians, Buddhists, Hindus, Muslims, and Jains. Instead of affirming what I'd learned, though, Watson threw me a spit-

* In the BBC's miniseries *Rome,* Marc Antony says to Lucius Verenus, his aide-de-camp whose life isn't going well: "You're not going to turn to drink, are you? You Stoic types often do that when things don't turn out as you'd hoped."

ball. He says latter-day Stoics became decadent, licentious, lewd, dirty old men whose indulgences were at odds with their stentorian professions of restraint. Sages who commended self-discipline somehow allowed themselves all manner of fleshly pleasures, and man-boy love was the best form of Eros. Women were okay, even necessary for procreation, but the purest affection was expressed by older men for boys.

Homosexuality is one thing: I'm okay with it, as are you, but we don't want to emulate ancient precursors of the NAMBLA Society. Stoics smiled on promiscuity. Incest? Hey, why not! If it feels good, do it. Diddling nieces, nephews, and cousins makes me a bit squirmy. Learning about the Stoics' transgressive horniness made me sniff piously. But lechery wasn't where I parted company with the Stoics. Perhaps they were libertarians long before modernists rationalized not paying taxes or serving in the military. We parted company, Zeno and I, on the issue of supping on fellow men. Dr. Watson explained that Stoics were so open-minded that even cannibalism didn't bother them. That's taking an idea to its limits, eh wot? Discovering that the ancient Stoics had rationalized such deviant behavior made me rethink. Perhaps there's a reason we don't worship in Stoic temples or attend Stoic masses. Self-control is a good thing, but ersatz self-discipline that flouts reasonable social taboos is just self-indulgence masquerading as profundity.

So I've decided I'm not a Stoic. I'm an animal-and-vegetable-eating, monogamous American who forgives the failings of strong people, except for cruelty, spousal abuse, preemptive war making, an absence of a sense of humor, et cetera. Like all ideological extremes—ecoterrorism, neoconservatism, PETA, radical Islamism, and fundamentalist evangelism—stoicism pretends to modesty, but preens self-righteously.

Fuck that. I'm not a human-bone-devouring, nephew-and-niece-fondling Greco-Roman. I'll settle for old-fashioned democratic Presbyterianism, adding in some Buddhism and yoga, buttressed by walks in God's woods and a dash of Reform Judaism. There's not much stoicism in this goodie bag, on balance: just enough. From now on, when I'm in pain, I'll ask: What would Steve Lilly, dairy farmer emeritus, do?

27.

Enduring, Singing Endtime Songs, Rating War Movies

For twenty-five years, we've watched neighbors persevere without whining despite troubles that include enduring the worst weather in Judeo-Christendom. How do they endure so much guff with so little complaint? Solving this riddle could help me resist my own troubles. Steve Lilly has more reason to gripe than I do, but he doesn't. Could I ape his self-control? Perhaps.

Still, confronting demons, I looked for guidance where educated, self-absorbed people usually seek ideas: in books, and increasingly online. When no one was around, I tuned to the Love Channel and Turner Classics. Ted Turner cries. He's an old man's old man. Walker Percy explained the human condition: we never feel so alive as when a natural calamity boils our way. In twenty-page slices, I staggered with Cormac McCarthy's doomed drunks, cowboys, and endtime characters. His austerity kills me. Jim Crace took me into his infernal Pesthouse. Years ago, I loved *Castle Keep*. Sardonic writers keep me company, like the Waughs, the Amises, Graham Swift, Philip Roth, and Mark Twain. Bleak historians like Keegan,

MacPherson, and Ambrose remind us that it could be worse. It has been worse. One day, it will be even worse.

By contrast, perky positive thinkers drive me nuts. Although I'm an unhinged, sky-blue optimist, perhaps a hypomaniac, I'm not now and never was, never could be, never will be a sensitive New Age guy. No. I discovered the hard way after starting Beliefnet.com, communing with priests, rabbis, ministers, monks, yogis, New Agers, pagans, Wiccans, and gnostics. We webcast the U.N.'s Millennial Peace Summit. As time passed, my job reminded me that I'm not pious, religious, or spiritual, may the Goddess Jane bless those who are. Eventually, I quit, but it didn't take, and I ended up getting fired.

While dog-paddling through a gumbo of serious ideas and books, I noticed that I was already living in a petri dish bubbling with Yankee forbearance—as abundant as snow, spring peepers, or fall leaves. As a hedge, I still research, and I sing, lustily accompanying Dennis Leary as he bangs out "I'm an Asshole" and doing Randy Newman's "Political Science" a cappella:

Boom goes London, boom Paree
More room for you, more room for me

My anthem is Joe Walsh's "Life's Been Good":

They say I'm crazy but I have a good time
I'm just looking for clues at the scene of the crime
Life's been good to me so far

For your endtime apocalyptic medley, start with Tom Lehrer's atomic bomb dream, "Who's Next?" Pick any George Jones song, and at least one of Warren Zevon's 296 tunes, especially "I'll Sleep When I'm Dead" and "Keep Me in Your Heart When I'm Gone." Toss in Roger Miller's "Chug-a-Lug," followed by the Kingston Trio's uncharacteristically bleak "Some lovely day, someone will set the spark off, and we will all be blown away!" Add Amy Winehouse doing "Rehab" for post-ironic effect, and "Wind It Up," Gwen Stefani translating "The Lonely Goatherd" into hip-hop. Our universal codas: Dan Hicks's "O'Reilly at the Bar" and Tom Waits doing "The Piano Has Been Drinking."

28.

Remembering the Forgotten

Toughness is as vulgar as professional wrestling. Like other virile attributes (strength, power, aggression), courage can be crude. Our loutish Scottish counterparts, "Hard Men," fight one another, beat their wives, and are often jailed. (Gaoled.) Toughness hurts. Good sense dictates that Scots and Americans alike seek milder models for self-sufficiency. Before Angles, Gaels, Saxons, Celts, and Picts fought to be Britain's tuffest tribe, the Greeks ranked courage above prudence, justice, and temperance. William Ian Miller says courage is "the spiny side of caring for others." (Love as cactus?) "Courage is reckoned the greatest of all virtues," Dr. Johnson said, "because, unless a man has that virtue, he has no security for providing any other." More than love or sex, courage is history's favorite theme.

"Courage comes embedded with a theory of manhood," Miller says. "In many cultures, as chastity was to women, so courage was to men, the virtue at the center of their gendered identity. . . . Courage made the man, cowardice unmanned him and got him called a woman."

Courage is to toughness as reticence is to chastity. In ancient texts, "tough" referred to sinew, tendon, iron, and bone. In science, toughness resists force. Courage is the elite's toughness. "Few doubt that the miner and longshoreman are tougher, more likely to be courageous than the accountant and adman," Miller says. Archaeologists, physical creatures, are tougher than English professors, or at least they're cast that way. Sixty-five-year-old Indiana Jones—okay, Harrison Ford—could kick the ass of the strongest, meanest member of the Modern Language Association. Think tankers are probably as physically tough as English professors, but in pictures, they're fat, double-chinned goobers. Yet Miller reminds us that many poets—including King David, Lord Byron, and Siegfried Sassoon—displayed courage in war. In the end, sadly, Miller says, we respect the elegant nerve of Eton's graduates, but ignore gritty working-class Tommies. We grant aristocrats extra credit for overcoming refined breeding. The same prejudice gives officers too many medals and snubs enlisted men.

"By using the word 'tough,' " Miller writes,

> we withhold some of the virtue that goes with courage. . . . Toughness, a semblance of courage, has been thrust on them. Since when does the hand get praised for being callused, although surely that callused hand is more worthy than the soft hands of he who quits after he gets his first blister. . . . Now we are more willing to see Spartan toughness as the meritorious end of a regime of self-denial, dedication, and commitment. . . . For the most part, we collapse toughness into courage and we see no need to distinguish the two . . . except when we want to determine whose courage is more praiseworthy, the intrepid enlisted man's or his equally

brave officer's, the street-fighter's or the corporate whistle-blower's.

This makes my head hurt. It's tough to contrast "tough" with "courageous." Differentiating between them is as fruitless as cutting into the entrails of a joke in order to decode its humor, or seeking a dead man's soul from an autopsy report. Toughness *is what it is*. If a rose is a rose by any name, and smells as sweet, a tough guy stands pungent, bristling, defying you to define or limit him—or challenge his courage.

One Memorial Day, I addressed my neighbors by the Plain Cemetery, a hundred yards from the little Civil War soldier, evoking my dead mates. The truth was that I didn't remember the fallen too well. I should have, I know: I sent them to their deaths. I didn't kill them, not that, but my orders were proximate causes of their ends. I'd known each for less than a week before they bought their respective farms. I'd made Cloud walk point though he was due to return home soon. I ignored his anguish. I wanted to believe the patently false myth that Native Americans had mystical talents. He argued that he was just a regular guy off the Rez with no tracking skills, but I told him that I'd heard he was good at this stuff. It was his duty to warn us.

Cloud sensed, no, Cloud *knew* something would happen. Yet he did his job. For his conscientiousness, he was shot many times. He'd dreaded this ambush but was powerless to prevent it. His gifts were jujus. Everyone in my platoon had believed in his magic but Cloud, who died within a few minutes. The second man in line, squad leader Schaefer, was shot through five joints: knees, a wrist, an elbow, and a hip. As a savage bonus, he was hit in the gut, too. The third man in line was shot in a foot, a wound that would get him home; the fourth man, hit in a buttock, took a joyful trip to the, um, rear. Sixth and seventh in line: Doc Froemming and me, unscathed.

Days later, I was hit with shrapnel and shot. In Intensive Care, I awoke facing poor Schaefer. Maybe he should be on this list of the deceased. Schaefer had argued: don't put Cloud on point. When I rejoined Delta, I assigned newcomers Cumbry and Hartry, kids from Detroit and the Texas piney woods, to a dangerous listening post. They'd scurry home if they sensed movement. They were killed too quickly to learn survival skills. Other people with whom I served were blinded, paralyzed, mutilated, or killed, like Gunnery Sergeant McCants and his boss. I wasn't responsible. Nor did I make Private Finder walk into a booby trap, or order that sad-ass gunner to throw a grenade at his buddies. Doc Froemming, the bravest man I served with, had a moment of bad karma. Not my fault. Cloud, Cumbry, and Hartry were teenagers, each one younger by far than our cherished daughter is today. Their deaths went unnoticed except by families and fellow grunts. We knew them vividly, but today, we hardly remember them except on official mourning days. I thought I'd remember every tiny detail about them, but I've forgotten too much about them and too little about me. I recall my sparse brave moments and terrifying weak ones. I thought the experience of war was so compelling, a horrible unending movie, that it was etched into my brain like acid, each cruel episode eating deeper than a photograph. But the truth is that the clearest memories I hold on to about these men are their deaths. I remember my pain more clearly than I recall them alive, in three dimensions, before they became casualties.

On Memorial Day, we honor all our kids who fought in Korea, the Gulf War, World War II, World War I, the Spanish-American War, the War Between the States, Afghanistan, and Iraq; all those damned wars. Today, the nation, secure, complacent, though ostensibly at war, knows few warriors, fallen or living. Names chiseled neatly on walls and plaques don't seem real. They're idealized, overdramatized, and yet forgotten. They're symbols of . . . something?

Tombs of the fallen become the refuges of the scoundrels who sent them away, men who pin flags on their breasts and cry crocodile tears. We must send more men to die because we've already sent men who died. The logic? Yet even when we can't recall their faces, conjure their heroics, or feel their mortal terrors, we must remember them, not because they were Trojans, Hussars, or gladiators, but because they did what they had to do. They were our boys, our friends, and our buddies. They smoked cigarettes, they ate bully beef, chipped beef, K-rations, C-rations, LRRP rations, or MREs, and they died. Maybe I'm blowing smoke, professing survivor guilt, false emotion, decades late. I can go a year without thinking about my guys. That's the problem: the forgetting. War is dirty even when we fight for rare just causes, when our enemies present transparent danger. Okay: these aren't news flashes, but as we remember their sacrifices, we must remember their suffering. For some of us, even lucky survivors, war lasts an eternity. When we send our kids to fight, we should be sure that we have reason, and not send them to inscrutable conflicts to die alone. I'm deeply sorry about Cloud, Cumbry, and Hartry.

A DEAD PRESIDENT, FAKE NAM VETS, AND ME

The funeral ceremonies and military pageantry for President Reagan (Captain, World War II, Theatrical Company) made me cry. Strange: I wasn't a big Reagan fan. Maybe it was the drugs, perhaps misplaced self-pity, but watching the guards do their precise, solemn work made me wistful. With certain cues, sentimental waves of patriotism wash over me. A parade can start it. "Taps" does it too. Watching veterans trudge from our Town Hall to the cemetery on Memorial Day does it, but mostly, the parade embarrasses me. The military bearing of our aging veteran contingent is shot to hell. We limping fogies stand more or less at attention as colors are raised, a wreath is laid, and rifles resound. Chins tremble. Eyes mist. We remember: kind of.

Similar emotions have overcome ex-warriors for centuries. French soldiers who marched with Napoleon across Europe, creating l'Empire only to be defeated by Russia's horrific winter—they forgot their suffering later, as *le drapeau tricolore* paraded grandly down the Champs Elysées. Awful memories abated as "La Marseillaise" echoed. Old men cried for lost youth and dead comrades. Decades after our doughboys plodded through the Marne, lacing their faded puttees and buckling their old Sam Browne belts as they prepared for Armistice Day parades made them remember their pride in service, not the squalid, horrendous details of trench warfare.

On some level, veterans who don't know Siddhartha from Sid Vicious sense that a well-drilled soldier is a Zen monk. A soldier standing at attention, bearing arms, looking sharp, lives in a momentary, contented mental zone. Civilians unencumbered by military service don't know that the core of military drill is, well, comforting. That's part of the warrior's problem. You know violent aggression produces adrenaline. You know bullets, bombs, and grenades kill and excite, if you aren't dead yourself. But do you also know that drill is hypnotizing? Calming? Sedating? Not likely. Sure, grunts gripe about Mickey Mouse parade duty, but inside, we love it. Something lodged like shrapnel in old soldiers craves the starched selflessness of military protocol. However, if you admit you like this stuff, you give your friends reason to doubt your sanity: as they should, because ceremony and drill lead to compliance, compliance becomes obedience, and pretty soon, you're wearing a helmet, charging into a storm of lead, delivering your own fusillade. Death happens.

The tug of patriotism is still so strong that some intelligent, accomplished men invent fictitious military careers to place themselves in the warriors' pantheon. Over lunch with me in Northampton, Joe Ellis established that his military service had been more worthy than mine. Beloved by his Mount Holyoke students, he'd been a platoon leader with the 101st Airborne. His platoon had cleared the mess at My Lai, he told his students. Wow! I'd just driven by, ignorantly. Commanding General William Westmoreland asked Joe to be his aide. So I deferred to Joe, who grinned benignly through pipe-stained teeth. As two patriotic combat veterans, we supported the Clintonian call to national service.

To my amazement, in 2001, *The Boston Globe* revealed that Ellis hadn't seen a minute of combat or waded through a single Southeast Asian hectare, much less delved into My Lai's bloody ditches. In 1968, Ellis had been a history teacher at West Point—legitimate duty that didn't require embellishment, one would think—but some fortunate souls, never in harm's way, regret not hearing the whir of hot metal and standing the test of brutal confrontation.

In 1975, without inventing a spurious combat narrative, James Fallows captured the challenge aging warless men face in a *Washington Monthly* article called "What Did You Do in the Class War, Daddy?" When he got his draft notice, like Warren Zevon and a million other American boys, Fallows feigned illness. He lost weight and looked cadaverous at his physical. Looking back, however, he regretted missing the bracing experience of being shot at. Most of Fallows's more conservative peers had breezed past recruiting stations without qualms, as we've established. Twenty, thirty years later, they decided: oh, yeah, somebody shoulda saved Vietnam! If only soft Democrats hadn't pulled the plug!

Don't get me wrong. Jim Fallows is admirable for rethinking his duty, and Joe Ellis is a great historian who served his country honorably. Despite his self-inventions, he's a better man than the ideologues who endangered the nation, failing to understand that war is something best avoided, rarely, if ever, to be undertaken preemptively. Padding your résumé is light-years removed from urging your nation to make war, making a billion enemies because of your false counsel. One is merely false courage: the other, abject treachery.

THE FUTURE

Surprisingly, my medical outlook brightened in the spring of 2008. Chemotherapy had shrunk my tumors, Dr. Smith happily told me. Six months earlier, a CT scan had revealed a new lesion, but it, too, had diminished under caustic baths. Chemical treatment augmented by targeted therapy would continue indefinitely. *Still!* What a lovely word! Some unpleasant things happened, too, beginning with a yearlong case of total alopecia. Eventually, I was hairless from head to toes. Instead of follicles, I sported rashes, pimples, and sores, and I was often nauseated. My feet developed infections. Three minor operations ensued. Hey: it was all good. One's hair comes back, and then goes again. Hair! Who needs it? I'm a fuzzy chia pet. Medical marijuana worked, too!

However, in late summer 2008, tumors were spreading, growing diffuse, no longer concentrated in four well-defined spots. Determining ruefully from CT scans that the treatments were killing me faster than the disease, Dr. Smith suspended therapies shortly after a new side effect, full-blown osteoporosis, manifested itself, making my bones as frail as fine porcelain. In April, I broke my right leg after slipping down one lousy stair-step. Surgery screwed my right tibia and fibula together. When that leg healed, I fell from my brand-new motor scooter—Look, Ma! A hundred miles per gallon! Oops—breaking four ribs, a clavicle, and my left tibia. At the time, I was hurtling along at maybe three miles an hour, tops, so slowly I could have used my damaged leg as a brake in the dirt road if it had occurred to me. Ah, me.

Still, I outlasted noble Randy Pausch, gallant Tony Snow, and Ted Koppel's friend Leroy Sievers, who blogged and podcasted on NPR.org about his two-year tangle with metastatic colon cancer. Now I'm hoping to outlast P. J. O'Rourke, recently diagnosed with anal cancer. It's on, O'Rourke!

Is it weird that my competitive spirit spills over into the ICU? Yes. It is. But even if I fail to gain immortality, it gives me solace to know that my friends will have to come to what I *hope* will be my bibulous wake—yet I won't have to celebrate *their* lives. Is there a worse contemporary social event than a death-denying, Kumbaya-singing "Celebration of Life"? A worse way to pass time than to join a passel of numb, bereaved people, all pretending that the dead one lives on?

"Don't mean nothin'," we said in the day, balefully dismissing every inexplicable, terrible, or terrifying thing we'd seen, heard, and done. Don't mean a thing.

We're *dead,* you idiots. Have a drink, have a laugh, and get on with it.

About the Author

ROBERT NYLEN was born on April 15, 1944, in Oak Ridge, Tennessee. He was educated at Bucknell University and the Wharton School at the University of Pennsylvania. He served as a combat infantry officer with the First Air Cavalry Division in Vietnam, earning two Purple Hearts and a Bronze Star. He was an entrepreneur, and a media consultant, and a lifelong student of history and lierature. He died on December 23, 2008, at home in Ashfield, Massachusetts, not long after this book was completed.

About the Type

This book was set in Sabon, a typeface designed by the well-known German typographer Jan Tschichold (1902–74). Sabon's design is based upon the original letter forms of Claude Garamond and was created specifically to be used for three sources: foundry type for hand composition, Linotype, and Monotype. Tschichhold named his typeface for the famous Frankfurt typefounder Jacques Sabon, who died in 1580.